STICKS and SKEWERS

STICKS and SKEWERS
ELSA PETERSEN-SCHEPELERN

photography by
WILLIAM LINGWOOD

TIME
LIFE
BOOKS

Alexandria, Virginia

TIME® LIFE BOOKS

Time-Life Books is a division of Time Life Inc.

TIME LIFE INC.
President and CEO: Jim Nelson

TIME-LIFE CUSTOM PUBLISHING
Vice President and Publisher Neil Levin
Senior Director of Acquisitions and Editorial Resources Jennifer Pearce
Director of New Product Development Carolyn Clark
Director of Trade Sales Dana Coleman
Director of Marketing Inger Forland
Director of New Product Development Teresa Graham
Director of Custom Publishing John Lalor
Director of Special Markets Robert Lombardi
Director of Creative Services Laura McNeill
Project Manager Jennie Halfant
Technical Specialist Monika Lynde

Printed and bound in China by Toppan Printing Co.
10 9 8 7 6 5 4 3 2 1

TIME-LIFE is a trademark of Time Warner Inc., and affiliated companies

Library of Congress Cataloging-in-Publicaton Data
Petersen-Schepelern, Elsa.
    Sticks & Skewers / Elsa Petersen-Schepelern : photography by
William Lingwood
        p. cm.
        title: Sticks and skewers.
        ISBN 0-7370-2034-2 (hardcover)
        1. Skewer cookery. I. Title: Sticks and skewers. II. Title.

    TX834 .P48 2000
    641.7'6--dc21   99-040074

First published in the United Kingdom in 2000 by
Ryland Peters & Small, 51–55 Mortimer Street, London W1N 7TD

Books produced by Time-Life Custom Publishing are available at a special bulk discount for promotional and premium use. Custom adaptations can also be created to meet your specific marketing goals. Call 1-800-323-5255.

Acknowledgments

Particular thanks to Shona Adhikari and Chef Manjit Gil of Delhi's Bokhara Restaurant in the Maurya Sheraton Hotel for unlocking the secrets of successful tandoori cooking. My thanks to my sister Kirsten and to my nephews Peter Bray and Luc Votan (for his expert advice on Vietnamese food). Thanks also to Helen, Bridget, and Norah for beautiful props and delicious food styling, to Paul Tilby for his splendid design (as usual), and to William Lingwood for his wonderful photographs.

Notes

All spoon measurements are level unless otherwise stated.

Barbecues, ovens, and broilers should be heated to the required temperature before adding the food.

Specialty Asian ingredients are available in large supermarkets, Thai, Chinese, Japanese, and Vietnamese shops, as well as Asian stores.

Designer Paul Tilby
Food Editor Elsa Petersen-Schepelern
Editor Maddalena Bastianelli
Production Patricia Harrington

Food Stylist Bridget Sargeson
Stylist Helen Trent

CONTENTS

SATAYS, BROCHETTES, KABOBS, and SPIEDINI

Around the world, cooks and chefs have devised interesting and delicious ways to prepare foods to be cooked on skewers. It makes a small quantity go a long way—and allows marinades and other flavorings to penetrate further into the main ingredients. (All those toasty barbecued edges are a bonus.)

Cher's character in the movie *Mermaids* must be the patron saint of food on sticks. She was incapable of serving ordinary food—instead, piling amazing concoctions of multiple ingredients on skewers. However I think the fewer ingredients on a stick, the better. Each one cooks at a different rate, so my idea of hell is to have well-cooked meat interspersed with half-raw bell peppers and onions—or the opposite; perfectly cooked vegetables and meat burnt to a cinder. But, if you must mix them, partially cook firm ingredients before threading and use just a few kinds.

When you've threaded the skewers, you can leave them, covered with marinade and foil or a lid, for an hour or two in the refrigerator. Acidic ingredients such as vinegar, tomatoes, or lemon juice will help preserve the food a little, as well as tenderizing and flavoring it. (But don't wait around—cook the skewers as quickly as possible!)

Preparing your barbecue   If you're cooking on a barbecue (a traditional stick-cooking method) take care to prepare it properly. Methods vary, according to the kind of barbecue, but in general, before you start to cook, the coals should be ash-grey, radiating heat with no flame visible, otherwise the food will be charcoal outside and raw inside. Start the fire 30–45 minutes before you plan to cook. To make sure that food, especially chicken and pork, is well cooked, space the pieces well apart on the stick—or, if you like rare beef or lamb, clump the chunks together.

Preparing the skewers   If using wooden skewers, always soak them in water for at least 30 minutes first, to stop them bursting into flames.

Other cooking methods   If you don't have a barbecue, you can still skewer! A broiler, stovetop grill pan (sometimes called a griddle), or an oven will all work well—just heat them to grilling speed first.

As a true pumpkin aficionado, I am picky about my pumpkins. I don't approve of the watery-fleshed kind with orange skins. It has to be blue-grey or dark green for me, having been brought up with an Australian variety called the Queensland Blue. This type has a good, firm texture, suitable for skewering, plus wonderful taste and brilliant color.

PUMPKIN, SWEET POTATO,
and SWEET PEPPER KABOBS

2 ORANGE OR RED BELL PEPPERS, HALVED AND SEEDED

1 lb. PEELED AND SEEDED FIRM-FLESHED PUMPKIN (4 cups, CUBED)

1 lb. PEELED ORANGE SWEET POTATO (ABOUT 2–3 SMALL)

OLIVE OIL OR MUSTARD OIL, FOR BRUSHING

BLACK SEEDS, LIGHTLY BRUISED, FROM 6 GREEN CARDAMOM PODS (OPTIONAL)

SEA SALT AND FRESHLY GROUND BLACK PEPPER

About 8 metal or bamboo skewers (if bamboo, soak in water for 30 minutes)

SERVES 4

Preheat the broiler. Broil the halved peppers, skin-side up, until the skin blisters, then put in a saucepan and cover tightly. Let steam for 10 minutes, then scrape off the skin. Cut the peppers into 1-inch squares and the pumpkin and sweet potato into 1-inch cubes, then thread them alternately onto the skewers.

Light an outdoor grill or preheat the broiler. Brush the vegetables with olive oil or mustard oil and grill or broil for 15 minutes or until cooked through and browned at the edges. (Halfway through the cooking time, sprinkle with the cardamom seeds, if using.) Test for tenderness and cook for 5 minutes longer if necessary*.

Serve with meat or poultry or, for vegetarians, on a bed of beans.

Note: To save time, the pumpkin and sweet potato may be parboiled for 5 minutes before threading.

VEGETABLES

EGGPLANT and CHEESE BROCHETTES
with TOMATO and ROSEMARY SALSA

It's very important to cook eggplants properly and, since they will take longer to cook than the cheese, they should be partially cooked before threading. Baby eggplants, unlike some of the modern hothouse varieties, still retain the tendency to bitterness and should be salted before cooking. You should slice them, sprinkle with salt, and set aside for about 30 minutes. Rinse and pat dry before cooking. Salting vegetables like eggplants, cucumbers, and zucchini also removes some of the water, softens the flesh and intensifies the flavor. Choose a cheese that doesn't melt easily, like Italian provolone. My favorite is Greek haloumi cheese, but it is almost impossible to find in the US.

Using a mandoline or sharp knife, slice the eggplants thinly lengthwise. Salt, rinse, and pat dry as described in the recipe introduction. Preheat a stovetop grill pan, brush with oil, add the eggplant slices, and grill on both sides until almost completely cooked, pressing down with a spatula as you do, so the flesh is marked in lines.

Remove and cool a little. Do the same to the slices of cheese, browning them on all sides. Cut into 1-inch squares, thread onto skewers, threading the eggplant zig-zag fashion around the cheese.

Mix the honey with the lime juice and salt and brush the brochettes on all sides. Cook until the edges are crisp.

Mix the salsa ingredients together and serve with the skewers and yogurt, if using.

8 BABY EGGPLANTS OR 2 LONG, THIN EGGPLANTS

OLIVE OIL, FOR BRUSHING

8 oz. NON-MELTING CHEESE, SUCH AS PROVOLONE OR FARMER'S CHEESE (OR GREEK HALOUMI OR INDIAN PANEER IF AVAILABLE), CUT INTO ½-INCH SLICES

3 tablespoons HONEY, WARMED

FRESHLY SQUEEZED JUICE OF 3 LIMES

SEA SALT AND FRESHLY GROUND BLACK PEPPER

1 cup PLAIN YOGURT, TO SERVE (OPTIONAL)

TOMATO AND ROSEMARY SALSA

4 MEDIUM TOMATOES, COARSELY CHOPPED

1 tablespoon CHOPPED FRESH ROSEMARY LEAVES, PLUS 4 SMALL SPRIGS, TO SERVE

8 metal or bamboo skewers (if bamboo, soak in water for at least 30 minutes)

SERVES 4

20–24 BABY POTATOES, ABOUT 1 inch IN DIAMETER

4–8 SPRIGS OF ROSEMARY, ABOUT 6 inches LONG

OLIVE OIL, FOR BRUSHING

SEA SALT AND FRESHLY GROUND BLACK PEPPER

1 metal kabob skewer

strips of foil for wrapping leaves

SERVES 4

Wash the potatoes well, then spin them dry in a salad spinner (this will roughen the surface, giving a more crunchy exterior).

Parboil the potatoes in salted water for 10 minutes. Drain, plunge into cold water, then pierce through with a metal skewer.

Trim the rosemary sprigs so the woody part is smooth and just a few leaves remain attached at the end. Wrap the leaves in a twist of foil.

Light an outdoor grill or preheat a broiler. Remove the skewer and replace with a trimmed rosemary sprig, threading 3–5 potatoes on each one.* Brush with oil, sprinkle with salt and pepper, and grill or broil for 10–15 minutes, turning once, or until cooked through and well browned.

*__Note:__ *The sticks can be prepared ahead to this point.*

ITALIAN POTATOES
on ROSEMARY STICKS

Woody herbs like bay and rosemary can be used as skewers for meats and vegetables, giving gorgeous flavor to the whole dish. They are especially good with lamb, the natural companion for rosemary.

GRILLED SUGAR-GLAZED CHERRY TOMATOES
with HERB DRIZZLE

These tomatoes are wonderful with meats like pork, but even better on their own, crushed into a split baguette, with lots of arugula leaves.

20 CHERRY TOMATOES

1 tablespoon SUGAR

3 tablespoons VIRGIN OLIVE OIL

¼ cup CHOPPED FRESH OREGANO

SEA SALT AND FRESHLY GROUND BLACK PEPPER

TO SERVE

4 SMALL BAGUETTES, SPLIT LENGTHWISE

¼ cup FRESHLY GRATED PARMESAN CHEESE

WILD ARUGULA LEAVES

4 wooden skewers, soaked in water for at least 30 minutes

SERVES 4

Light an outdoor grill or preheat a broiler. Thread the tomatoes onto 4 soaked wooden skewers. Melt the sugar and oil in a saucepan and stir in the oregano, salt, and pepper.

Brush the skewers with the sugar-herb oil. Grill or broil for 10 minutes or until the tomatoes are hot and the skin blistered.

Serve with meats or in split baguettes with Parmesan, arugula, and a little of the sugar-herb oil.

MEDITERRANEAN VEGETABLE SKEWERS
with GARLIC and HERBS

I have always been worried about skewers threaded with meat and vegetables together. They cook at different speeds, so something is always bound to be badly cooked. I like to cook the vegetables on separate skewers, and partially cook the difficult ones first, like pepper and onion (and the bacon too), until almost tender.

OLIVE OIL, FOR BRUSHING

1 LARGE ONION, QUARTERED LENGTHWISE THEN SEPARATED INTO PETALS

1 RED OR YELLOW BELL PEPPER, HALVED AND SEEDED

4 GARLIC CLOVES, HALVED

4 SLICES BACON OR SMOKED PANCETTA, CUT INTO 1-INCH SQUARES

12 MUSHROOMS, 1 inch IN DIAMETER

¼ cup CHOPPED FRESH TARRAGON, PARSLEY OR ROSEMARY

6 MEDIUM PLUM TOMATOES, HALVED AND SEEDED

8 FRESH BAY LEAVES

SEA SALT AND FRESHLY GROUND BLACK PEPPER

4 metal or long bamboo skewers (if bamboo, soak in water for 30 minutes)

SERVES 4

Preheat the boiler. Brush a heavy-bottom skillet with the oil, add the onions, and sauté gently until softened and lightly browned. Remove to a plate. Put the pepper halves under the broiler and cook until the skins char. Transfer to a saucepan, cover, and let steam for 10 minutes. Add the garlic and bacon or pancetta to the skillet and cook until the bacon is lightly browned. Remove the bacon to the plate. Add the mushrooms to the skillet and sauté until lightly browned. Transfer the mushrooms to the plate and let cool a little. Leave the garlic in the skillet.

Scrape the blistered skin off the peppers and cut the flesh into squares. Save any pepper juices and add to the skillet with 1 tablespoon olive oil and the chopped herbs and garlic. Keep warm so the herbs and garlic infuse the oil.

Thread the mushrooms, tomato halves, onion petals, garlic pieces, bay leaves, bacon, and pepper squares onto metal or soaked bamboo skewers. Brush with the oil and sprinkle with salt and freshly ground pepper. The dish can be prepared ahead to this point.

Light an outdoor grill or preheat a stovetop grill pan or broiler. Grill or broil the skewers until toasty and brown on all sides, 5–10 minutes, or until tender.

Remove to a serving platter and drizzle with the herbed oil mixture. Serve with roasted or grilled meats or bean dishes, or in split baguettes or pita breads.

CHILI SHRIMP BROCHETTES

Grilling shrimp in their shells produces absolutely amazing flavor. Threading them onto skewers means you can turn the shrimp easily without burning yourself. A hands-on dish!

12 LARGE UNCOOKED SHRIMP
OR 20 MEDIUM-SIZED

3–5 SCALLIONS, HALVED LENGTHWISE
AND BLANCHED FOR 1 MINUTE IN
BOILING WATER (OPTIONAL)

CHILI LIME MARINADE

4 RED CHILIES, SEEDED AND CHOPPED

2–4 GARLIC CLOVES, CRUSHED

¼ cup CORN OR PEANUT OIL

GRATED ZEST AND JUICE OF 3 LIMES

SEA SALT FLAKES

BREADCRUMBS, TOASTED IN A DRY
SKILLET (OPTIONAL)

*12–20 bamboo skewers, soaked in water
for at least 30 minutes*

SERVES 4

Push a toothpick into the neck of each shrimp between head and shell and carefully hook out the black vein. Alternatively, cut down the back shell and draw out the vein. If preferred, remove the legs. You can also shell the shrimp completely if you like.

To make the marinade, crush the chilies, garlic, and salt using a fork or mortar and pestle. Put in a wide dish, add the oil, lime zest and juice, and breadcrumbs, if using, and mix well. Put the shrimp into the chili mixture, pressing it into the backs if they have been cut. Marinate for up to 30 minutes if time allows.

Light an outdoor grill or preheat a broiler or stovetop grill pan. For each shrimp, insert a soaked bamboo skewer from the head end, pushing out the point where the back starts to curve. Tie the tail close to the chest with a blanched scallion leaf, if using. Brush with marinade and grill or broil for 3–5 minutes on each side until the shells are brown and crispy and the flesh opaque.

FISH and SEAFOOD

To make the Chili Onion Marmalade, put the onions, oil, bay leaf, chilies, if using, and sugar in a wide, heavy-based skillet over a moderate heat. Cover and simmer over a low heat for about 15 minutes until the onions begin to soften (a pinch of salt will help the process). Stir every few minutes. Remove the lid, then add the vinegar, crème de cassis, and allspice, if using. Cook gently, without stirring, until the onions have become translucent, about 15–20 minutes more. Remove, cool, and transfer to a lidded container until ready to use. The marmalade will keep in the refrigerator for 1–2 days.

Light an outdoor grill or preheat a broiler or stovetop grill pan. Trim the scallops if necessary and cut any large ones in half crosswise to make 2 disks. Heat the oil in a skillet, add the scallion pieces and pancetta, and cook briefly on both sides until part-cooked but not crisp. Cool slightly.

Put a piece of scallion on top of a scallop and wrap with a piece of pancetta. Secure with a soaked bamboo skewer, piercing the scallop through the diameter of the disk, if possible, so it will cook flat.

Broil the scallops under a hot broiler or over a medium charcoal fire until the scallops are opaque and the onions and bacon lightly browned at the edges. Do not overcook or the scallops will shrink and be tough.

Put the dressing ingredients in a wide, shallow bowl and beat with a fork. Add the salad leaves and toss to coat.

To serve, put small piles of leaves on 4 plates, add a spoonful of Chili Onion Marmalade, and divide the kabobs between the plates. Sprinkle with pepper and, if you like, drizzle a little dressing over each scallop before serving.

Scallops and bacon are a surprisingly delicious marriage of flavors. The Chili Onion Marmalade is very good (omit the chili if you like) and can be served with other recipes in this book.

SCALLOP and BACON KABOBS
with CHILI ONION MARMALADE

CHILI ONION MARMALADE

2 lb. ONIONS, ABOUT 6 MEDIUM, FINELY SLICED

¼ cup OLIVE OIL

1 FRESH BAY LEAF

4 LARGE CHILIES, SEEDED AND FINELY SLICED (OPTIONAL)

1 tablespoon SUGAR

A PINCH OF SALT (OPTIONAL)

1 tablespoon RED WINE VINEGAR

1 tablespoon CRÈME DE CASSIS (OPTIONAL)

¼ teaspoon GROUND ALLSPICE (OPTIONAL)

SCALLOPS

12 MEDIUM SCALLOPS OR 8 LARGE

1 tablespoon OLIVE OIL

5–6 SCALLIONS, CUT INTO 1-inch LENGTHS

4–8 SLICES SMOKED PANCETTA

FRESHLY GROUND BLACK PEPPER

ARUGULA, BABY FRISÉE, AND OTHER SALAD LEAVES, TO SERVE

LIGHT DRESSING

2 tablespoons OLIVE OIL

1 teaspoon WHITE RICE VINEGAR

1 tablespoon CHOPPED FRESH FLATLEAF PARSLEY

SEA SALT AND FRESHLY GROUND BLACK PEPPER

12–16 bamboo skewers, soaked in water for at least 30 minutes

SERVES 4

Wash the fish, pat dry, and make 2–3 deep slashes into the thickest part on each side, cutting through to the bone. This will help the marinades penetrate the flesh.

Put 4 cups water in a flat-bottomed container, add the ingredients for the first marinade, and stir. Add the fish and press down until well covered. Set aside for 30 minutes. (Indian cooks do not like very fishy flavors, so the first marination is designed to remove those flavors and to make the fish taste fresh and clean.)

To prepare the second marinade, put a layer of damp cheesecloth in a strainer, add the yogurt, and set aside for 15 minutes to drain. (If you use thick yogurt, you can omit this step.) Put the strained yogurt into a bowl, beat in the egg yolk, then all the other ingredients.

Remove the fish from the first marinade and press with your fingers to wring out the liquid. Rub the yogurt mixture all over the fish, pressing into the slashes in the sides. Cover and set aside to marinate in the refrigerator for 1 hour.

Preheat the oven to 400°F, or the broiler, or light an outdoor grill. Push a long metal skewer into each fish, from head to tail. Cook for 8 minutes. Remove from the heat and put in a heatproof bowl, pointed end down, for 3 minutes to let the moisture drip away. Baste with melted butter or ghee and cook for 3 minutes more, or until done.

Remove from the heat and serve with salad leaves, chunks of lemon or lime, and finely sliced onion (cut it lengthwise through the root for the authentic Indian look).

TANDOORI BARBECUED FISH

Chef Manjit Gil, from Delhi's famous Bokhara Restaurant, is perhaps the world's finest Indian chef. He says the secret to successful tandoor cooking is to cook the food in two stages, letting the meat or fish drain before the final stage.

4 WHOLE FISH SUCH AS SNAPPER OR POMFRET, ABOUT 1 lb. EACH, SCALED, CLEANED, WITH FINS TRIMMED

¼ cup MELTED BUTTER OR GHEE

FIRST MARINADE

2 tablespoons SALT

¼ cup WHITE MALT OR RICE VINEGAR

2 tablespoons LEMON JUICE

SECOND MARINADE

⅓ cup PLAIN YOGURT

1 EGG YOLK

1 inch FRESH GINGER, PEELED AND GRATED

3 GARLIC CLOVES, CRUSHED

1 teaspoon AJWAIN (LOVAGE SEED) OR CELERY SEED (OPTIONAL)

1 tablespoon GROUND RED PEPPER

2 teaspoons GROUND TURMERIC

1 teaspoon SALT

1 teaspoon GARAM MASALA OR CUMIN

1 tablespoon GRAM FLOUR (CHICKPEA FLOUR) OR CORNSTARCH

¼ cup LIGHT CREAM

TO SERVE

FRESH SALAD LEAVES

4 LEMONS OR LIMES, CUT IN CHUNKS

1 RED ONION, SLICED LENGTHWISE

4 long metal kabob skewers

SERVES 4

Monkfish is a firm-fleshed fish, which can take rough treatment such as barbecuing. But, like all fish, cook it just long enough for the flesh to become opaque. A smoky pancetta-style bacon will help hold it together and give extra pizzazz to its rather mild flavor. The sauce is gorgeous with many fish dishes.

MONKFISH BROCHETTES
with LEMON SOY BUTTER

LEMON SOY BUTTER

¼ cup UNSALTED BUTTER

1 tablespoon SAKE OR VODKA

JUICE OF 1 LEMON

1 tablespoon TAMARI SOY SAUCE

1 inch FRESH GINGER, PEELED AND SLICED

2 GARLIC CLOVES, CRUSHED

MONKFISH BROCHETTES

¼ cup SUNFLOWER OR PEANUT OIL

8 THIN SLICES SMOKED PANCETTA, HALVED CROSSWISE

1 lb. MONKFISH FILLETS

FRESH BAY LEAVES, HALVED LENGTHWISE (OPTIONAL)

TO SERVE

BABY SALAD LEAVES

BOILED NEW POTATOES

about 8 metal or bamboo skewers (if bamboo, soak in water for 30 minutes)

SERVES 4

Light an outdoor grill or preheat a broiler or stovetop grill pan. Put the Lemon Soy Butter ingredients in a small pan and heat until frothing and well mixed.

Heat the oil in a skillet, add the pancetta, and sauté gently until cooked but not crisp. Cool.

Cut the monkfish into 1½-inch cubes. Brush with some of the oil, then wrap each cube in a piece of bacon. Thread the packages onto the skewers, alternating with pieces of bay leaf, if using.

Broil the brochettes under a hot broiler or over a hot fire, turning them over after 1–2 minutes, until the bacon is crispy and the fish just cooked, about 3 minutes in all. No longer, or the fish will overcook.

Serve the fish on a pile of baby salad leaves with the Lemon Soy Butter strained over the top and boiled new potatoes on the side.

FRESH TUNA SPIEDINI
with LEMON WEDGES, BAY LEAVES, and CRACKED PEPPER

Make this chunky Mediterranean dish with tuna, swordfish, or salmon, all of which have assertive flavors, strong enough to flourish with bay leaves and lemon. Tuna and salmon are best cooked slightly pink in the middle.

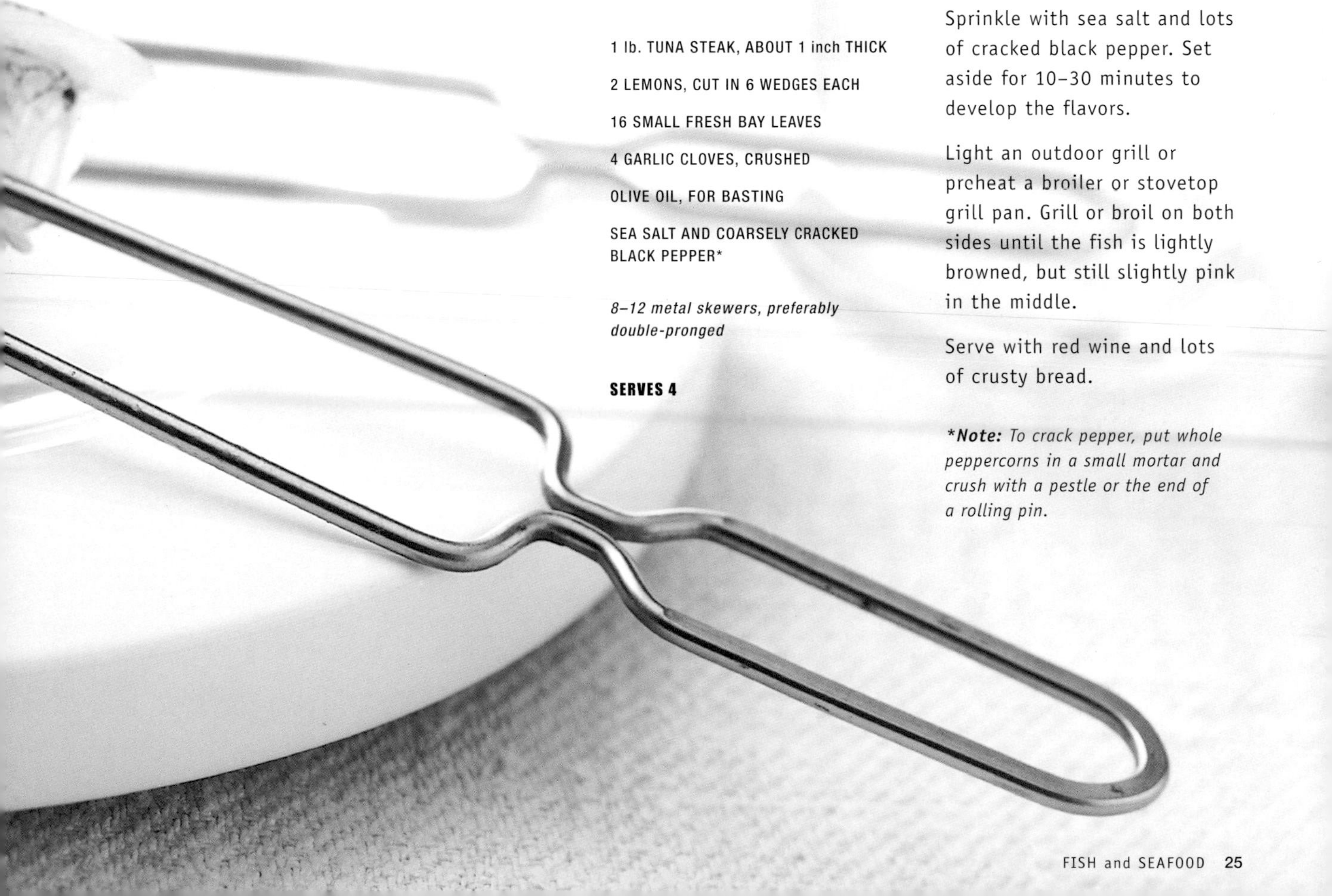

1 lb. TUNA STEAK, ABOUT 1 inch THICK

2 LEMONS, CUT IN 6 WEDGES EACH

16 SMALL FRESH BAY LEAVES

4 GARLIC CLOVES, CRUSHED

OLIVE OIL, FOR BASTING

SEA SALT AND COARSELY CRACKED BLACK PEPPER*

8–12 metal skewers, preferably double-pronged

SERVES 4

Cut the tuna steaks into cubes. Onto each skewer, thread 1 wedge of lemon, 2 bay leaves, and 2 chunks of tuna.

Mix the garlic and oil in a bowl and brush over the skewers. Sprinkle with sea salt and lots of cracked black pepper. Set aside for 10–30 minutes to develop the flavors.

Light an outdoor grill or preheat a broiler or stovetop grill pan. Grill or broil on both sides until the fish is lightly browned, but still slightly pink in the middle.

Serve with red wine and lots of crusty bread.

***Note:** To crack pepper, put whole peppercorns in a small mortar and crush with a pestle or the end of a rolling pin.*

This mixture can be cooked on other kinds of skewers, but lemongrass gives delicious flavor. Thai spice pastes can be bought ready-made, but if you can't find them, use the recipe given here.

LEMONGRASS STICKS

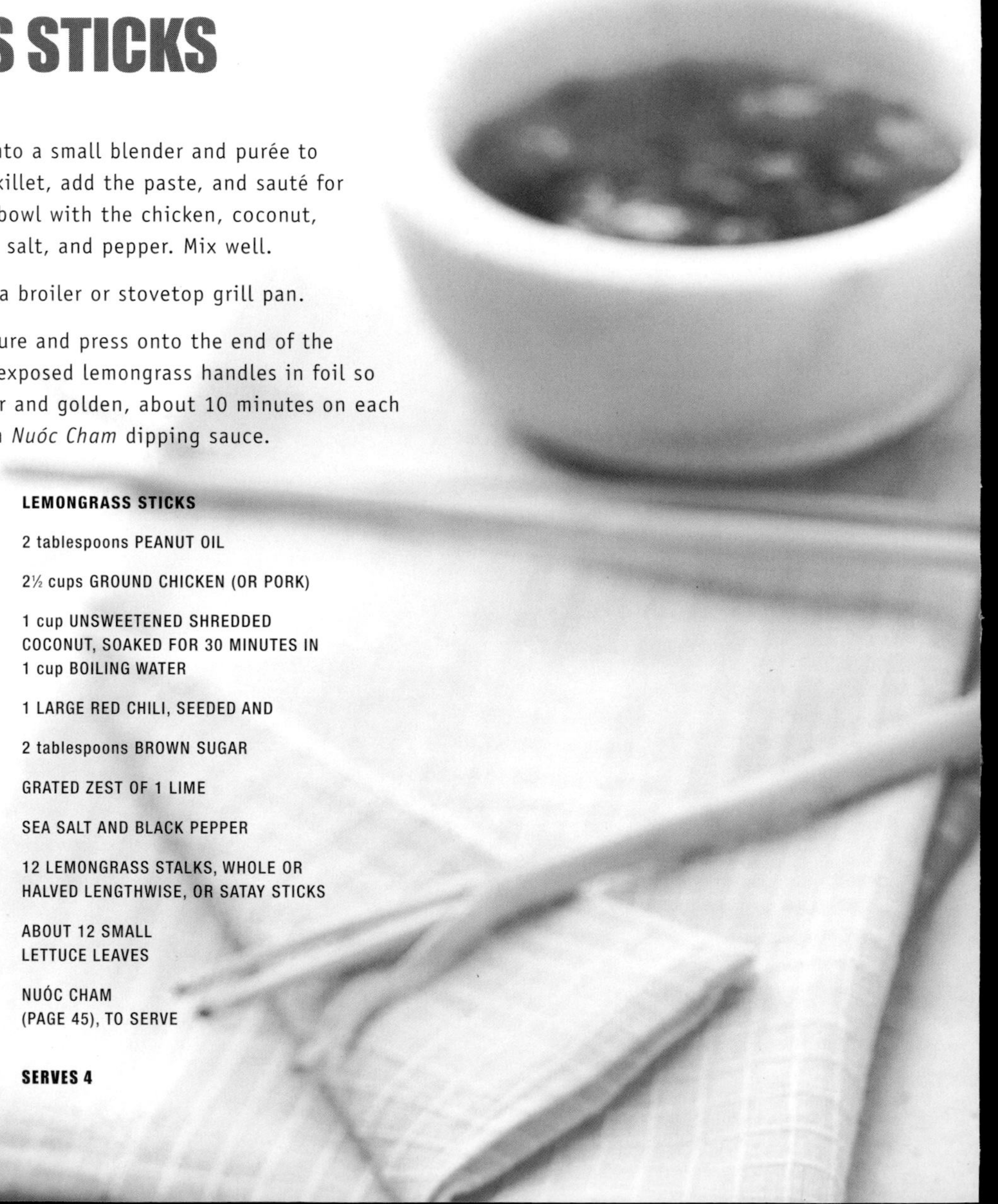

Put the spice paste ingredients into a small blender and purée to a paste. Heat the oil in a small skillet, add the paste, and sauté for 5 minutes. Cool, then put into a bowl with the chicken, coconut, chopped chilies, sugar, lime zest, salt, and pepper. Mix well.

Light an outdoor grill or preheat a broiler or stovetop grill pan.

Take 1–2 tablespoons of the mixture and press onto the end of the lemongrass or skewers. Wrap the exposed lemongrass handles in foil so they don't burn. Cook until tender and golden, about 10 minutes on each side. Serve in lettuce leaves, with *Nuóc Cham* dipping sauce.

SPICE PASTE

1 SHALLOT OR SMALL ONION, SLICED

6 GARLIC CLOVES, SLICED

2 RED CHILIES, SEEDED AND SLICED

1 inch FRESH GINGER, PEELED AND CHOPPED

1 teaspoon GROUND TURMERIC

2 teaspoons CORIANDER SEEDS, CRUSHED

1 teaspoon BLACK PEPPERCORNS, CRUSHED

6 ALMONDS, CRUSHED

1 tablespoon FISH SAUCE (OR SOY)

2 WHOLE CLOVES, CRUSHED

LEMONGRASS STICKS

2 tablespoons PEANUT OIL

2½ cups GROUND CHICKEN (OR PORK)

1 cup UNSWEETENED SHREDDED COCONUT, SOAKED FOR 30 MINUTES IN 1 cup BOILING WATER

1 LARGE RED CHILI, SEEDED AND

2 tablespoons BROWN SUGAR

GRATED ZEST OF 1 LIME

SEA SALT AND BLACK PEPPER

12 LEMONGRASS STALKS, WHOLE OR HALVED LENGTHWISE, OR SATAY STICKS

ABOUT 12 SMALL LETTUCE LEAVES

NUÓC CHAM (PAGE 45), TO SERVE

SERVES 4

POULTRY

Put all the yakitori sauce ingredients in a saucepan, stir, bring to a boil, boil hard for 3–5 minutes, then remove from the heat.

Light an outdoor grill or preheat a broiler or stovetop grill pan. Broil the halved peppers until the skin blisters, then put in a saucepan and cover tightly. Let steam for 10 minutes, then scrape off the skin. Cut the peppers into 1-inch square pieces.

Grill or blanch the leeks or scallions, then cut into 1-inch sections. Thread 2 quail eggs onto 6 skewers and 2 mushrooms on another 6, with scallion tops interspersed. Set aside.

Thread 8 skewers with chicken, pepper squares, and leek or scallion. Grill all the skewers over a very hot fire or under a very hot broiler (put the skewers as close to the heat as possible). Cook for 2 minutes on each side until the juices begin to flow, then transfer to the saucepan of sauce, sticks upward.

Remove and cook for 1 minute on each side, then dip into the sauce again. Each time you dip, let excess sauce run off back into the pan. Cook again, until tender but not dried out.

Remove to a serving platter and serve sprinkled with pepper.

Though yakitori is traditionally made with green peppers, I prefer ripe ones, so use red or yellow instead. My supermarket sells a long, pointed kind, about 10 inches long, which are easy to peel. Many people don't precook the vegetables, but the meat cooks long before they do, so I think it's important to give them a head-start. You can buy yakitori sauce from the supermarket, but homemade is better.

YAKITORI CHICKEN

YAKITORI SAUCE

½ cup SAKE OR VODKA

⅔ cup DARK SOY SAUCE

3 tablespoons MIRIN (SWEET RICE WINE) OR SHERRY

2 tablespoons SUGAR

CHICKEN SKEWERS

4 LARGE RED OR YELLOW PEPPERS, HALVED AND SEEDED

8 BABY LEEKS OR 12 SCALLIONS, HALVED LENGTHWISE AND BLANCHED

8–12 BONED CHICKEN THIGHS, EACH CUT INTO 3 (ABOUT 1-inch CUBES)

FRESHLY GROUND BLACK PEPPER OR JAPANESE PEPPER

VEGETARIAN ALTERNATIVES

12 HARD-COOKED QUAIL EGGS, SHELLED

12 CLOSE-CAPPED MUSHROOMS, ABOUT 1-inch DIAMETER

about 20 wooden or bamboo satay sticks, soaked in water for 30 minutes

SERVES 4

SCALLION CHICKEN SKEWERS

I think chicken thighs have more flavor than breasts. Use them for this simple, quick and easy Korean kabob.

Thread 1 piece of chicken and 1 piece of scallion onto each skewer. Mix the marinade ingredients together in a flat, shallow dish. Add the skewers and turn to coat.

Cover and chill for 3 hours or overnight, turning in the marinade from time to time.

Light an outdoor grill or preheat a broiler. Cook for about 5 minutes on each side or until done.

Variations

Beef is also good cooked in the same way. Cut 1 lb. beefsteak into narrow strips, then thread one end of each strip onto a soaked bamboo skewer, alternately with the scallions. If you like, add a splash of sake to the marinade. Marinate as in the main recipe, then cook until the meat is as rare or well-done as you prefer.

Prepare scallops in the same way, but omit the scallion. Cook for a shorter time, just until the scallops become opaque, or they will shrink and become tough.

*Note: To make ginger purée, break fresh ginger into large pieces and soak in a bowl of water for about 30 minutes. Peel and purée in a blender, adding a splash of water if necessary. Freeze in ice cube trays and use from frozen. One cube equals about 1 tablespoon purée.

8–12 CHICKEN THIGHS, SKINNED AND BONED, CUT INTO 3–4 PIECES EACH

ABOUT 12 SCALLIONS, CUT INTO 1-inch PIECES

GINGER MARINADE

2 GARLIC CLOVES, CRUSHED

2 tablespoons GINGER PURÉE* OR GRATED FRESH GINGER

ABOUT ¼ cup FISH SAUCE OR SOY SAUCE

1 tablespoon SESAME OIL

1 tablespoon SESAME SEEDS, TOASTED IN A DRY SKILLET

1 tablespoon SUGAR

1 tablespoon CORN OIL

24–36 wooden or bamboo satay sticks, soaked in water for 30 minutes

SERVES 4

SPATCHCOCKED CHICKEN
with ROASTED GARLIC, POTATOES, and ONIONS

Spatchcocking—splitting a bird down the back then pressing it flat—produces a delicious, crisp dish with lots of flavor. People love eating this dish with their fingers, so provide lots of paper napkins or hot towels.

4 POUSSINS OR CORNISH GAME HENS

2 teaspoons SEA SALT

2 tablespoons PAPRIKA

OLIVE OIL (SEE METHOD)

4 SPRIGS OF THYME

4 WHOLE HEADS OF GARLIC, TOPS SLICED OFF

12 SMALL RED POTATOES

2–3 RED ONIONS, CUT INTO WEDGES

8 flat metal kabob skewers

SERVES 4

Put the birds on a board, cut each one down either side of the backbone, then remove and discard it. Open out the carcasses, pressing down hard on the joints with the flat of your hand until they crack out flat. Fold the legs and wings close to the body. To keep the birds flat, thread 2 skewers crosswise, running diagonally from the drumstick, through the breast, then the wing. Mix the salt with the paprika.

Put the birds, skin-side up, in a large roasting pan, brush with olive oil, and sprinkle with the salt mixture. Add the thyme, garlic heads, potatoes, and onion wedges and drizzle generously with oil. The dish can be prepared ahead to this point and kept in the refrigerator ready for last-minute cooking.

Preheat the oven to 400°F. Put the pan in the oven and roast for 15 minutes. Turn the birds over, reduce the heat to 375°F, and continue cooking for 15 minutes more. Turn them over again and cook until done, with crisp crunchy edges, about 45 minutes to 1 hour in total. Test with the point of another skewer—the juices should run clear with no trace of pink.

Serve the birds and vegetables on a large platter.

TANDOORI CHICKEN

This delicious, authentic tandoori chicken was taught to me by Chef Manjit Gil, responsible for the Northwest Frontier cooking in Delhi's splendid Bokhara restaurant. Color in all things has great significance in India, and though tandooris are often a lurid red or yellow, modern chefs, in India and the West, now avoid food colorings. Tandoori dishes are cooked on skewers, but these are removed before serving in a restaurant. If you cook them in small quantities, they can be served on the skewers instead.

Cut the chicken into pieces about 1 x 1½ inches. Pat dry. To make the first marinade, put the salt, ginger, garlic, and vinegar in a bowl. Stir well, add the chicken, stir, and set aside for 15 minutes.

Put the cheese, egg, chopped chilies, cilantro, cornstarch, and half the cream in a blender or food processor and pulse to mix.

Remove the chicken from the first marinade and squeeze gently to remove excess moisture. Put into a clean bowl and add the second marinade. Turn in the mixture and massage it in with your fingers. Stir in the remaining cream and set aside for 30 minutes. Light an outdoor grill, preheat a broiler, or preheat the oven to 400°F.

Fold the chicken pieces in half and thread onto the ends of soaked wooden skewers, 2–3 pieces per skewer. Cook for about 8 minutes until half-cooked. (If cooking in the oven, put a tray on the shelf underneath to collect the drippings.)

Remove the skewers from the heat and set them upright in a bowl for 5 minutes so excess moisture can drain away.

Remove the chicken pieces from the skewers, unfold them, and re-thread them flat, leaving a gap between the pieces. Baste with melted butter or oil and return to the heat until done, about 8 minutes. Sprinkle with the juice of 1 lemon and serve with finely sliced onions (you can salt them first to soften), the remaining lemon, cut in wedges, and torn salad leaves.

1½ lb. BONELESS, SKINLESS CHICKEN

MELTED BUTTER OR OIL, FOR BRUSHING

FIRST MARINADE

1 tablespoon SALT

1 inch FRESH GINGER, PEELED AND GRATED

3 GARLIC CLOVES, CRUSHED

2 tablespoons WHITE MALT OR RICE VINEGAR

SECOND MARINADE

⅓ cup GRATED PROCESSED CHEESE OR MILD MONTEREY JACK

1 SMALL EGG, BEATEN

4 GREEN CHILIES, SEEDED AND CHOPPED

1 LARGE BUNCH FRESH CILANTRO, CHOPPED (ABOUT ½ oz.)

1 tablespoon CORNSTARCH

3 tablespoons LIGHT CREAM

TO SERVE

2 LEMONS

FINELY SLICED RED ONIONS

SALAD LEAVES

8 long wooden or bamboo skewers, soaked in water for 30 minutes

SERVES 4

Thais do the world's best stick food. From the finest restaurant to the simplest street hawker's stall, they seem incapable of turning out anything but great food.

THAI CHICKEN SATAYS

Thread the chicken strips, zig-zag fashion, onto soaked satay sticks. Mix the marinade ingredients in a bowl, add the sticks, turning them until well coated. Chill for 1 hour, turning occasionally.

To make the sauce, put the peanuts, if using, in a dry skillet and toast until light brown. Crush coarsely and reserve. Soak the dried chilies in boiling water for 30 minutes, then transfer to a spice mill (clean coffee grinder) or blender and add the shallots or onion, garlic, almonds, and lemongrass or lemon juice. Work to a paste.

Heat the corn oil in a wok or skillet, add the chili mixture, and sauté gently for 5 minutes, stirring several times. Add the coconut milk and simmer, stirring constantly (keep stirring, and don't cover the pan, or the coconut milk will curdle). Add the tamarind paste or lime juice, sugar, salt, and peanuts or peanut butter. Simmer for about 2 minutes, then cool a little and serve in a bowl, topped with cilantro leaves.

Light an outdoor grill or preheat a broiler. Remove the chicken satays from the marinade and cook for 2 minutes on each side, or until cooked through and lightly browned at the edges.

Note: *If the sauce sits for any length of time, you may need to thin it a little with hot water before serving.*

4 LARGE BONELESS CHICKEN BREASTS, SKINNED AND CUT CROSSWISE INTO ¼–½-inch STRIPS

3 tablespoons CORN OIL

COCONUT MARINADE

2 tablespoons THAI 7-SPICE OR 1 tablespoon CHINESE 5-SPICE

1 tablespoon BROWN SUGAR

1 tablespoon LIME JUICE

1 inch FRESH GINGER, PEELED AND GRATED

1 tablespoon FISH SAUCE

½ cup CANNED COCONUT MILK

SATAY SAUCE

½ cup UNSALTED PEANUTS OR PEANUT BUTTER

5 DRIED RED CHILIES

8 SMALL SHALLOTS OR 1 MILD ONION

1 GARLIC CLOVE, CRUSHED

8 ALMONDS, COARSELY CHOPPED

1 STALK LEMONGRASS, FINELY CHOPPED, OR JUICE OF 1 LEMON

2 tablespoons PEANUT OIL

1 cup CANNED COCONUT MILK

2 teaspoons TAMARIND PASTE OR FRESH LIME JUICE

1 teaspoon BROWN SUGAR

SALT

A FEW CILANTRO LEAVES, CHOPPED, TO SERVE

20 wooden or bamboo satay sticks, soaked in water for 30 minutes

SERVES 4

Satays are popular Southeast Asian snacks, and each country has its favorite accompaniments. *Nuóc Cham* is Vietnamese, satay sauce is Thai, Malay, or Indonesian. (*Satay* means "three".)

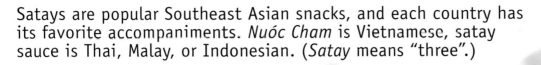

CHICKEN SATAYS
MARINATED in GINGER and TAMARIND

Mix the tamarind marinade ingredients together in a bowl or pitcher.

Cut the chicken into slices, ½ inch wide, then cut those slices into strips, ½ inch wide. Thread them, zig-zag fashion, onto soaked wooden or bamboo skewers. Put the skewers in a shallow dish and pour over the marinade. Set aside for 30 minutes.

Light an outdoor grill or preheat a broiler. When ready to cook, drain the satays, pour the marinade into a saucepan, bring to boiling point, then simmer, stirring, for 15 minutes. Grill or broil the satays until cooked through.

Serve with the hot tamarind marinade and *Nuóc Cham* or Satay Sauce. (A traditional Vietnamese serving treatment is to serve with a "table salad" of shredded carrot, mint and Asian basil leaves, soaked rice noodles, and lettuce leaves for wrapping.)

TAMARIND MARINADE

1 tablespoon GINGER PURÉE (PAGE 30) OR 1 inch FRESH GINGER, PEELED AND GRATED

3 GARLIC CLOVES, CRUSHED

½ cup FISH SAUCE OR SOY SAUCE

2 tablespoons TAMARIND PASTE OR JUICE OF 2 LIMES

⅔ cup CANNED COCONUT MILK

2 tablespoons PEANUT OIL

CHICKEN SATAYS

4 CHICKEN BREASTS, SKINNED AND BONED

NUÓC CHAM (PAGE 45) OR SATAY SAUCE (PAGES 37 OR 53), TO SERVE

12–20 long wooden or bamboo satay sticks, soaked in water for 30 minutes

SERVES 4

I prefer duck breasts with the crispy skin still attached, but feel free to discard it before cooking if you like.

DUCK BREAST SATAYS
with PEPPER LEMON MARINADE

Cut the duck breasts diagonally into strips about ¼ inch wide. Thread onto soaked bamboo sticks or metal skewers. Mix the remaining ingredients together in a bowl, add the skewers, turn to coat, and let marinate for about 30 minutes. Meanwhile, light an outdoor grill or preheat a broiler to a high heat.

When ready to cook, drain the skewers and grill or broil until done to your liking (duck is nicer a little rare). Meanwhile, bring the marinade to the boil, simmer for 5 minutes, then transfer to a dipping bowl. Serve the satays with the dip.

Mediterranean alternative

Brush the duck skewers with red pesto before cooking. Serve as part of a plate of tapas, with a glass of ice-cold sherry.

2 LARGE DUCK BREASTS, WITH OR WITHOUT SKIN

½ cup SWEET SOY SAUCE, SUCH AS INDONESIAN KECAP MANIS

½ teaspoon GROUND CORIANDER

1 teaspoon FRESHLY GROUND BLACK PEPPER

JUICE OF 1 LEMON

2 MEDIUM SHALLOTS, FINELY SLICED

12–20 bamboo satay sticks, soaked in water for 30 minutes, or metal skewers

SERVES 4

CHILI MARINADE

⅔ cup RED WINE

JUICE OF ½ LEMON OR 1 LIME

3 tablespoons OLIVE OIL

1 RED CHILI, SEEDED AND DICED

2 GARLIC CLOVES, CRUSHED

1 ONION, VERY FINELY CHOPPED

1 teaspoon SALT

1 tablespoon SUGAR

1 tablespoon COARSELY CRUSHED BLACK PEPPER

TURKEY KABOBS

²1 lb. TURKEY ESCALOPES

BABY SALAD LEAVES, TO SERVE

PAPAYA SALSA

1 SMALL RIPE PAPAYA, PEELED AND SEEDED

1 RED PEPPER

1 RED CHILI, SEEDED AND DICED

1 tablespoon GRATED FRESH GINGER

6 BABY CORNICHONS (GHERKINS), FINELY SLICED

½ CUP TORN FRESH CILANTRO LEAVES

GRATED ZEST AND JUICE OF 3 LIMES

SEA SALT AND FRESHLY GROUND BLACK PEPPER

8 metal kabob skewers

SERVES 4

A recipe filled with New World flavors. Turkey is a low-fat meat that deserves to be served other than at Christmas and Thanksgiving. The fruity salsa is full of sweet flavors and spicy notes of chili and ginger—serve it also with other dishes in this book. Delicious!

CHILI TURKEY KABOBS
with PAPAYA SALSA

Put the marinade ingredients in a bowl and beat with a fork. Cut the turkey into 1–1½-inch cubes, add to the marinade, cover, and chill overnight.

When ready to cook, drain the turkey and thread onto metal skewers. Put the marinade in a small saucepan and bring to a boil. Simmer for 5 minutes and reserve.

To make the salsa, cut the papaya into ½-inch dice. Peel the pepper with a vegetable peeler (don't worry if you don't get all the peel), then seed and cut into ½-inch dice. Put in a small serving bowl, add the other salsa ingredients, and mix well.

Light an outdoor grill or preheat a broiler to medium hot. Cook the turkey skewers about 3–4 inches from the heat for 3–4 minutes, turning and basting the meat with the reserved marinade, or until the turkey is cooked all the way through.

Serve with a few salad leaves and the salsa. Warmed soft flour tortillas would also be a delicious accompaniment.

SINGAPORE PORK SATAYS

In Southeast Asia, satays are served as snacks, or with other dishes as part of a meal, not as an entrée. For a party or barbecue, prepare a selection of different satays and sauces and serve them all together.

2 lb. BONELESS PORK LOIN

1 tablespoon CORIANDER SEEDS

½ teaspoon GROUND TURMERIC

1 teaspoon SALT

1 tablespoon BROWN SUGAR

1 STALK LEMONGRASS, FINELY SLICED

5 SMALL SHALLOTS, FINELY CHOPPED

½ cup SUNFLOWER OR PEANUT OIL

TO SERVE

1 CUCUMBER, QUARTERED LENGTHWISE, SEEDED, THEN SLICED CROSSWISE INTO CHUNKS

DIPPING SAUCE, SUCH AS SATAY SAUCE (PAGE 37 OR 53), NUÓC CHAM (PAGE 45), OR CHOPPED CHILI MIXED WITH SOY OR FISH SAUCE

20 wooden or bamboo satay sticks, soaked in water for 30 minutes

SERVES 4

Cut the pork across the grain into ¾-inch slices, then into cubes.

Heat the coriander seeds in a dry skillet until aromatic. Put into a spice mill (or clean coffee grinder) and grind to a powder. Put into a large bowl, then add the turmeric, salt, and sugar.

Put the finely sliced lemongrass and shallots in the spice mill or a blender and work to a paste (add a little water if necessary). Add to the bowl and stir well. Stir in 2 tablespoons of the oil.

Add the cubes of meat and turn to coat in the mixture. Cover and marinate in the refrigerator for 2 hours or overnight.

Light an outdoor grill or preheat a broiler. When ready to cook, thread cubes of pork onto soaked satay sticks, 2 on each, leaving a little space between the pieces. Brush with oil and grill or broil until done. (Pork must be cooked right through—and not at too high a heat, or it will be tough.)

Thread a piece of cucumber onto the end of each skewer and serve with dipping sauce.

PORK, LAMB, and BEEF

Put the pork, garlic, lemongrass, cilantro, chilies, brown sugar, fish sauce, and egg in a food processor and work to a paste. Chill for at least 30 minutes.

Take 1–2 tablespoons of the mixture and, using wet hands, form into a ball. Repeat until all the mixture has been used. Press a soaked chopstick or skewer through the middle of each ball and thread 2–3 balls onto each stick. Pat until snug, then chill.

To make the *Nuóc Cham*, work the garlic, chili, and sugar to a purée in a spice mill (clean coffee grinder) or with a mortar and pestle. Add the chopped lime and any collected juice, then purée again. Stir in the fish sauce and about ½ cup water. Reserve.

Toast the peanuts for serving in a dry skillet, then crush coarsely and reserve. Soak the noodles in hot water for about 15 minutes, drain, then boil for 1 minute. Drain and reserve.

Light an outdoor grill or preheat a broiler. Grill or broil the pork balls until cooked right through (break one open to check). Serve, sprinkled with the nuts, with a "table salad" of lettuce, mint, and basil. To eat, remove from the sticks, wrap in lettuce, add carrots, noodles, peanuts, and herbs, roll up, and dip in *Nuóc Cham*.

Note: Fish sauce is delicious and traditional. If unavailable, use soy sauce diluted with water.

VIETNAMESE PORK BALL BROCHETTES

These traditional kabobs are called brochettes, the result of the French colonial period, but the flavors are distinctly Vietnamese, especially the herbs, salad, and *Nuóc Cham*—the delicious, piquant, salty, spicy condiment used as an all-purpose dipping sauce.

2½ cups GROUND PORK, WITH SOME FAT

4 GARLIC CLOVES, CRUSHED

2 STALKS LEMONGRASS, FINELY SLICED

1 BUNCH CILANTRO, CHOPPED

2 RED CHILIES, SEEDED AND DICED

1 tablespoon BROWN SUGAR

1 tablespoon FISH SAUCE*

1 EGG, BEATEN

NUÓC CHAM

2 GARLIC CLOVES, CRUSHED

1 RED CHILI, SEEDED AND CHOPPED

1 tablespoon SUGAR

½ LIME, SEEDED AND CHOPPED (PEEL INCLUDED)

1½ tablespoons FISH SAUCE*

TO SERVE

¼–½ CUP CHOPPED PEANUTS

1 SMALL BUNDLE RICE STICK NOODLES

16–20 SMALL LETTUCE LEAVES

2 CARROTS GRATED INTO STRIPS

LEAVES FROM 1 BUNCH FRESH BASIL

LEAVES FROM 1 BUNCH FRESH MINT

12–16 short wooden chopsticks or bamboo skewers, soaked in water for 30 minutes

SERVES 4

AFGHAN LAMB KABOBS
with GINGER, RED WINE, and BAY LEAVES

All through Pakistan and Afghanistan, restaurants and roadside barbecue stalls produce iron skewers of lamb, chicken, and occasionally beef. The skewers are terrifying—about a yard long—and served in great bundles in the middle of the table with huge piles of delicious fresh naan bread. Muslim cooks wouldn't use wine or the ginger, for that matter, but I think it improves the flavor enormously. Beef is also good cooked this way.

1 SMALL LEG OF LAMB, ABOUT 3 lb.

6 tablespoons GINGER PURÉE* (PAGE 30), OR 2 inches FRESH GINGER, GRATED

½ BOTTLE RED WINE, OR TO COVER

2 FRESH BAY LEAVES, BRUISED

GHEE, MUSTARD OIL, OR OLIVE OIL, FOR BRUSHING

SEA SALT

NAAN BREAD OR FLOUR TORTILLAS

CUCUMBER RAITA (OPTIONAL)

1 CUCUMBER, SEEDED, SLICED, SALTED, THEN RINSED AND PATTED DRY

1 TOMATO, SEEDED AND DICED

1 ONION, FINELY SLICED

½ cup PLAIN YOGHURT

SALT AND FRESHLY GROUND BLACK PEPPER

12 long metal kabob skewers

SERVES 4

Ask the butcher to cut the leg of lamb across the bone into thick slices, about 1¼ inches wide. Remove and discard the central bone from each slice, then cut the meat into 1¼ inch cubes.

Put in a bowl, add the ginger, and turn to coat. Add the wine and bay leaves, cover, then marinate in the refrigerator for 1 hour or up to 2 days.

Remove from the marinade and pat dry. Thread onto metal skewers, brush with melted ghee or oil, and sprinkle with sea salt.

Mix the raita ingredients together in a small bowl and set aside.

Light an outdoor grill or preheat a broiler until very hot. Grill or broil the kabobs for about 5 minutes on each side, until the meat is crisp and brown outside and still pink inside. Serve with the raita and warmed naan bread or tortillas.

Note: To make your own ginger purée, see the recipe note on page 30.

What did we do before food processors? Spent all day grinding things like the meat for these kibbehs (now a work of seconds in the wonder machine). I use the small part for chopping onions, then tip them into the larger part to mix them with the meat.

MIDDLE EASTERN KIBBEH KABOBS
with TABBOULEH, HUMMUS, and PITA

Put the onions in a small food processor (these chop onions better than the large ones). Pulse to the equivalent of coarsely grated. Add the parsley and chop again. Transfer to a large processor, with the lamb mince, spices, and seasoning and pulse to a smooth paste.

Pat 16 flat metal skewers completely dry. Take a ball of mixture, about 2 tablespoons, and put on the end of the skewer, about ¾ inch from the end. Press it along the skewer to make an oval or cylinder about 4 inches long. (Since the mixture can easily fall off the skewers, try putting the skewers inside a hinged grill rack.)

Light an outdoor grill or preheat a broiler or stovetop grill pan. Grill or broil the kabobs for about 2 minutes on each side until crisp on the outside and tender inside.

Put on a large serving platter with a pile of warmed pita bread beside and separate bowls of sliced onion, salad leaves, hummus, and yogurt mixed with dried mint, if using. (Traditionally, the meat is pulled off the skewers with the bread.)

2 ONIONS, QUARTERED

A LARGE HANDFUL OF PARSLEY, STEMS REMOVED (ABOUT 3 oz.)

2½ cups GROUND LAMB (OR BEEF)

½ teaspoon GROUND CINNAMON

½ teaspoon GROUND SAFFRON

SEA SALT AND COARSELY CRUSHED BLACK PEPPER

TO SERVE

PITA BREAD

SLICED RED ONION

GREEN SALAD LEAVES

HUMMUS

PLAIN YOGURT

1 teaspoon DRIED MINT (OPTIONAL)

about 16 flat-sided metal skewers

hinged metal grill rack, oiled (optional)

SERVES 4

1 SMALL LEG OF LAMB, ABOUT 3 lb.

GARLIC MARINADE

6 GARLIC CLOVES, CRUSHED

3 tablespoons EXTRA-VIRGIN OLIVE OIL

GRATED ZEST AND JUICE OF 1 LEMON

A PINCH OF FRESHLY GROUND CINNAMON

A PINCH OF FRESHLY GROUND CLOVES

SEA SALT AND COARSELY CRUSHED
BLACK PEPPER

TO SERVE

WARMED FLATBREADS, SUCH AS
LAVASH, VILLAGE BREAD, PITA BREAD,
OR FLOUR TORTILLAS

TABBOULEH SALAD

HUMMUS

CHILI SAUCE (OPTIONAL)

CHOPPED FRESH TOMATO

*8 metal or bamboo skewers (if bamboo,
soak in water for 30 minutes*

SERVES 4

Ask the butcher to cut the lamb into slices across the bone, about 1 inch wide. Remove the bone from the middle and separate the meat across the natural separations. Cut into cubes.

Mix the garlic marinade ingredients in a bowl, then add the lamb and turn to coat well. Cover and leave for 2 hours or overnight in the refrigerator. Turn occasionally if possible.

Light an outdoor grill or preheat a broiler. Remove the lamb from the marinade and thread onto metal skewers. Grill or broil for about 5–7 minutes on each side.

Serve rolled up in warmed lavash or other flatbread with tabbouleh, hummus, chili sauce, if using, and chopped tomatoes.

Greek and Lebanese Australians make these wraps with grilled fillets from the loin of the lamb. This can be a little expensive outside lamb-growing areas, so I have used slices from the leg. Village bread or lavash are thin scarf-like sheets of flatbread. Use pita or flour tortillas if unavailable.

SOUVLAKI LAMB
with HUMMUS and TABBOULEH SALAD, WRAPPED in WARMED FLATBREAD

This marinade and sauce can be used for other satay skewers such as chicken, duck, and (not very Indonesian) pork. Some chilies are milder than others, so choose the variety and number of chilies to suit the palates of your guests. You can also use the Satay Sauce on page 37.

INDONESIAN BEEF SATAYS
with PEANUT SATAY SAUCE

Cut the beef crosswise into thin strips, about ⅛ inch thick and 2 inches long.

To make the coconut marinade, mix the coconut milk, lime juice, chili, lemongrass or lemon, garlic, coriander, cumin, cardamom, fish sauce, lime zest, and sugar in a bowl. Add the beef strips and stir to coat. Cover and chill for 2 hours or overnight to develop the flavors.

To make the Satay Sauce, grind the peanuts in a blender or food processor until coarse. Heat the oil in a wok, add the garlic, chilies, and onion and stir-fry until golden. Add peanuts, sugar, lime juice, coconut milk, and soy sauce. Bring to a boil and simmer, stirring, until thickened.

Preheat a broiler. Drain the beef, discarding the marinade. Thread the beef, zig-zag fashion, onto soaked wooden or bamboo skewers and broil or cook in a skillet (brushed with a film of peanut oil) until browned and tender. Serve, sprinkled with peanuts, if using, and satay sauce.

Note: The sauce recipe makes about 2 cups, which is enough for 2–3 other kinds of satays to be served at the same meal.

1 lb. BONELESS BEEF SIRLOIN

½ cup PEANUTS, CRUSHED, TO SERVE (OPTIONAL)

COCONUT MARINADE

½ cup CANNED COCONUT MILK

JUICE OF 2 LIMES (ABOUT ⅓ cup)

2 FRESH RED CHILIES, FINELY CHOPPED

3 STALKS LEMONGRASS OR 1 LEMON, FINELY CHOPPED

3 GARLIC CLOVES, CRUSHED

2 teaspoons GROUND CORIANDER

1 teaspoon GROUND CUMIN

1 TEASPOON GROUND CARDAMOM

2 tablespoons FISH SAUCE

GRATED ZEST OF 1 LIME

1 teaspoon SUGAR

SATAY SAUCE*

1½ cups ROASTED PEANUTS

1 teaspoon PEANUT OIL

1 GARLIC CLOVE, CRUSHED

2 RED CHILIES, SEEDED AND DICED

1 ONION, FINELY SLICED

1 tablespoon BROWN SUGAR

1 teaspoon LIME JUICE

1 cup CANNED COCONUT MILK

1 tablespoon SWEETENED SOY SAUCE, SUCH AS INDONESIAN KECAP MANIS

12 long bamboo skewers, soaked in water for 30 minutes

SERVES 4

FAJITA MARINADE

1½ tablespoons OLIVE OIL

1½ tablespoons LIME JUICE

A PINCH OF SEA SALT FLAKES

2 teaspoons TABASCO OR CHILI OIL

½ teaspoon CRUSHED CHILIES

4 GARLIC CLOVES, CRUSHED

BEEF KEBABS

1½ lb. SKIRT STEAK, CUT INTO
1-inch CUBES

2 RED ONIONS, CUT INTO WEDGES

2 RED PEPPERS, SEEDED AND CUT
INTO 1-inch SQUARES

CORN OIL, FOR BRUSHING

TOMATO SALSA

3 TOMATOES, SEEDED AND DICED

1 SHALLOT, CHOPPED

2 tablespoons CHOPPED CILANTRO

JUICE OF 1 LIME

1 tablespoon CHOPPED JALAPEÑO CHILI

SALT AND FRESHLY GROUND
BLACK PEPPER

TO SERVE

DRIED CHILI FLAKES

12 FLOUR TORTILLAS, WARMED

GUACAMOLE

SPRIGS OF CILANTRO

12 metal kabob skewers

hinged metal grill rack, oiled (optional)

SERVES 4

Mix the marinade ingredients in a flat, shallow dish, add the meat cubes, and turn to coat. Cover and chill for at least 2 hours or overnight.

Heat a stovetop grill pan. Brush the onions and peppers with oil, add to the pan, and cook until browned on all sides. Mix the salsa ingredients together in a small bowl.

Light an outdoor grill or preheat a broiler. Thread the meat onto half the skewers and the pepper and onion onto the remaining skewers. Put the skewers in a hinged grill rack and grill or broil until crispy brown. Remove from the heat and sprinkle with chili flakes.

Serve with warmed tortillas, guacamole, cilantro, and salsa.

In Spanish, a *fajita* is a belt or band—in food terms, fajitas are marinades, usually applied to large pieces of skirt steak, but also wonderful with skewers and with other ingredients such as chicken or seafood.

BEEF FAJITAS
with CHILI SPRINKLE

I grew up on a pineapple farm and, to us professionals, the dinky little disks you see in cans or in restaurants were for the birds! Pineapples come with their own, albeit rather prickly, handle. You just slice off the skin with a machete, hold the fruit by the top, and munch away. If we were being very civilized, the peeled pineapples would be cut into wedges like these. Perfect for cooking, juicing, or eating daintily with a knife and fork.

PINEAPPLE STICKS
with SUGAR-LIME SAUCE

To make the sauce, put the lime juice and sugar in a small saucepan, bring to a boil, and stir until the sugar dissolves.

To make the Coconut Cream, beat the cream with the confectioners' sugar until soft peaks form, then fold in the coconut cream, if using.

Cut the pineapple quarters into 2–3 wedges lengthwise. If preferred, slice off the core sections, then cut each wedge into slices about ½ inch thick. Thread long metal skewers through each wedge and brush with the lime mixture.

Light an outdoor grill or preheat a broiler. Grill or broil until the fruit is tinged dark brown. Serve drizzled with any leftover sauce, accompanied by the whipped coconut cream.

SUGAR-LIME SAUCE

JUICE OF 1 FRESH LIME (2 tablespoons)

½ cup BROWN SUGAR

WHIPPED COCONUT CREAM

1 cup HEAVY CREAM

2 tablespoons CONFECTIONERS' SUGAR

2 tablespoons CANNED COCONUT CREAM (OPTIONAL)

PINEAPPLE STICKS

1 PINEAPPLE, PEELED AND QUARTERED LENGTHWISE (REMOVE THE PRICKLY EYES WITH THE POINT OF A KNIFE)

8 metal kabob skewers

SERVES 4

To make the batter, beat the egg in a small bowl with ⅔ cup cold water. Sift the flour into a second bowl and gradually stir in the egg mixture to form a smooth batter.

Peel the bananas and cut them at an angle crosswise into pieces about 1 inch long.

Half fill a large bowl with ice cubes and cold water and set beside the stove. Film a serving plate with oil and set beside the water.

To make the Sugar Syrup, put the oil in a saucepan with the sugar and 3 tablespoons water. Heat, stirring, until the sugar dissolves, then heat gently, without stirring, until the mixture reaches hard crack stage—300°F on a candy thermometer or when a drop of syrup, dropped into the bowl of water, hardens instantly.

Fill a wok one-third full of the oil and heat to 375°F or until a piece of bread browns in 30 seconds.

Stick soaked cocktail sticks or French fry forks* into the banana pieces, dip the fruit into the batter, then put into the hot oil and cook for 1 minute. (Work in batches of 4–6.) Remove from the oil with a slotted spoon and dip into the sugar syrup, holding the stick with tongs. Sprinkle with sesame seeds, then immediately drop them, one by one, into the ice water. The syrup hardens instantly into a crackly glaze. Transfer to a serving plate and serve sprinkled with confectioners' sugar or more sesame seeds.

*Note: Alternatively, the sticks may be inserted after cooking.

FRITTER BATTER

1 EGG

¾ cup ALL-PURPOSE FLOUR

BANANAS

3–4 JUST-RIPE BANANAS

3 tablespoons SESAME SEEDS, TOASTED IN A DRY SKILLET

PEANUT OR SUNFLOWER OIL, FOR FRYING

¼ cup CONFECTIONERS' SUGAR, FOR DUSTING (OPTIONAL)

SUGAR SYRUP

1 tablespoon PEANUT OIL

⅔ cups SUGAR

about 20 wooden cocktail sticks or chip forks, soaked in water for 30 minutes

SERVES 4

Hugely popular, this traditional Chinese dish depends for its success on the sugar syrup staying at precisely the same temperature. Use a candy thermometer (available from good kitchen stores) to help you—and remember, practice makes perfect.

CHINESE BANANA FRITTERS

When I was little, toffee apples were always very red and crisp—my favorite was the tiny, white-fleshed Lady in the Snow. Pick one of the small apples now sold in supermarkets—you get more toffee for your apple! Use wooden chopsticks to make skewers.

TOFFEE APPLES

8–12 SMALL RED APPLES

2½ cups BROWN SUGAR

¼ cup UNSALTED BUTTER

2 tablespoons VINEGAR

1 tablespoon CORN SYRUP

a baking sheet, greased

8–12 short wooden chopsticks

SERVES 8–12

Soak the apples in cold water for 10–30 minutes. Rinse, then dry completely with paper towels.

Put the sugar in a saucepan with the butter, vinegar, corn syrup, and ⅔ cup water. Heat gently, stirring, until the sugar dissolves. Boil hard for about 5 minutes, stirring occasionally to stop the mixture sticking. Continue boiling until the mixture reaches hard ball stage—250°F on a candy thermometer or when a teaspoon of syrup, dropped into cold water, hardens instantly into a ball. If it doesn't, continue boiling until it does.

Push thick wooden sticks, such as chopsticks, into the apples, then dip them into the toffee, twirling them around for a few seconds. Remove and leave on the greased baking sheet, sticks upward, until the toffee hardens—about 10 minutes. Serve immediately, or wrap the toffee apples in cellophane and tie with ribbons.

YOUR CHOICE OF:

2–3 RIPE MANGOES, PEELED AND PITTED

JUICE OF 1 SMALL LEMON

2 tablespoons SUPERFINE SUGAR

1 BASKET STRAWBERRIES, ABOUT
2½ CUPS QUARTERED

8 RIPE APRICOTS, HALVED AND PITTED

ICE-CREAM:

1 cup MILK

3 EGG YOLKS

⅔ cup SUGAR

1 cup HEAVY WHIPPING CREAM

12–24 wooden treat sticks

MAKES ABOUT 12 LARGE OR 24 SMALL

You can buy plastic frozen treat molds with attached plastic sticks. I prefer wooden sticks, then you can use any kind of container as a mold, ranging from egg cups to popover pans.

FROZEN FRUIT POPS

If using mangoes, purée the flesh in a blender with the lemon juice and sugar. Chill. If using strawberries or apricots, put in a saucepan with the lemon juice, sugar and ¼ cup water, bring to a boil, and simmer until soft. Strain into a bowl and chill.

To make the ice-cream, heat the milk to just below boiling point. Put the egg yolks in a bowl and beat until creamy. Beat in ¼ cup hot milk, then the remaining milk, a little at a time. Stir in the sugar and transfer to a bowl set over simmering water. Cook, stirring, until the mixture coats the back of a spoon. Do not let boil. Remove from the heat, dip the bowl into cold water, then cool.

Stir in the cream, add your choice of fruit, then churn, in batches if necessary.* Spoon into frozen treat molds and insert the sticks. If using makeshift molds, such as small paper cups or popover pans, put a treat stick in the middle.

Freeze, then serve as required to greedy small people.

__Note:__ Alternatively, partially freeze in a shallow metal pan, whizz in a food processor, then freeze again.

INDEX

P.R
mary celular
1787
909 - 0056

malml

508 - 373 - 8117

mary   5834
887 - 888 - 583
5839

Tools & Techniques

Handyman Club Library™
Handyman Club of America
Minneapolis, Minnesota

Tools & Techniques

CREDITS

Mike Vail
Vice President, Products & Business Development

Tom Carpenter
Director of Books & New Media Development

Mark Johanson
Book Products Development Manager

Dan Cary
Photo Production Coordinator

Chris Marshall
Editorial Coordinator

**Steve Boman, Paul Currie,
Mark Johanson**
Writers

Steve Anderson
Contributing Writer

Bill Nelson
Series Design, Art Direction and Production

Mark Macemon
Lead Photographer

Ralph Karlen
Photography

John Nadeau
Technical Advisor and Builder

Craig Claeys
Contributing Illustrator

Charlie Swenson
Technical Consultant

Dan Kennedy
Book Production Manager

ISBN 1-58159-025-3

Handyman Club of America
12301 Whitewater Drive
Minnetonka, Minnesota 55343

Table of Contents

Tools & Techniques

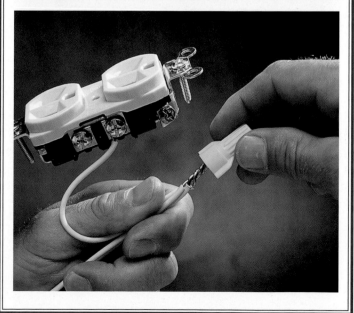

Introduction

If you were allowed only one home reference book in your library, this might well be the volume to choose. From tool use and basic woodworking tips to plumbing, wiring and metalworking, you'll find a little bit of everything in the fully packed pages that follow.

The information to be found in this book is not here by accident. Over the years, we've learned a lot about the Members of the Handyman Club of America—partly because many of us who worked to make this book are club Members ourselves. We've attempted the same projects, faced the same problems and challenges, and asked the same questions.

The first section of this book deals with a subject that's close to all our hearts: the workshop. The workshop is both a source of pride and a welcoming retreat for the handyman. Our search to make it harder-working, more efficient and more comfortable is a never-ending quest. It's the place where we produce our greatest accomplishments and encounter our greatest frustrations. The workshop information you'll find here covers a wide range of topics: from good advice about organizing your too-limited shop space to tips for laying out projects quickly and accurately, to sound skill-building and helpful hints for using just about every tool you own. And practically every little nugget of information is accompanied by a beautiful color photo or illustration so you can see for yourself. Setting up shop, measuring and layout, cutting, drilling, shaping, fastening, finishing and metalworking are the primary skills you can develop with the help of this book.

The second section of this book deals with a subject that can be hard to get excited about, but every handyman must face eventually: plumbing. In this brief but very complete treatment, you'll discover the basics of handling the most common plumbing materials: how to sweat copper pipe, how to weld PVC tubing, how to make a dielectric connection between different metal types, and much, much more. You'll also find plenty of useful information to help with the plumbing projects you're most likely to take on. You'll see how a drain/waste/vent system is laid out and how a bathroom sink is hooked up. You'll even find out the real secret behind a question that's puzzled many of us for years: how does a toilet really work?

And finally, this book concludes with a section on wiring that will help take the fear out of doing electrical projects and repairs. We've included all the basics you need to know about cable, making connections, and handling wiring materials safely. And we've added specific information on electrical circuits and how to hook up common electrical fixtures found in everyone's home.

Whether you're a weekend handyman or an experienced tradesman, you'll learn many new and useful things about your workshop and your home simply by taking the time to examine and read this book—we think you'll agree that it's time well spent.

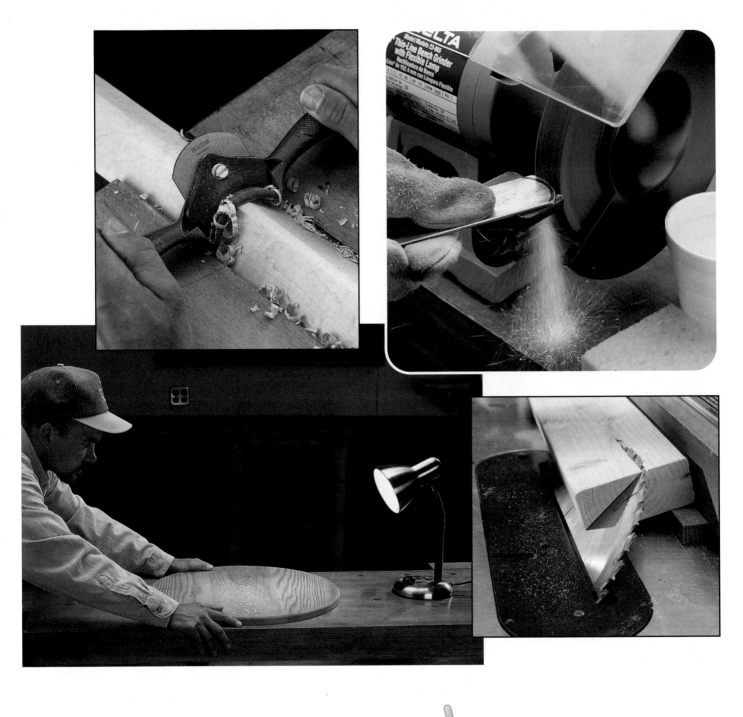

Workshop

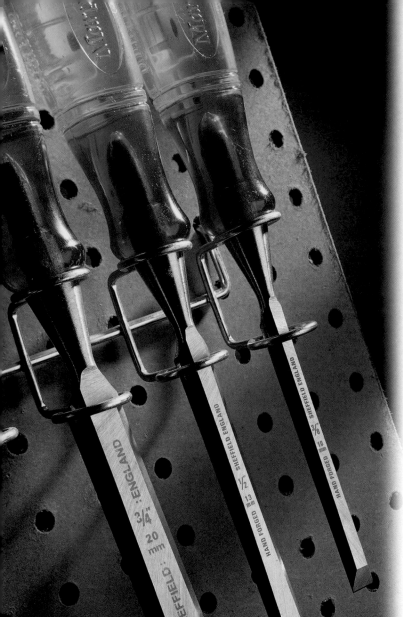

General workshop info

A workshop is constantly evolving. It begins with the selection of a space: half of a double garage, a room in the basement or, if possible, a separate outbuilding. Preparing the space for use as a workshop takes some work and planning. In almost all cases, you'll need to increase the electrical service to the area by adding dedicated 20 amp lines for your major tools, and perhaps 240 volt service for a state-of-the art table saw, radial-arm saw or shaper. You'll need to assess the ventilation and perhaps add a window or a vent fan. If possible, a built-in dust collection system should be installed before you start setting up the working shop. A finishing area (perhaps a spray booth) and storage needs also should be addressed.

Over time, tools are added. First, a few essential tools like a table saw or radial-arm saw, a drill press, and an assortment of hand tools and portable power tools. As you gain more experience and your interests become more defined, additional tools, like a router and router table and specialty tools such as a lathe or shaper are thrown into the mix. Meanwhile, your supply of hardware, jigs and building materials will continue to grow (and will require efficient storage).

Whether your workshop is a drop-down worksurface in the laundry room or a gleaming, 2,000 square foot shrine, you'll need to develop and follow good tool maintenance and shop upkeep practices.

Power tools you'll need (by experience level)

Beginner

- Circular saw with combination blade
- Jig saw
- Power sander, pad-type
- Small workbench or setup table
- Corded drill (reversible with variable speed)
- Cordless drill/driver with basic bits and accessories
- Shop vacuum

Intermediate

Add:
- Reciprocating saw
- Table saw
- Power miter saw
- Hammer drill
- Drill press
- Belt sander
- Random-orbit sander
- Router & router table
- Bench grinder
- Dust collection system
- Tool sharpening center
- Scroll saw
- Biscuit joiner

Advanced

Add:
- Jointer
- Air compressor and air tools
- Power planer
- Sanding station
- Band saw
- Sliding compound miter saw
- Lathe
- Spray booth and HVLP sprayer
- Shaper
- Welding equipment

Typical garage workshop layout (double garage)

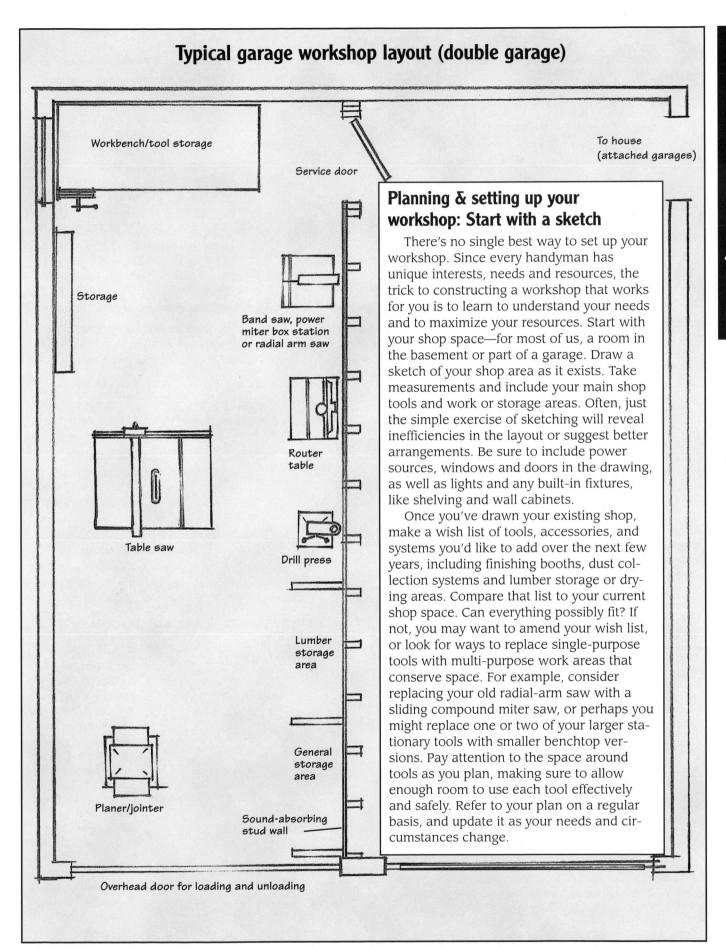

Workbench/tool storage

Service door

To house
(attached garages)

Storage

Band saw, power
miter box station
or radial arm saw

Router
table

Table saw

Drill press

Lumber
storage
area

General
storage
area

Planer/jointer

Sound-absorbing
stud wall

Overhead door for loading and unloading

Planning & setting up your workshop: Start with a sketch

There's no single best way to set up your workshop. Since every handyman has unique interests, needs and resources, the trick to constructing a workshop that works for you is to learn to understand your needs and to maximize your resources. Start with your shop space—for most of us, a room in the basement or part of a garage. Draw a sketch of your shop area as it exists. Take measurements and include your main shop tools and work or storage areas. Often, just the simple exercise of sketching will reveal inefficiencies in the layout or suggest better arrangements. Be sure to include power sources, windows and doors in the drawing, as well as lights and any built-in fixtures, like shelving and wall cabinets.

Once you've drawn your existing shop, make a wish list of tools, accessories, and systems you'd like to add over the next few years, including finishing booths, dust collection systems and lumber storage or drying areas. Compare that list to your current shop space. Can everything possibly fit? If not, you may want to amend your wish list, or look for ways to replace single-purpose tools with multi-purpose work areas that conserve space. For example, consider replacing your old radial-arm saw with a sliding compound miter saw, or perhaps you might replace one or two of your larger stationary tools with smaller benchtop versions. Pay attention to the space around tools as you plan, making sure to allow enough room to use each tool effectively and safely. Refer to your plan on a regular basis, and update it as your needs and circumstances change.

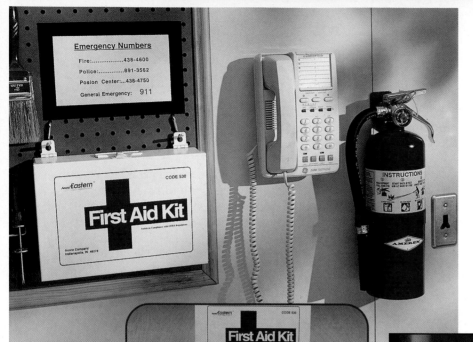

Create an emergency area

The workshop is perhaps the most accident-prone area of your home. Sharp blades, heavy objects, dangerous chemicals and flammable materials are just a few of the factors that increase the risk of accidents in the shop. While good housekeeping, respect for your tools and common sense will go a long way toward reducing the risk of accidents, you should still be prepared in the event an accident occurs. Designate part of your shop as an emergency center. Equip it with a fully stocked first aid kit, fire extinguisher and telephone with emergency numbers clearly posted.

A well-equipped first aid kit should contain (as a minimum) plenty of gauze and bandages, antiseptic first aid ointment, latex gloves, a cold compress, rubbing alcohol swabs, a disinfectant such as iodine, and a first aid guidebook.

The ABC's of fire extinguishers

Fire extinguishers are rated by their ability to combat fires of varying causes. An extinguisher rated "A" is effective against trash, wood and paper fires. "B" will extinguish flammable liquid and grease fires. "C" can be used on electrical fires. For the workshop, choose a dry chemical extinguisher with an "ABC" rating.

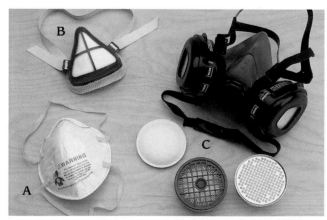

Protect against dust and fumes. A particle mask (A) is a disposable item to be worn when doing general shop work. A dust mask (B) has replaceable filters and flexible facepiece to keep out finer particles, like sawdust and insulation fibers. A respirator (C) can be fitted with filters and cartridges to protect against fumes and very fine particles, especially when working with chemicals.

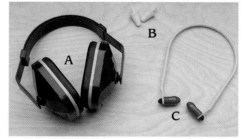

Protect your hearing when operating power tools or performing other loud activities. Ear muffs (A) offer the best protection, followed by expandable foam earplugs (B) and corded ear inserts (C).

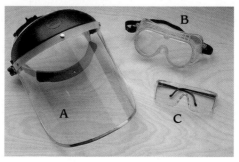

Eye protection should be worn at all times in the workshop. A face shield (A) is worn when doing very hazardous work, such as operating a lathe. Safety goggles (B) and glasses (C) should have shatterproof polycarbonate lenses.

Workshop First Aid Tips

Note: *None of these treatments should be considered a substitute for medical attention. They are intended as guidelines on how to react to workshop mishaps. Whenever anyone is injured, contact a doctor as soon as possible.*

Situation | ## Treatment

Deep gash/excessive bleeding

1) Maintain firm pressure on the wound with a clean cloth.
2) Dress with a gauze bandage.
3) If bleeding persists, and wound is a non-fracture, elevate the affected area so it is above the heart.

Deep puncture wound

1) Clean wound with soap and water.
2) Loosely cover wound with gauze bandage.
3) Apply insulated ice bag or cold compress to reduce swelling, relieve pain and impair absorption of toxins.
4) Be aware that internal bleeding may occur.

Stab wound/embedded object

1) Leave the embedded object in place. Do NOT remove it.
2) Apply a clean cloth or gauze pad to the area around the wound.
3) Prevent movement of the object by wrapping it with gauze.

Amputation

1) Maintain constant pressure with a clean cloth.
2) Carefully wrap severed item in gauze that has been moistened with either water or saline solution.
3) Place severed item in a sealed plastic bag.
4) Place this bag into a larger bag containing water and ice (never let severed part come in direct contact with ice).

Burn

1) If the burn is more severe than first-degree (skin that is red or slightly swollen) it should not be treated at home. See a doctor immediately.
2) For minor burns, immerse the affected area in cold water for five minutes. Gently apply a cold, wet cloth to areas that are unable to be immersed. Change the cloth frequently.

Electric shock

1) Quickly and safely break victim's contact with affecting current (disconnect plug or shut off breaker).
2) ALL electrical burns should be considered severe. Internal tissue may be affected more severely than the minor damage appearing on the skin. 911 should be called immediately if the electrical shock has caused any of the following: erratic heartbeat, severe jolt, abnormal tingling, unconsciousness (momentary or prolonged), muscle spasms or aches, fatigue, headaches or a visible burn.

Chemicals in eyes

1) Do not rub or irritate the affected eye.
2) Flush with warm water.

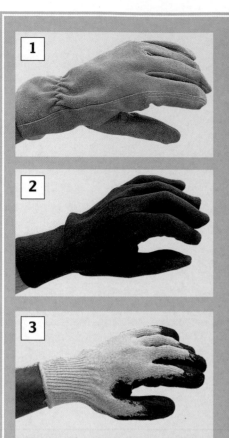

Get a grip on glove selection

Always wear the proper glove for the task at hand. Maintain a supply of good-condition gloves of the following types, and add special purpose gloves as needed.

1 Heavy work gloves for handling building materials and general interior and exterior wear

2 Jersey or heavy cotton gloves for yardwork and general wear

3 Rubber-dipped masonry gloves for working with concrete and mortar

4 Disposable plastic gloves for painting and light finishing and for handling hardwoods, like cherry, that are sensitive to oils in skin

5 Neoprene rubber gloves for working with caustic chemicals, such as chemical paint stripper, and for working around electrical current

6 Household-type rubber gloves for painting and finishing and for working with cleansers

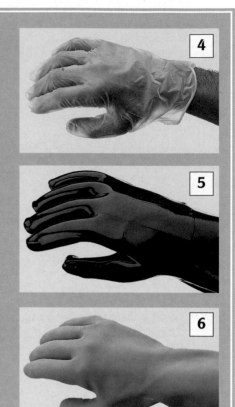

Remove-to-lock keys protect against unauthorized or unsupervised tool use

Many power tools, particularly stationary tools, come equipped with a removable lock key that is inserted into the ON/OFF switch of the tool. The tool cannot be turned on if the key is not in place. Store the lock keys in a convenient place that's out of sight from the tool.

Extension Cord Ratings

To make certain that your power tools run safely and at peak performance, use only extension cords that are rated to handle the amperage of the tool.

Cord Length	Gauge	Maximum Amps
25 ft.	18	10
25 ft.	16	13
25 ft.	14	15
50 ft.	18	5
50 ft.	16	10
50 ft.	14	15
75 ft.	18	5
75 ft.	16	10
75 ft.	14	15
100 ft.	16	5
100 ft.	12	15
125 ft.	16	5
125 ft.	12	15
150 ft.	16	5
150 ft.	12	13

Tips for dust collection & dust collection systems

Dust from workshop activities poses many threats to safety and to producing good results. It is a fire hazard, a health hazard when breathed in, and a general irritant. It is responsible for ruining countless carefully applied finishes, and if uncontrolled it will shorten the life span of your power tools. A good dust collection system is a must in any workshop. It can be as simple as a shop vac with a dust filter used locally, but the best solution is to construct a network of hoses connected permanently to your stationary shop tools and powered by a quality dust collector.

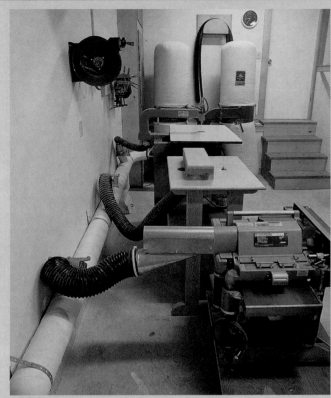

The two-stage dust collector in the background of this workshop photo is connected to all of the stationary power tools in the shop with dedicated 4 in. or larger hoses mounted to the walls and positioned to be out of the way when work is taking place.

A tool vac is a relatively new entry is the dust collection field. It's similar to a shop vac in size and power. Tools are connected to the power source through a receptacle mounted on the tool vac. This allows the vac to shut on and off automatically as the tool is used.

How to ground a dust collection system

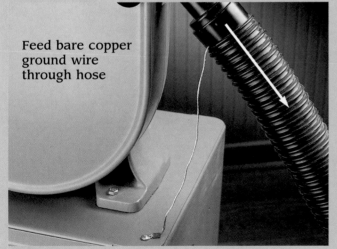

Feed bare copper ground wire through hose

1 Due to the dangers of sparking caused by static electricity, a dust collection system should be electrically grounded so the built-up electricity can escape. Attach a strand of bare copper wire to the metal cabinet of each stationary tool in the dust collection system (assumes that tools are grounded through the power supply system). Drill a small guide hole into the hose port near the tool and feed the wire into the hole.

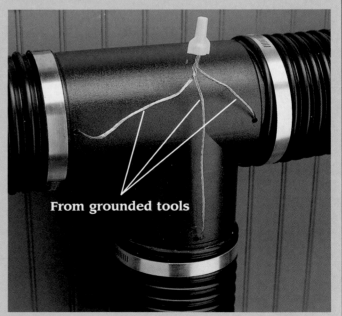

From grounded tools

2 Drill exit holes at hole connectors and pigtail ground wires together with a wire nut. You may need to caulk around the wire openings to maintain the vacuum seal.

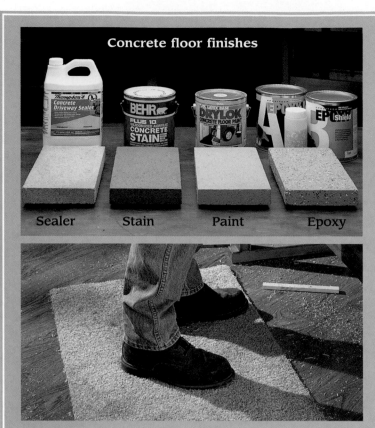

Concrete floor finishes

Sealer   Stain   Paint   Epoxy

Don't ignore the floor

If you stop and think about it, you have more direct contact with the floor of your shop than any other part. So it only makes sense to make sure your shop floor is safe, clean and comfortable. Start with the floor finish. If your shop has an unfinished concrete floor, there are several finishes you can apply to make it more attractive and easier to clean (photo, above left). *Concrete sealer* is a clear product that helps the concrete resist staining and creates a "slick" surface that's easier to sweep but isn't slippery; *concrete stain* is essentially sealer with a coloring agent for visual appeal; *concrete paint* seals and beautifies the floor, but because the product has more body it will fill small voids and cracks, eliminating areas where dirt, mildew and even insects can collect; *epoxy paint* is a two part finish that prevents moisture seepage up through the floor, resists stains and spills, and has a very attractive appearance. Regardless of the floor type or surface treatment, sweep and clean it regularly, and provide a cushion for your feet at work areas in the form of a rubber floor mat or even old carpet scraps (photo, lower left).

Tips for keeping a tidy workshop

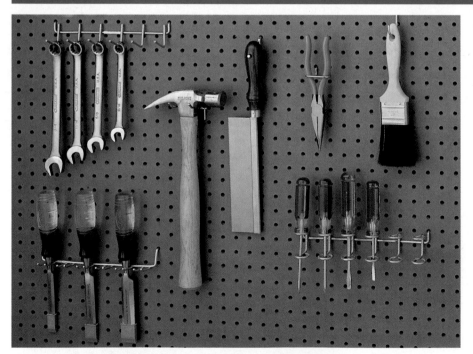

Pegboard tool hangers: A workshop standard

Perforated hardboard (pegboard) is the wallpaper of the workshop. In addition to general pegboard hooks, you can purchase whole systems of hanging devices in many sizes and configurations to effectively support and organize specific tools. Use tempered hardboard if available.

An attractive cleanup tool

Screws, washers, drill bits and other small metal parts have a way of disappearing into the nearest heap of sawdust or shavings as soon as you turn your back. Find and rescue them easily and safely with a shop magnet.

General tips for shop tool maintenance

Engrave identification marks onto shop tools

Every handyman knows that borrowed tools often end up on permanent loan. Keep tabs on your shop tools by engraving your name or initials into the tool casing with a rotary tool or carving tool. In addition to reminding your friends and family members where the tool came from, identification marks may help you recover your tools in the event of a robbery.

Make a habit of keeping every blade sharp

Some people enjoy the art of coaxing a razor-sharp blade onto knives and chisels, but for most of us it's just another shop chore that's easily ignored—especially with less glamorous tools, like the pruning shears being sharpened with a grinding bit and rotary tool above. To help make sure the sharpening and tool maintenance actually happen, dedicate one day or weekend every year to tool maintenance, including sharpening.

Maintain a well-dressed grinding wheel

The bench grinder is one of the most important tools in any shop for keeping other tools up and running at peak performance levels. But it too requires occasional maintenance. Over time, the grinding wheel or wheels build up resins and other gunk that settle into the grit of the wheel, where they harden each time you use the grinder. If you notice that your wheel has a brown, burnished appearance, it's time to *dress the wheel.* This procedure can be accomplished with a dressing tool, like the one shown at right, or simply with a stick made of silicone carbide. Simply apply the dressing tool or carbide stick to the spinning grinding wheel and inspect the wheel visually until the surface is clean and fully restored.

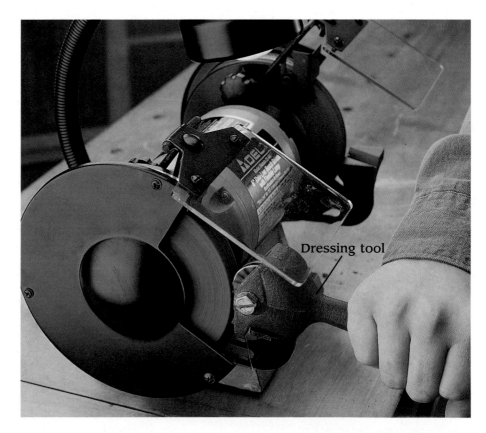

Dressing tool

Woodworking woods

Choosing the best wood species for your project goes a long way toward ensuring success. Different species naturally lend themselves better to the types of machining required for a project, as well as the overall look. For example, project parts that incorporate decorative edge profiles may be easier to shape using soft wood, but ultimately harder, more straight-grained wood will stand up better over time. Cost and local availability are also important determining factors. If you're building outdoors, cedar is generally an inexpensive wood choice in the Upper Midwest, but on the West Coast redwood is typically more economical, and in the South you'll likely save money by building with cypress. When choosing wood, pay particular attention to the tone of the wood when a finish is applied. To get a good idea what the finished color will be, simply dampen a small section of a planed board with mineral spirits or rubbing alcohol.

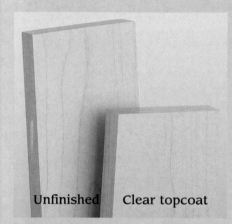

Walnut has rich, dark tones when topcoated. Grain is relatively straight. Moderately easy to work. Moderate to expensive. Species shown is black walnut.

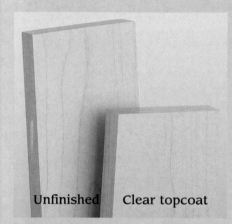

Maple is a light-colored hardwood with straight, tight grain. Hardness makes it durable but somewhat difficult to work. Inexpensive to moderate. Species shown is hard maple.

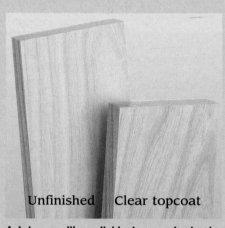

Ash is a readily available, inexpensive hardwood. Its color and grain are not distinguishing, but it can be finished to replicate more expensive hardwoods.

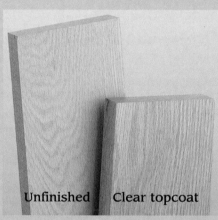

Red oak is one of the more inexpensive and prevalent wood species in today's marketplace. Has dramatic grain figure and warm red color. Fairly easy to work.

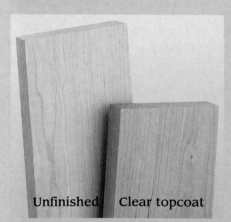

Cherry has a deep, reddish brown color when finished (color varies greatly between heartwood and sapwood). It is hard and tends to be brittle. Occasionally splotchy when finished. Moderate to expensive. Species shown is black cherry.

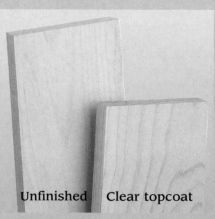

Pine is a very general species term used to refer to most coniferous softwood. It ranges from white to yellow according to species. Generally easy to work with strong grain patterns. Inexpensive to moderate. Species shown is ponderosa pine.

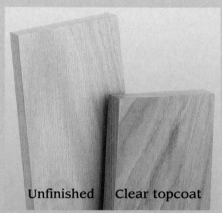

White oak is a versatile hardwood with a distinctive appearance. Used extensively in furniture-building, as well as in boatbuilding. It is moderate in price (quartersawn tends to be higher cost). Moderate workability.

Plywood grades & characteristics

Plywood is generally graded according to the veneer on both the front and back panels, as well as the exposure durability type. For example, Exterior C-D plywood would have one side conforming to the "C" grade, and the other side conforming to the "D" grade, with an "Exterior" exposure rating. The following charts explain American Plywood Association veneer grades, along with exposure durability types.

Veneer Grade	Characteristics
N	A smooth, natural-finish select heartwood or sapwood veneer that is free of open defects. It will not allow more than six repairs (wood only) per 4 × 8-ft. panel. Well matched for both grain and color.
A	A smooth, paintable veneer that does not permit more than 18 neat repairs per sheet. In less demanding applications, it may be used with a natural finish.
B	A solid surface veneer that allows shims, circular repair plugs and tight knots up to 1 in. Repairs of some minor splits permitted.
C-Plugged	An upgraded "C" veneer that limits splits to ⅛-in. width, and does not permit knotholes or borer holes in excess of ¼ × ½. Some broken grain allowed. Synthetic repairs permitted.
C	A veneer with tight knots to 1½ in. Can have knotholes up to 1 in. across the grain, or up to 1½ in. if the total width of knots and knotholes is within specified limits. Wood or synthetic repairs are okay. Permits discoloration and sanding defects that do not impair its strength, while limiting splits and stitches.
D	Allows knots and knotholes to 2½ in. width across the grain within specified limits. Permits limited splits and stitches. This grade limited to Interior or Exposure 1 panels.*

*Exposure Ratings are:

Exterior: Fully waterproof bond designed for applications subject to permanent exposure to moisture.

Exposure 1: Fully waterproof bond, but not intended for permanent exposure to weather or moisture.

Exposure 2: Interior type with intermediate glue. Intended for protected construction applications where slight exposure to moisture can be expected.

Interior: Designed exclusively for interior applications.

Grade stamps

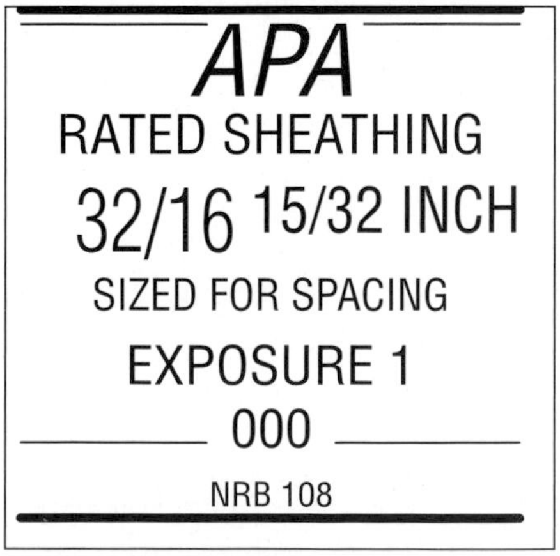

APA
RATED SHEATHING
32/16 15/32 INCH
SIZED FOR SPACING
EXPOSURE 1
000
NRB 108

MILL 03
WC LB ® NO.2
DOUG FIR **S·DRY**

Plywood grade stamps indicate the actual thickness of the material (sometimes to within 1/32 in.) The stamp also indicates whether the plywood is exterior rated.

Dimension lumber is rated by species, general quality (lower numbers indicate higher quality) and the mill where the lumber originated.

Nominal vs. actual board sizes

Nominal size	Actual size
1 × 1	¾ × ¾
1 × 2	¾ × 1½
1 × 3	¾ × 2½
1 × 4	¾ × 3½
1 × 6	¾ × 5¼
1 × 8	¾ × 7¼
1 × 10	¾ × 9¼
1 × 12	¾ × 11¼
2 × 2	1½ × 1½
2 × 3	1½ × 2½
2 × 4	1½ × 3½
2 × 6	1½ × 5¼
2 × 8	1½ × 7¼
2 × 10	1½ × 9¼
2 × 12	1½ × 11¼

Shop furnishings you can build

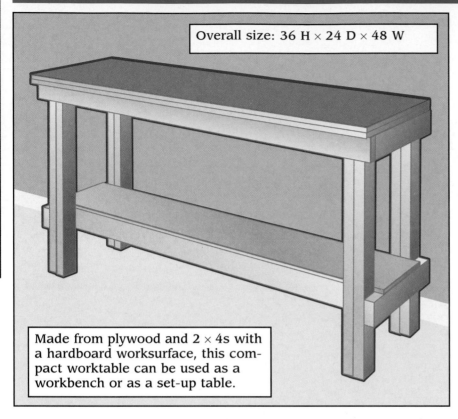

Overall size: 36 H × 24 D × 48 W

Made from plywood and 2 × 4s with a hardboard worksurface, this compact worktable can be used as a workbench or as a set-up table.

Workbench/set-up table

The workbench/set-up table project shown here is the kind of workshop furnishing that may not get a lot of attention but would be sorely missed if you were forced to do without it.

To build this workbench/set-up table, start by cutting the legs, rails and stretchers to length from 2 × 4 stock. Group the eight legs into four pairs, and attach the rails at the top and 8 in. up from the bottoms of the legs. Use wood glue and drive 3 in. deck screws through the rails and into the leg pairs, making sure everything is square. Then, fasten the bottom stretchers to the inside edges of the leg pairs, with their ends flush against the lower rails. Fasten the top stretchers on the outside edges of the leg pairs, overlapping the ends of the top rails. Cut and glue the two subtop panels together, and attach them to the top rails and stretchers, then cut and glue the worksurface to the subtop assembly. After the glue has dried, you may want to trim around the edges of the worksurface with a router and piloted roundover or flush-cutting bit. Finally, cut and attach the shelf to the lower rails and stretchers with 1½ in. deck screws.

Exploded view

Join subtop panels with glue and 3 in. deck screws driven down into rails and stretchers

Attach hardboard worksurface to subtop with wood glue

All 2 × 4 joints formed with wood glue and 3 in. deck screws

Secure shelf to rails and stretchers with 1½ in. deck screws (countersunk)

Workbench/set-up table cutting list

Key	No.	Part	Size	Material
A	1	Worksurface	¼ × 24 × 48	Hardboard
B	2	Sub-top	¾ × 24 × 48	Plywood
C	2	Stretcher (top)	1½ × 3½ × 48	Pine 2 × 4
D	2	Stretcher (bottom)	1½ × 3½ × 45	Pine 2 × 4
E	4	Side rails	1½ × 3½ × 19	Pine 2 × 4
F	1	Shelf	¾ × 12 × 48	Plywood
G	8	Legs	1½ × 3½ × 34¼	Pine 2 × 4

Materials:
(6) 2 × 4 × 8 ft. pine studs
(3) ¾ × 2 × 4 ft. plywood handy panels OR
two ¾ × 4 × 8 ft. sheets plywood
(1) ¼ × 2 × 4 ft. tempered hardboard handy panel

Wood glue, deck screws (1½, 3 in.)

Shop furnishings you can build

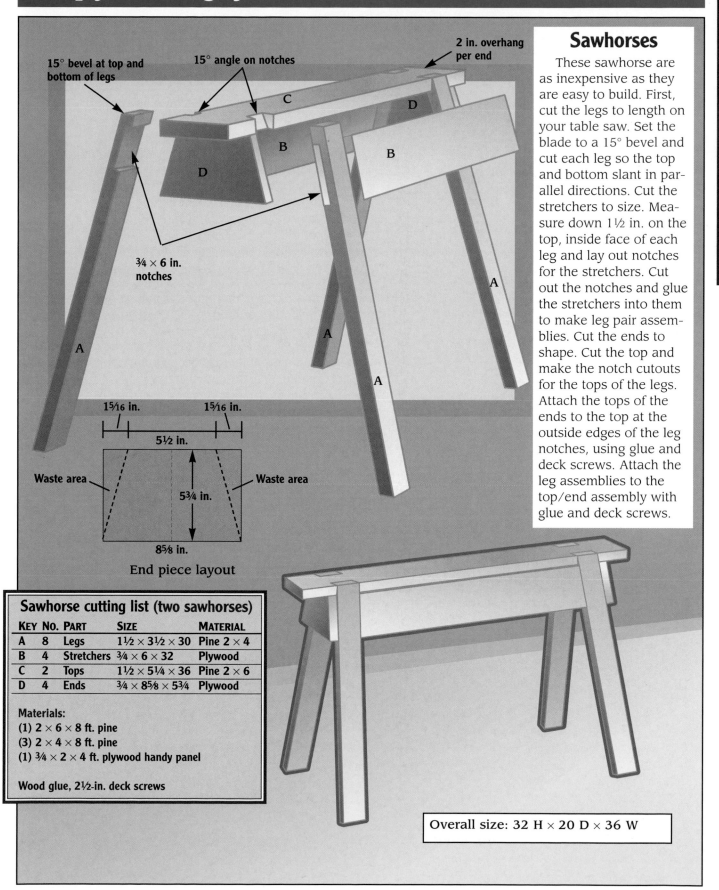

15° bevel at top and bottom of legs

15° angle on notches

2 in. overhang per end

C

D

B

D

B

A

A

A

A

A

¾ × 6 in. notches

1⁵⁄₁₆ in.   1⁵⁄₁₆ in.

5½ in.

Waste area   Waste area

5¾ in.

8⁵⁄₈ in.

End piece layout

Sawhorses

These sawhorse are as inexpensive as they are easy to build. First, cut the legs to length on your table saw. Set the blade to a 15° bevel and cut each leg so the top and bottom slant in parallel directions. Cut the stretchers to size. Measure down 1½ in. on the top, inside face of each leg and lay out notches for the stretchers. Cut out the notches and glue the stretchers into them to make leg pair assemblies. Cut the ends to shape. Cut the top and make the notch cutouts for the tops of the legs. Attach the tops of the ends to the top at the outside edges of the leg notches, using glue and deck screws. Attach the leg assemblies to the top/end assembly with glue and deck screws.

Sawhorse cutting list (two sawhorses)

KEY	NO.	PART	SIZE	MATERIAL
A	8	Legs	1½ × 3½ × 30	Pine 2 × 4
B	4	Stretchers	¾ × 6 × 32	Plywood
C	2	Tops	1½ × 5¼ × 36	Pine 2 × 6
D	4	Ends	¾ × 8⁵⁄₈ × 5¾	Plywood

Materials:
(1) 2 × 6 × 8 ft. pine
(3) 2 × 4 × 8 ft. pine
(1) ¾ × 2 × 4 ft. plywood handy panel

Wood glue, 2½-in. deck screws

Overall size: 32 H × 20 D × 36 W

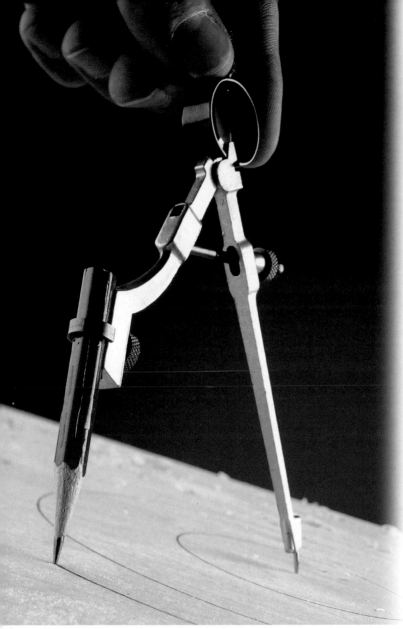

Measuring, Marking & Layout

Successful workshop projects start with careful, accurate measuring, marking and layout. The most critical elements in these steps of the process are good planning, accurate measuring and using sharp marking tools that create readable lines. The level of precision needed varies according to the intricacy and complexity of your project. Rough carpentry (for example, putting up stud walls or installing floor underlayment or roof decking) requires a certain amount of care, but generally you can achieve satisfactory results using tape measures, framing squares and a lumber pencil as a marking tool. Trim carpentry (installing moldings and decorative trim) requires a higher degree of accuracy, so you'll want to involve steel rules, levels, and angle gauges in the process. A good sharp pencil will usually give you marking lines of acceptable accuracy. Fine woodworking carries the highest standard of accuracy. You'll want to use marking gauges, compasses, and any of a wide selection of specialty measuring tools to create well-made projects. Generally, a marking knife or a scratch awl is the marking tool of choice for fine woodworking.

In this chapter you'll find a wealth of tips and tool information to help you get professional measuring, marking and layout results as quickly and efficiently as possible.

Tape measure tips

To obtain accurate readings from a tape measure, start measuring at the 1-in. mark. The end hook on a tape measure often has some play in it, which can alter measurements slightly. And even a secure hook may be bent or caught against a splinter or bump. Don't forget to subtract one inch from the final reading. Steel rules are generally more accurate than tape measures, but they too can become worn or nicked—for best results, sight from the 1-in. mark on any measuring device.

Using the end hook as a starting point when taking measurements with a tape measure can be unreliable, as illustrated by the photo above.

Rating marking tools:
Four degrees of accuracy

Choosing the best marking tool for your project is a matter of weighing the amount of tolerance you're willing to accept against the readability of the lines you scribe—as well as the ease and speed with which the tool can be used. *Marking knives* create highly accurate lines because the flat blade rides flush against a straightedge and cuts through wood fibers and grain contours that can cause a pencil to waver. They're the tool of choice for most fine woodworking projects. *Scratch awls* also cut through fibers and grain, but the round shaft causes the point to be offset slightly from the straightedge. Lines scored with a scratch awl are easier to see because they're wider, which is especially helpful when marking softwoods. *Pencils* are popular marking tools for rough carpentry and some woodworking tasks. A regular pencil sharpened to a fine point will create a fairly precise, readable line. Lumber pencils require less frequent sharpening and create dark, highly readable lines.

Marking knife

Scratch awl

#2 pencil

Lumber pencil

Tips for scribing & laying out

Use a white pencil to mark dark-colored wood, like hardboard or walnut.

Attach medium-grit sandpaper to your toolbox to make a convenient and safe sharpener for lumber pencils.

Use a grease pencil to mark metal, plastic and other materials that can't be marked clearly with a pencil.

Use a sliding T-bevel to transfer angles to your workpiece.

Transfer grid drawings to your workpiece by drawing a scaled grid, then recreating the pattern using the grid as a reference.

Make a sturdy template from hardboard or another durable material when making multiple parts with the same profile.

Three ways to scribe parallel lines

ROUGH CARPENTRY: To create a fast and reasonably accurate line parallel to the edge of a board, use your fingers as a marking gauge. Hold a pencil firmly at the desired mark and glide your hand along the length of the board, using your bent knuckles as an edge guide.

TRIM CARPENTRY: A much more accurate parallel line can be transferred with a combination square and a pencil. Measure the distance you need, place the square against the edge of the board, and glide the square and the pencil together along the length of the cut.

WOODWORKING: The most accurate parallel lines can be drawn with a marking gauge. Measure the distance and firmly glide the tool the length of the cut.

A quick note on the speed square

Created for use in roof construction, *speed squares* allow you to mark angles quickly and accurately in any workshop or construction situation. By pivoting the speed square against one edge of the workpiece, you can mark cutting lines angled by degree or by slope. The slope angles can be found by sighting along the row of numbers labeled *Common numbers.* These numbers represent the number of inches of slope per foot when the pivot end of the square is pressed against the edge of the board and the Common number is aligned on the same edge of the workpiece as the pivot. The degree marks are used in the same manner. Be sure to mark lines along the *marking edge* of the speed square. In the photo to the right, a 2 × 4 is being marked for a 25° cut.

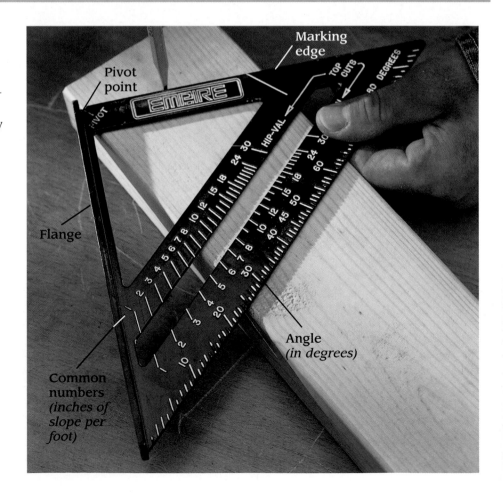

Marking edge

Pivot point

Flange

Common numbers *(inches of slope per foot)*

Angle *(in degrees)*

Two options for tracing a wall contour

When installing built-in cabinets or wall shelving, you may need to trim the end of a shelf, countertop or trim piece to follow the line of a wall that's out of square. Rather than relying on trial-and-error to get the workpiece to fit snugly into an out-of-square corner, transfer the contour of the wall to make a cutting line on the workpiece.

Using a spacer. Cut a small, square piece of scrap hardboard and set the end of the board against the walls. Press the scrap-wood spacer against the wall, and drag it along the profile of the wall, following with a pencil as you go.

Using a compass. Simply set the compass so the legs are about an inch apart, then follow the wall profile with the point, tracing along with the pencil in the other compass leg to make cutting lines.

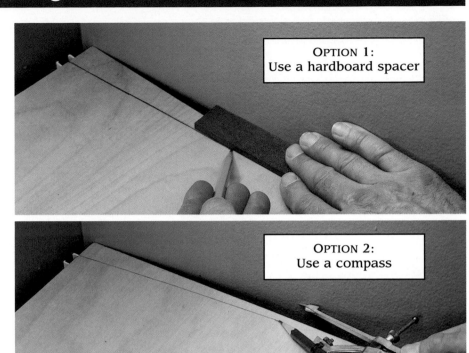

OPTION 1:
Use a hardboard spacer

OPTION 2:
Use a compass

How to find miter angles for base molding

1 To determine the correct length and cutting angle for base moldings, first lay masking tape on the floor at the corner. Use a scrap piece of molding to extend a line beyond the corner for each wall.

2 Press the blade of a sliding T-bevel against one wall and adjust the blade angle so the handle of the tool runs through the point where the lines on the masking tape intersect. Trace the line for reference, then transfer the angle of the T-bevel to your miter box. You can also use the baseboard outlines to measure the length for each trim piece.

An easy way to divide evenly

When you need to divide a board into equal sections, don't worry about performing elaborate mathematical calculations (such as dividing a 7¾-in.-wide board into four equal portions). Instead, just lay a ruler on the board and angle it until it measures a distance easily divisible by the number of cuts. Make certain one edge of the ruler is on the "0" mark. In the example to the left the ruler is angled so that the 12 in. mark touches the far edge of the board. Dividing the board into four pieces is easy: Just mark the board at inches 3, 6 and 9. Repeat the procedure farther down the board and use the marks to draw parallel cutting lines on the board.

Use a marking gauge

Mortise cuts must be extremely precise. To mark the cuts properly, use a marking gauge, available at good hardware stores. As with any marking tool, hold it firm and steady.

Build a center-marking jig

Build a simple center-marking jig with a scrap piece of 2 × 4 and doweling. The gauge can be as wide as you like. Just be certain that the dowels are an equal distance from the center pencil hole. On the reverse side of the jig, insert two dowels 1 in. from the center hole. This side will allow you to find the center on narrow pieces up to 1⅝ in. wide. When using the jig, angle it so both dowels are pressing firmly against the side of the board you are marking.

Find the center of a circle

Clamp a combination square or other straightedge to a framing square. The edge of the straightedge should be flush with both the inside and outside corner of the square where the two legs meet. Position the framing square so each leg is at a flush tangent to the workpiece, then trace the edge of the straightedge past the center of the workpiece at two or more spots. The point where the lines meet is the centerpoint.

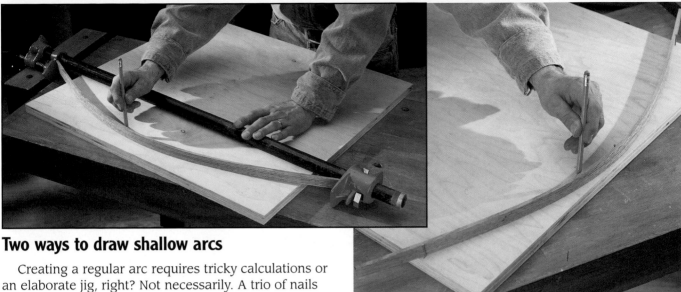

Two ways to draw shallow arcs

Creating a regular arc requires tricky calculations or an elaborate jig, right? Not necessarily. A trio of nails and a strip of wood will do the job. Tack one nail at each endpoint of the arc, and tack the third nail at the apex of the arc, spaced evenly between the endpoints. Cut a thin strip of plywood or hardboard that's at least a few inches longer than the length of the arc. Bend the strip between the the nails as shown in the above, right photo. Trace along the inside edge of the strip to draw

your shallow arc. A variation of this method is simply to insert the wood strip between the jaws of a pipe clamp and tighten the clamp until the strip bows to form an arc of the radius you're seeking (See photo, above left). This method is not as accurate, but it won't leave any nail holes in the workpiece.

Make a simple trammel for drawing circles

A trammel is a marking device that pivots around a centerpoint to create a circle. You can buy fancy milled steel woodworking trammels, or you can make your own with a thin strip of hardboard. Just drive a nail through one end of the strip, then measure out from the nail toward the other end an amount equal to the radius of the circle. Mark a centerpoint for drilling a pencil guide hole at that point (usually, 3/8 in. dia.). Tack the nail at the center of the workpiece, insert the pencil into the guide hole, then make a single revolution around the nail with the pencil to draw the circle.

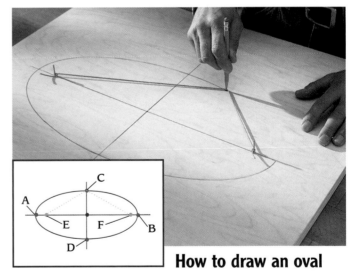

How to draw an oval

Draw perpendicular lines to mark the length and width of the oval. Measuring out from the point of intersection, mark endpoints for the length (A, B) and the width (C, D). Set a compass or trammel to draw an arc that's half as long as the length of the oval. With the point of the compass or trammel at one endpoint for the oval width (C or D), scribe hash marks on the length line (points E, F). Tack nails at points E and F. Tie a string to the nails so the amount of string between the nails is the same as the distance from A to F. Pull the string taut with a pencil tip and trace the oval.

Squares & squaring

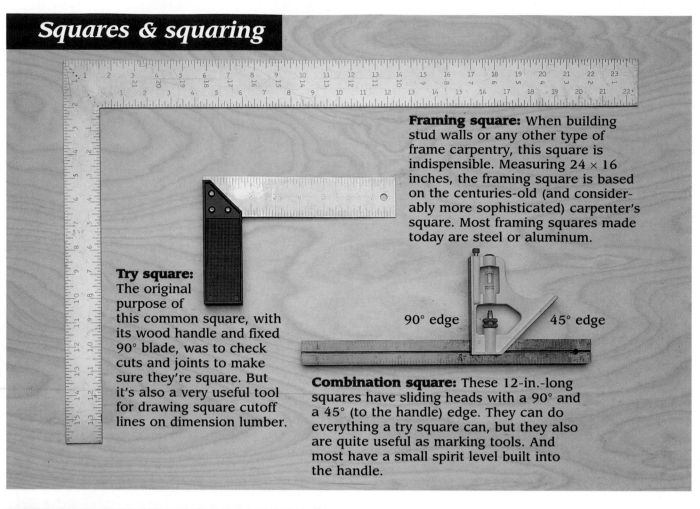

Framing square: When building stud walls or any other type of frame carpentry, this square is indispensible. Measuring 24 × 16 inches, the framing square is based on the centuries-old (and considerably more sophisticated) carpenter's square. Most framing squares made today are steel or aluminum.

Try square: The original purpose of this common square, with its wood handle and fixed 90° blade, was to check cuts and joints to make sure they're square. But it's also a very useful tool for drawing square cutoff lines on dimension lumber.

90° edge   45° edge

Combination square: These 12-in.-long squares have sliding heads with a 90° and a 45° (to the handle) edge. They can do everything a try square can, but they also are quite useful as marking tools. And most have a small spirit level built into the handle.

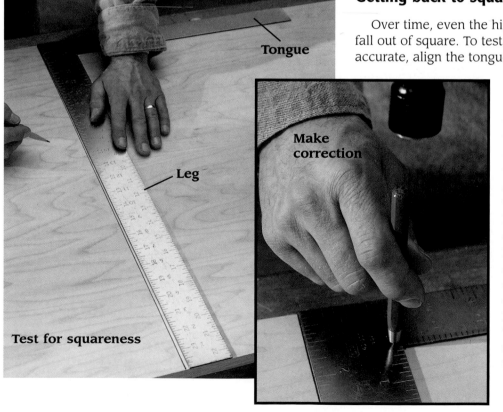

Tongue

Leg

Make correction

Test for squareness

Getting back to square one

Over time, even the highest quality steel squares can fall out of square. To test if your steel square is still accurate, align the tongue of the square with the edge of a wide board and trace a line along one side of the leg. Flip the square over and check to see if the leg is still parallel to the line. If not, the square is out of square. You may be able to correct the problem with a steel punch and a hammer. If the square's inside angle is less than 90°, punch a small depression near the square's inside corner. Check the angle, and continue to punch small depressions near the inside corner until the angle is correct. If the inside angle is more than 90°, punch small depressions on the outside corner of the square.

Measure the diagonals to test frames & casework for square

Drawers, frames, cabinet carcases, tabletops... any workshop project that depends on square corners should be tested repeatedly while it's under construction to make sure that it's still in square. A quick and reliable way is to measure the distance between outside corners on opposing sides of the project. If the measurements are equal, the project is square. If not, you'll need to make adjustments. If your project is a glued-up box or frame, as shown to the right, make adjustments by pushing or pulling on one clamp, while keeping the other steady.

Level up, plumb down

Transferring a point from a floor to a ceiling (or vice versa) is an important skill to have when doing frame carpentry. To mark a point on the floor (sole plate) that's directly below a point on the ceiling (cap plate) simply suspend a plumb bob from the higher point and mark the location of the tip when the plumb bob comes to rest. To find the point directly above another point, raise a straight board from the lower point and adjust its position with a level until it's exactly plumb, then mark the higher point.

Is your level level?

You'll flip for this test

To find out if your spirit level is truly level, set it on a smooth, flat surface (like a piece of fiberboard) and shim beneath the surface with wood shims until the bubble in the lower vial reads level. Then, flip the level and check to see if the bubble in the upper vial gives a similar reading. If not, one of the vials has fallen out of calibration. You can also perform a similar test with the end vials that are used to check for plumb.

But the solution may be simple

Many spirit levels sold today are designed with replaceable vials. If the old vials are removable, you can avoid tossing out an otherwise good level by locating a replacement vial and replacing the old with the new.

A Gallery of Levels

The 4-foot level

Whether its made from mahogany, laminated wood, plastic resin or extruded aluminum, the 4-ft. level is the cornerstone of many building trades. They're used for everything from plumbing stud walls (as shown here) to leveling concrete block to installing cabinets or grading soil. No tool collection is complete without one.

The line level

Used mostly in masonry, this simple devices clips onto a mason's string so the string can be leveled to establish grade or course height.

The post level

When installing fence posts, attach a post level to the post top with a rubber band, and adjust the post until the level tells you it is plumb and level.

The water level

The water level is an ancient device used to find level points that are far apart or separated by obstructions. The original water levels consisted of two glass vials connected by tubing. The tubing was filled with colored water and the vials attached to the two points being leveled. The height of the water in each vial would always be equal. The new-fangled electronic version of a water level shown here is used for leveling fences, grading soil and setting concrete forms. The electronic module shown to the right is set at the desired height of the project. Then, the end of the level hose (See opposite page) is raised or lowered at the fence post or form brace locations. When level is achieved, the module emits a loud buzzing noise.

The electronic level

In addition to spirit level vials, the electronic levels give digital read-outs so you can set slopes that are accurate to within 1/10 degree. Many also sound alerts when level is achieved.

The torpedo level

This 9-in.long spirit level is as portable as they come—you can even carry one in your pocket. Some torpedo levels, like the one shown here, come with magnetized bodies, which are especially useful in plumbing applications. They're well suited for tight quarters, but if precision is important, try to use a longer level.

The 2-foot level

A shorter version of the 4-ft. level, these tools also feature a center vial for establishing level and end vials for establishing plumb. They're slightly less accurate due to their shorter length but can fit into many spaces that are too small for the 4-ft. version.

The laser level

Once a fantasy tool for most handymen, laser levels have dropped in price in recent years, and for the first time some models are in the "affordable" range. They project a level laser beam up to 250 ft., allowing you to make highly accurate level readings for outdoor or indoor projects. Most come with a swiveling base so level lines can be projected 360°. If you're undertaking a large-scale building project but don't want to spend the money on a laser level, they can be rented at most rental stores and some building centers.

Cutting is a fundamental process that's critical to the success of just about any project you're likely to undertake in your workshop. It's essentially a three-part task: laying out the cutting line (See *Measuring, marking & layout*); setting up for the cut; and executing the cut. Setting up involves choosing the best tool and blade for the job, then adjusting the tool or position of the workpiece to ensure an accurate cut.

There are really only two ways of cutting: either you apply a tool to the workpiece (as with most portable and hand tools), or you apply the workpiece to the tool (as with table saws and other tools where the cutting instrument remains in one spot throughout the cut). When applying the tool to the workpiece, use a combination of straightedges, cutting guides and clamps to achieve accurate cuts. When applying the workpiece to the tool, you normally rely on the built-in fences and scales of the tool to guide the cut.

The basic types of cuts undertaken in workshops include: *cross-cutting* (making a straight cut across the grain of a board); *rip-cutting* (reducing the width of a board by cutting it lengthwise with the grain); *miter-cutting* (cross-cutting at an angle with the saw blade perpendicular to the workpiece) and *bevel-cutting* (making a nonperpendicular cut). In addition to these basic cuts, this section also includes information on mortising and cutting non-wood materials. For information on cutting metal, see pages 84 to 94.

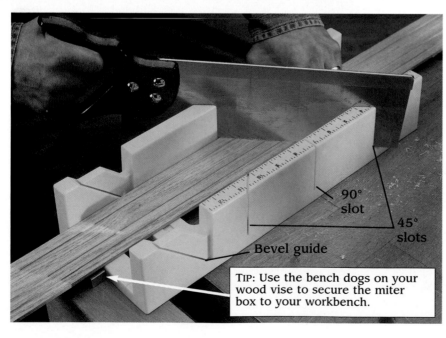

90°
slot

45°
slots

Bevel guide

TIP: Use the bench dogs on your wood vise to secure the miter box to your workbench.

Back to the basics:
Make quick & accurate miter cuts by hand

With the recent explosion in popularity of the power miter saw, the hand miter box has become almost a forgotten tool. But for making a few quick miter cuts, you may want to revisit this handy and age-old device. A simple, inexpensive miter box with precut slots for 45° and 90° can be stored in a tool box or under your workbench, then clamped in place in no time at all. And with the precut slots, no setup time is required. To use the hand miter box, hold your workpiece firmly in place, or clamp it in place, and pull the backsaw in firm, short strokes.

Guide keeps hand saws in line

This easy-to-build cutting guide will ensure straight, accurate cuts with a hand saw. Simply join two pieces of scrap plywood at a right angle, making sure the heads of the fasteners are recessed. Add a piece of scrap wood at the front of the jig to make a lip for holding the jig tightly against your workpiece.

Lip

Team of hand saws can handle any cut

Choosing the right tool for the job is especially important when using hand-powered tools. The collection of hand saws shown above can perform just about any cutting task you're likely to encounter in your workshop.

(A) 8- to 10-tpi cross-cut saw for general cutting of dimension lumber or sheet goods; *(B) Back saw* for miter-cutting; *(C) Hack saw* for cutting metal; *(D) Wallboard saw* for making cutouts in wallboard and other soft building materials; *(E) Flush-cutting saw* for trimming wood plugs and through tenons; *(F) Dovetail saw* (saw shown is smaller version called "Gentleman's saw"); *(G) Japanese saw* (cuts on the pull stroke)for quick trim-carpentry cutting; *(H) Fret saw* for making delicate scrolling cuts; *(I) Coping saw* for curved cuts in trim carpentry.

Band saw & jig saw blades

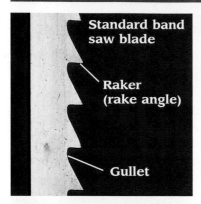

Standard band saw blade

Raker (rake angle)

Gullet

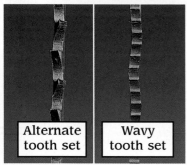

Alternate tooth set | **Wavy tooth set**

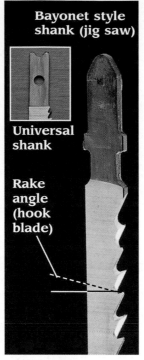

Bayonet style shank (jig saw)

Universal shank

Rake angle (hook blade)

Straight blades for jig saws, band saws, scroll saws and reciprocating saws vary by number of teeth per inch (tpi), the set of the teeth, the rake angle of the teeth, and the width and thickness of the blade. The type of metal used to make the blade and the presence of carbide or other hardened steel tips affect the longevity (and the price) of the blades. Blades for some tools have numerous tooth configurations: for example, band saw blades can be purchased with *standard teeth* (above), or *skip-tooth* and *hook-tooth* configurations.

Circular saw blades

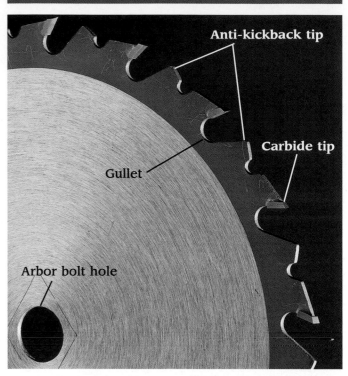

Anti-kickback tip

Carbide tip

Gullet

Arbor bolt hole

Circular saw blades are fitted onto portable circular saws, table saws, radial-arm saws and power miter saws. Select blades by matching the number of teeth per inch to the task at hand—but make sure the tpi number is for the correct blade diameter (anywhere from 3½ in. to 18 in. or so, with 7¼ in. the most common for portable circular saws, and 10 in. the most common for table saws, power miter saws and radial-arm saws).

Reciprocating saw blade types

Reciprocating saws are used to perform many different construction tasks. The size and shape of the blades used changes dramatically according to use. Keep a complete set of blades in your saw case.

A good set of reciprocating saw blades includes: (A) 6 in., 18 tpi blade for heavy metal; (B) 6 in., 10 tpi blade for general cutting; (C) 9 in., 6 tpi blade for fast cuts and general roughing in; (D) 12 in., 8 tpi blade for cutting timbers and other thick materials; (E) 6 in., 4 tpi blade for fast, rough wood-cutting; (F) 6 in., 5 tpi blade for fast, cleaner cuts; (G) 3⅝ in., 14 tpi blade for curved cuts in hard woods.

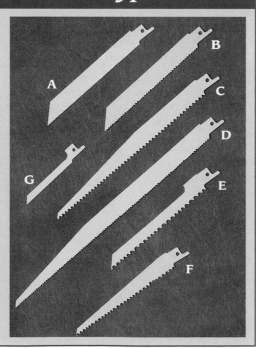

Common circular saw blade styles (right) include: (A) General purpose combination blade (good for ripping); (B) Thin-kerf anti-kickback blade (note expansion slots); (C) Roofer's blade (for portable circular saws); (D) Trim-cutting blade (for clean, relatively fast cross-cuts); (E) Carbide-tipped cross-cutting blade (good for power miter saws). Generally, more teeth per inch produce cleaner, slower cuts.

Saw blade selection chart

Band saw

TASK	WIDTH (IN.)	PITCH	STYLE*	SET*
Scrollwork, joinery	1/8	14 tpi	ST	AB or R
Cutting light metal	1/8	14 tpi	ST	W
Tight curves	1/8	6 tpi	SK	AB
Smooth curves	3/16	10 tpi	ST	AB
General purpose	1/4	6-8 tpi	ST or SK	AB
Rip-cutting	1/4	4-6 tpi	H	AB or R
Gen. cross-cutting	3/8	8-10 tpi	ST or SK	AB or R
Fast cross-cutting	3/8	4 tpi	SK	AB
Resawing	1/2	4 tpi	H	AB

*Key ST=standard, SK=skip-tooth, H=hook-tooth, AB=alternate-bevel, R=raker, W=wavy

Jig Saw

TASK	MATERIAL	LENGTH	PITCH
Fast, rough carpentry	Wood	4 in.	6 tpi
General purpose	Wood	4 in.	8 tpi
Smooth finish	Wood	4 in.	10 tpi
Extra-smooth finish	Wood	3 in.	12-14 tpi
Light metal	Metal	3 in.	12-14 tpi
Thick metal	Metal	3 in.	24 tpi

Circular Saw

TASK	TYPE	TPI (8¼-IN./10-IN. DIA.)
General purpose	Combination	16-36/18-50
Trim carpentry	Cross-cut	40-64/60-80
Rough carpentry	Cross-cut	34-40/40-60
Smooth cross-cutting	Cross-cut	50-64/60-80
Rip-cutting	Ripping	16-36/18-24
Plywood and particle board	Plywood/panel	48-64/60-80
Light metal	Metal-cutting	58-64/60-72

Scroll Saw

TASK	TYPE	GAUGE	PITCH
General cutting	Scrolling	#5	15 tpi
Cutting without tear-out	Reverse-tooth fret	#7	11.5 tpi
Fine scrollwork	Scrolling	#7	12 tpi
Very tight curves	Spiral-tooth	#2	41 tpi
Fast cuts	Fret	#9	11.5 tpi

TIP: Give your blades a bath

Saw blades that aren't performing as well as you like don't necessarily need sharpening: they may just need a quick cleaning. Special pitch/resin removing compound or ordinary oven cleaner can be used to clean blades (be sure to wear gloves).

Coping base trim for an inside corner

1 Cut one mating board square, and cut the other at a 45° bevel, using a miter saw. The beveled board should be slightly longer than the finished length.

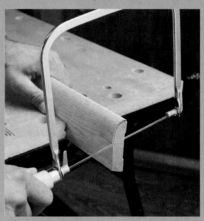

2 With the square-cut board flush in the corner, use a coping saw to trim the excess wood from the beveled end, leaving an end that's perpendicular but tapers up to follow the profile of the molding.

3 Apply the wood finish to both boards, then slip the beveled board into the corner so it overlaps the end of the square-cut board.

Cutting with circular saws

Cutting

Make & use a straightedge

Build an 8-ft. straightedge to cut plywood and paneling with your circular saw. The straightedge shown below has a ¼ in. plywood base, and a 1 × 2 cleat (you can also use a strip of plywood) that serves as a saw guide. After assembling the straightedge, position the circular saw with the foot tight against the cleat and trim off the excess portion of the plywood base. To use the straightedge, position the trimmed edge of the plywood base flush with your cutting line and clamp the straightedge to the workpiece.

Cutting line

Good-side-down for cleaner cuts

Portable circular saws cut on the upward rotation of the blade. To avoid tear-out on the better face of your workpiece, turn it good-face-down when cutting.

Two techniques for making plunge cuts

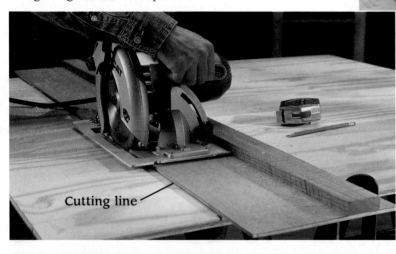

Use a jig saw: Tip the jig saw forward on the front edge of its foot. Align the tip of the blade with the cutting line, then turn on the saw and gently but firmly lower the blade into the cutting area. The blade will want to bounce, but by maintaining firm pressure on the front of the foot you can keep it under control until it enters the wood.

Use a circular saw: Place the front edge of the foot against the board, retract the blade guard and hold it in a raised position with your thumb. Turn on the saw and lower the blade into the wood, using the front of the saw foot as a fulcrum. Always wear safety goggles.

Rotary cutters use drilling action to make internal cuts

Spiral cutting tools are a cross between a jig saw or reciprocating saw and a power drill. The spiral-shaped cutting bit for the tool looks and acts like a drill bit, but, like a jig saw, it cuts straight or curved lines in building materials like drywall, tile, plaster, fiberglass and wood using different bits. A relatively new tool innovation, these compact cutters are especially useful in making internal cuts and cutouts. In the photo to the right, a spiral cutting tool is being used to cut holes for water supply pipes in a sheet of cement board.

Making curved cutouts

Minimum radius cuts for band saw blades

As a general rule, you should choose the widest band saw blade that can handle the job you're doing. But because the width of the blade limits the tightness of the curves you can cut, you should choose the wisest blade that can follow your tightest cutting radius.

BLADE WIDTH	SMALLEST RADIUS CUT
1/8"	3/16"
3/16"	3/8"
1/4"	5/8"
3/8"	1 1/4"
1/2"	3"
3/4"	5"
1"	8"

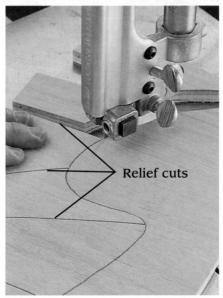

Relief cuts

Relief cuts prevent binding

When making a curved contour cut using a jig saw, band saw or scroll saw, make relief cuts from the edge of the workpiece to the cutting line, in the waste area, so waste can be removed as you cut.

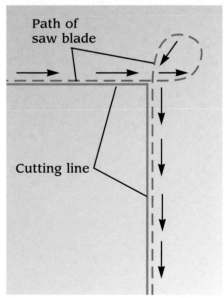

Path of saw blade

Cutting line

Cut a loop to make a square

Making square internal cuts can be a perplexing problem, but here's a simple solution: cut along one leg of the square, and keep cutting past the corner. Loop the saw blade back and cut the second leg.

Single-flute straight bit

Spiral upcut bit

Cut perfect circles with a router compass

Most handymen think of routers as primarily tools for cutting decorative profiles or perhaps an occasional dado or rabbet. But they can also be very effective tools for cutting stock to size and shape. When the right bits and techniques are used, they produce extremely clean edges that often require no sanding.

If you need to cut a square workpiece into a circular shape, a router compass is an excellent choice. Simply secure the router base to the wide end of the compass, set the adjustable center pin to the desired radius of the cut, and secure the pin at the center of the circle. For best results, make the cut in several passes of increasing depth. A single-flute straight bit or a spiral upcut bit can be used to remove large amounts of waste in the cutting area, without bogging down.

Tips for cutting with a power miter box

Bolt and nut won't let wood chips accumulate

Stopblock

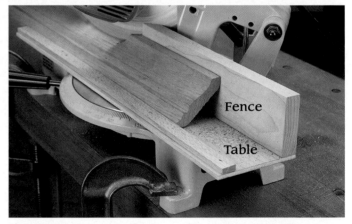

Fence

Table

Stopblock speeds up repetitive cuts

When making repetitive cuts with a power miter saw (or radial-arm saw), clamp a stopblock to the saw fence at the desired length. A lag screw driven squarely into the edge of the stopblock creates a solid surface for aligning the workpiece, while keeping wood chips from building up between the block and workpiece.

Jig takes the math out of beveling molding

Cutting miter-bevels in crown molding often involves tricky math and very precise angles. To simplify the task, use this jig. Join a straight board about 3 in. high to a strip of ¼-in. plywood about 6 in. wide. These will be the "fence" and "table" of the jig. Place a piece of crown molding into the "L" formed by the fence and table, and adjust it until the beveled sides are flush against the fence and table. Mark the position on the table, remove the molding and attach a wood strip at the mark. This strip will hold the molding at the proper angle for bevel-cutting miters.

Cutting

Proper setup is key to safe cutting with radial-arm saw

Over the years the radial-arm saw has earned a reputation as one of the most dangerous workshop tools. But for most cross-cutting operations, the tool can be a real workhorse that's as safe as any other tool you own. The most important aspect of cutting safely with a radial-arm saw is to secure your workpiece, while keeping your hands well clear of the saw blade. A pushstick with a birdseye cutout is a good choice for bracing smaller workpieces against the saw fence—it's particularly effective when used in conjunction with a stopblock that holds the free end of the workpiece in place. Once the workpiece is secure, start the saw and guide it through the cut with your right hand. Shut off the saw and allow the blade to stop spinning before removing the workpiece and returning the saw carriage back behind the fence.

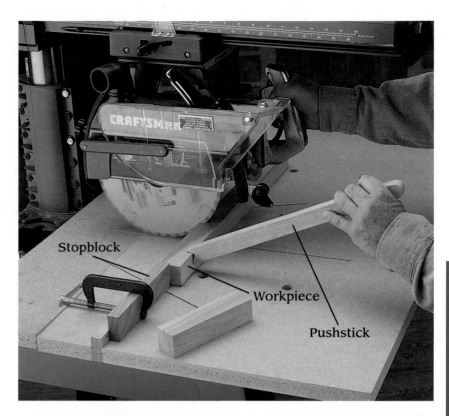

Stopblock

Workpiece

Pushstick

Resawing stock on a band saw

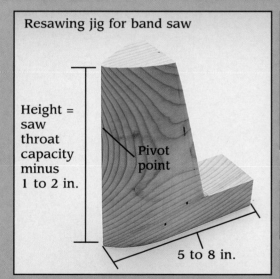

Resawing jig for band saw

Height = saw throat capacity minus 1 to 2 in.

Pivot point

5 to 8 in.

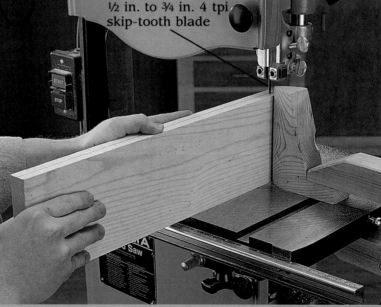

½ in. to ¾ in. 4 tpi skip-tooth blade

Resawing thick lumber into thinner strips for woodworking is a job best accomplished with a band saw. The simplest method is to attach a fence to the band saw table, parallel to the blade, and feed the stock through as you would when rip-cutting on a band saw. The downside to this method is that the saw blade tends to travel, following the grain of the wood, and resulting in an uneven cut that requires quite a bit of surface planing. One way to minimize the unevenness of the resaw cut is to use a jig like the one shown to the left. When clamped to the saw table so the pivot point is even with the cutting edge of the blade, the jig may be used as a guide to set the thickness of the cut. Because the pivot point is so narrow, you can adjust the feed direction of the board to compensate for blade travel, resulting in a more even cut. You'll still need to surface-plane the workpiece, but you'll waste less wood.

Relief block keeps cutoff pieces free and clear when cross-cutting

Use a relief block to prevent cutoff pieces from getting jammed between the fence and the blade when cross-cutting on the table saw. The relief block can simply be a piece of scrap wood clamped to the fence. Make sure the relief block is positioned behind the point where the workpiece will make first contact with the saw blade. Never stand directly behind the workpiece when feeding it into the blade.

Relief block

Blade guard removed for clarity

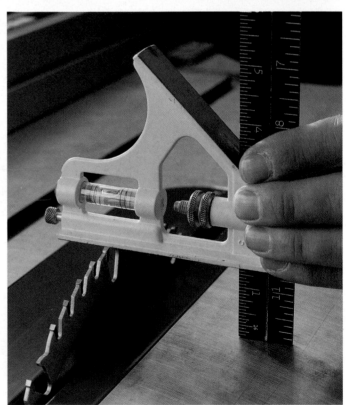

As a rule, take measurements

Don't trust the cutting scale on the table saw fence if you're making precise cuts. Instead, measure the distance from the cutting edge of the blade to the fence with a steel rule when setting up for your cut. Double-check the distance after securing the fence, and make a practice cut on scrap for added precision.

Get blade height just right

Use a combination square to set the height of a table saw blade. The bottom of the square should just be touching the tip of one of the teeth. Because tooth length is not always uniform, spin the blade by hand and make sure you're referencing off the tooth that will cut deepest (be sure to unplug the saw first).

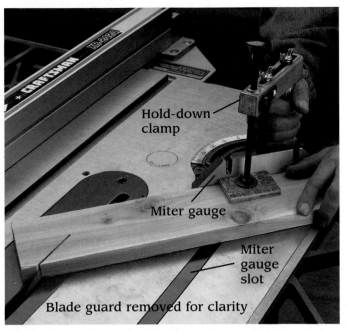

Shop vac blows cutoff pieces clear

Small cutoff pieces have a way of kicking out of the saw throat or becoming jammed around the blade. One way to keep these annoying trim pieces out of your way is simply to position your shop vac hose near the cutting area to blow clear small cutoff pieces. Be sure to leave ample clearance for the workpiece.

Add miter-gauge hold-down for quick, accurate miter-cutting

Make your miter gauge more reliable by adding a hold-down clamp to keep workpieces steady during miter cutting. Hold-downs are sold at most larger tool centers or may be purchased directly from the company that manufactured your table saw.

Wood fences make good sense

Adding a wooden auxiliary fence to your table saw (or just about any other tool) extends the life of both your saw fence and your saw blades by eliminating damaging metal-to-metal contact. An auxiliary fence that's taller than the saw fence also creates a good surface for clamping jigs, stopblocks and hold-downs. The fence shown here is made from hard maple and attached to the metal fence with T-bolts that fit into a slot in the saw fence so no screw heads protrude.

Reverse the miter gauge for panel cutting

Sheet goods and glued-up panels are often too wide to be fed into the blade with the saw's miter gauge. You can solve this problem by turning the gauge around so the head of the gauge is fed into the miter gauge slot first. Attach an auxiliary fence to the miter gauge to create a more stable surface for pressing against. You can also use a miter-gauge hold-down (See photo at top of page) to keep the panel steady.

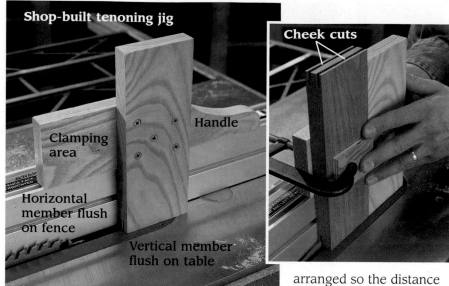

Shop-built tenoning jig

Clamping area

Handle

Horizontal member flush on fence

Vertical member flush on table

Cheek cuts

Sweet cheeks for tenons

Making the cheek cuts for tenons is clumsy and dangerous without a good tenoning jig—and the results are usually disappointing. This shop-built tenoning jig is easy to make from scrap wood and will help you produce tenons that fit on the first try. First, cut the vertical and horizontal members—the horizontal member should have a contour on the tail to create a handle, as shown above. Join the two members with wood screws, arranged so the distance from the bottom of the horizontal member to the bottom of the vertical member is equal to the height of your saw fence. Make sure the members are exactly perpendicular. To use the jig, clamp your workpiece to the jig and feed the workpiece into the blade, keeping steady pressure against the fence and the table (See photo, above right). Cut all the way through the workpiece and the jig. Always test your cuts on a scrap board before cutting your workpieces. Use your miter gauge to guide the workpiece when cutting the tenon shoulders.

Trim wedge and dowel ends with a flush-cutting saw

A flush-cutting saw with a very flexible blade is the ideal tool for trimming off the ends of tenon wedges or dowels. The saw shown above is a Japanese saw that cuts on the pull stroke.

The "poor man's mortising machine"

There are many methods you can use to cut mortises for mortise-and-tenon joinery. The best way is to purchase a special mortising machine or a mortising attachment for your drill press. But if you'd rather not spend the money on these expensive tools, the following method will produce clean mortises when done carefully. It's a little slower and takes some trial-and-error, but for the weekend woodworker who already owns a drill press, it's a good option.

1 Carefully lay out your mortise using a marking gauge or straightedge. Choose a drill bit the same diameter as the thickness of the mortise (⅜ in. is common), then remove the waste wood from the mortise by drilling overlapping holes using a depth stop.

2 Use a sharp chisel to clean up the sides of the mortise so they're flat and smooth. Make sure the flat face of the chisel is contacting the wood. Clean up the ends of the mortise with a chisel the same width as the thickness of the mortise.

A treat for steel tabletops

Apply rubbing or polishing compound to steel table-tops to smooth out the surface and remove rust. Then, wipe the top clean and apply a coat of car wax to seal the table and keep workpieces sliding smoothly.

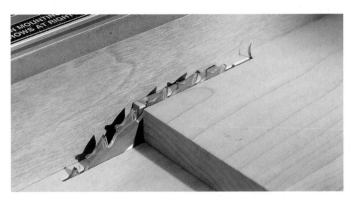

Create custom throat plates

When making trim cuts or cutting small workpieces, cover the throat opening of your saw by laying a piece of thin plywood over the throat and raising the spinning saw blade. Use a piece of scrap wood to hold the plywood down.

Increase your cutting angle

To make cuts with an angle greater than the maximum tilt of your saw blade, attach a spacer to your saw fence or to the workpiece.

Spacer

Handy jig for cutting tapers

An adjustable taper jig is a handy accessory for any table saw owner. The legs of the jig can be set to cut tapers according to angle or to slope.

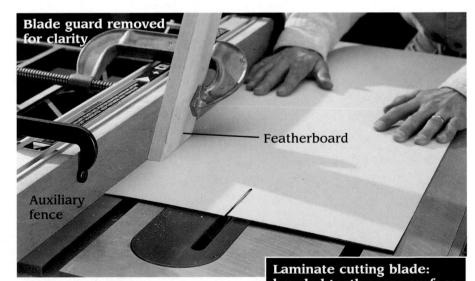

Taper jig

Blade guard removed for clarity

Featherboard

Auxiliary fence

Cutting laminate

Before cutting laminate on your table saw, attach an auxiliary fence that's flush with the tabletop so the laminate won't slide or wedge under the fence. A special laminate cutting blade (right) prevents chipping of the surface.

Laminate cutting blade: beveled teeth score surface of laminate to prevent chip-out from cutting teeth

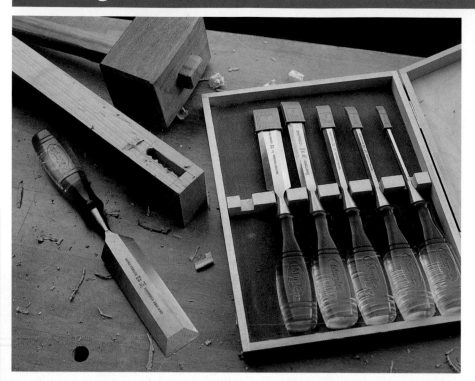

Cabinetmaker's chisels

Most of the wood chisels sold and owned today are bevel-edge cabinetmaker's chisels (See photo, left). Available in standard widths ranging from ¼ to 1½ in., they can handle a variety of everyday cutting tasks, including cutting mortises and paring tenons. If you're a serious woodworker who appreciates hand tools, you may want to look into a set of mortising chisels, which have thicker shanks and wider, shock-resistant handle butts. Better quality chisels are made with hardened steel that hold an edge for a long time. The main differences are in handle material, size and feel. If investing in a set of quality chisels, make sure the ones you choose feel comfortable and well balanced in your hand.

How to sharpen chisels

1 Grind off any nicks using a bench grinder with a medium-grit wheel (or a coarse-grit sharpening stone). Hold the tool on the flat portion of the tool rest, with the beveled side facing up. Hold the tip against the wheel and move it from side to side, keeping the cutting edge square. Cool the blade frequently with water to keep it from losing its temper. When all nicks are gone, turn the blade so the cutting edge is down. Adjust the tool rest so the blade touches the grinding wheel at a 25° bevel. Move the blade from side to side, keeping the blade at a 25° bevel. Continue to cool the blade regularly.

2 Place a few drops of light machine oil on a fine-grit sharpening stone. Place the back of the blade on the whetstone and draw it back and forth several times to remove any burrs.

3 Wipe the stone with a clean rag, and apply more oil. Turn the blade over, and hold it at a 25° angle so the bevel is flat against the stone. Draw the tool back and forth. Here, a bevel guide is used for a precise edge angle.

4 Put a micro-edge on the blade by lifting it slightly so just the tip touches the stone. Draw the blade lightly two or three times along the stone, until a slight burr can be felt along the back of the blade. Turn the blade over, hold it flat (as in step 2) and draw it one time along the stone to remove the burr. Done properly, this will give the chisel a razor-sharp edge.

1

25° angle

2

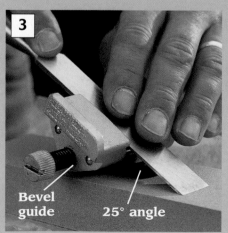

3

Bevel guide   **25° angle**

4

Cutting

The right way to cut hinge mortises

Installing hinges (or strike plates) is a frequently encountered task for the handyman, and as often as not we rely on the trial-and-error method—with mixed results. Here's the best way to cut a hinge mortise.

1 Remove the hinge pin (if it's removable) and position the hinge leaf or strike plate on the edge of the door or on the door jamb. Tack it into place with screws, then score an outline around the plate with a utility knife. This prevents the wood from splintering past the ends of the mortise.

2 Choose a chisel that's close to the same width as the mortise. With the beveled side of the chisel facing toward the mortise, tap the butt of the chisel handle with a wood or rubber mallet. Cut into the wood to a depth equal to the thickness of the hinge leaf or strike plate. Cut along all sides of four-sided mortises.

3 With the beveled edge of the chisel tip flat against the workpiece, make a series of relief cuts in the waste wood area of the mortise. Space the cuts ⅛ to ¼ in. apart (make closer cuts in harder woods). The cuts should be equal in depth to the finished depth of the mortise.

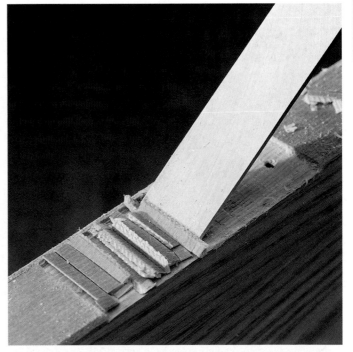

4 Clean out the waste wood by driving the chisel against the direction of the relief cuts. To avoid digging in too deep, try to keep the beveled edge of the tip flat in the mortise. Scrape the bottom of the mortise smooth. If you need to deepen the mortise, repeat the procedure—don't simply try to make deeper scraping cuts.

How to cut bricks & pavers

1 Install a masonry blade in your circular saw. Adjust the saw blade to cut about ¼ in. deep. When cutting multiple bricks or pavers, clamp them together for gang-cutting. Draw your cutting line and score it with the masonry blade. Wear eye protection at all times.

Masonry blade

2 Set each scored brick or paver on-edge on a semi-resilient surface (like a sheet of plywood). Position the blade of a wide brickset on the edge, aligned with the scored cutting line. Strike the brickset with a 3-lb. maul until the brick or paver cleaves along the cutting line.

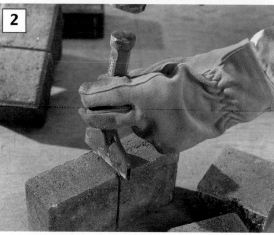

Wet saw

Option: Use a wet saw. If your project requires that you cut more than a dozen or so bricks or pavers, think seriously about renting a wet saw for the job. Available at most rental centers, wet saws are fast and easy to operate. Simply set the brick or paver on the tool bed with the cutting line aligned with the saw blade and lower the counter-weighted blade. Do not pull down forcefully on the blade.

How to cut tiles with a tile cutter

Push scoring tool forward

Scoring tool

Sizing gauge

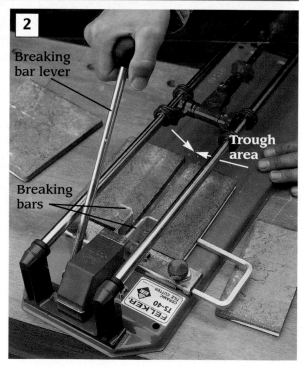

Breaking bar lever

Trough area

Breaking bars

1 Set the tile on the bed of the tile cutter so the cutting line is aligned with the point of the scoring tool. Some tile cutters, like the one above, are equipped with a sizing gauge so you can set the tool to make multiple cuts that are the same width. Lighter duty cutters often cut on the pull stroke, but the rented, heavy-duty model shown here cuts on the push stroke. Press down on the lever that lowers the scoring tool and push forward, scoring the cutting line.

2 Retract the scoring tool clear of the tile, then lower the lever that controls the breaking bars. These bars exert downward pressure toward the trough in the center of the bed, causing the tile to snap along the scored line.

Cutting

Glass data sheet

TYPE	CHARACTERISTICS	USES
Sheet	Lowest cost, noticeable waviness due to thickness variations	Windows, cabinet doors, general household use
Plate	Ground and polished to a degree much flatter than sheet glass	Large display windows, table tops, glass shelves
Tempered*	High impact strength and small, relatively harmless fragments when shattered	Patio doors, French doors, skylights, overhead windows

*Both sheet glass and plate glass may be tempered

Cutting Plexiglas

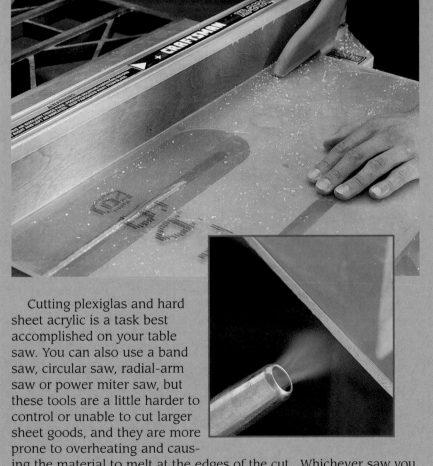

Cutting plexiglas and hard sheet acrylic is a task best accomplished on your table saw. You can also use a band saw, circular saw, radial-arm saw or power miter saw, but these tools are a little harder to control or unable to cut larger sheet goods, and they are more prone to overheating and causing the material to melt at the edges of the cut.. Whichever saw you use, use a blade with a high number of teeth per inch (tpi). The table saw above is equipped with a plywood cutting blade. If the material has a paper or poly facing, leave it on until the cut is finished. The edges of the cut can be sanded or rounded over with very fine sandpaper or emery cloth. For a clear edge, run the flame from a propane torch carefully along the edge (inset photo).

How to cut glass

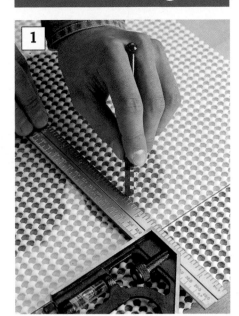

1 Set the sheet of glass on a soft, non-skid surface like the rug pad shown above. Lubricate the cutting wheel with lightweight machine oil. Using a straightedge as a guide, score a cutting line with a glass cutting tool. Press down firmly on the tool—the goal is to create a score line that breaks the glass surface in a single pass. Making multiple passes will result in a filed or very rough cut.

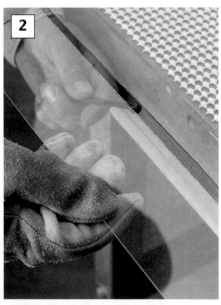

2 Slide the glass sheet to the edge of your worksurface so the scored line overhangs the edge. Wearing work gloves, apply gentle downward pressure to the waste section of glass. Then, tap lightly on the underside of the scored cutting line with the ball end of the glass cutting tool. This will cause the glass to fracture along the cutting line. Smooth the cut edge with emery paper.

Drilling

Drilling precise and uniform holes is an overlooked art form in most workshops. But the fact is, it doesn't take much longer to set up drilling guides that will help make your drilling projects virtually foolproof. Choosing the right tool and the right style of bit is also very important to drilling success. The basic selection of drill types includes:

• **Hand drills** (brace-and-bit, egg-beater style and others). These tools are becoming less common with the advent of the cordless power drill, but they're still nice to have around for drilling a few quick holes on-site (and the battery never runs down).

• **Corded portable drills.** These too have lost prominence to the cordless, but every shop should still be equipped with one of these workhorses. With few exceptions, they can still create more torque than cordless drills, and they're very reliable for large projects, like screwing down decking.

• **Cordless drills.** How did we ever get along without these tools? Technology continues to evolve, but generally a 12-volt model with an exchangeable battery pack will perform just about any workshop drilling task.

• **Drill press.** For power and precision, a drill press is unbeatable. For most tasks, a benchtop model will do the job. But if you do a lot of woodworking or metalworking, look for a floor-standing model with easily adjustable speed and a larger throat capacity.

A backer board prevents tear-out

Regardless of the type of drill and bit you're using, bits will cause splintering and tearout when they exit a board. To prevent this from happening, simply slip a backer board beneath the workpiece before drilling. Any piece of wood scrap can be used as a backer board. For a more permanent backer board, many woodworkers attach pieces of scrap wood to their drill press table with screws driven up through the guide holes in the table. In addition to preventing tearout, a wood auxiliary table on your drill press helps prevent damage that can occur to drill bits if they're inadvertently driven into the metal table.

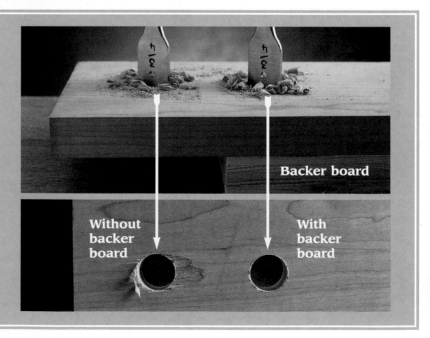

Backer board

Without backer board

With backer board

Drill press speeds

MATERIAL	HOLE DIA.	SPEED (RPM)
Plastic	1/16 in.	6000-6500
	1/4 in.	3000-3500
	1/2 in.	500-1000
Soft metal	1/16 in.	6000-6500
	1/4 in.	4500-5000
	1/2 in.	1500-2500
Steel	1/16 in.	5000-6500
	1/4 in.	1500-2000
	1/2 in.	500-1000
Wood	0-1/2 in.	3000-4000
	1/2-1 in.	2000-3000
	1+ in.	700-2000

Note: Multispur bits should be used at very low speed (250 to 700 rpm)

Portable drill types

Hand-held power drills are made in two basic handle styles: the *T-handle* and the *pistol grip*. If you use your drill for extended periods of time, the T-handle is probably a better choice because it's more balanced and won't cause fatigue as soon. The T-handle also is easier to control for precision drilling. Pistol-grip drills are preferred by people who work with harder materials because the design allows you to apply more downward pressure directly over the bit—but never press too hard.

Pistol grip

T-handle

Secure a sphere

Drilling holes into a wood sphere is easy with this homemade holder. Drill holes slightly smaller than the diameter of the sphere into the centers of two small pieces of scrap wood. Sandwich the sphere between the holes and secure with a woodscrew clamp.

Steady a cylinder

A block of wood with a V-groove will hold dowels and other cylinders steady during drilling. Simply set the blade on your table saw to 45° and cut 1-in.-deep grooves from opposite ends, forming a "V" in the center of the board. Adjust the width and depth of the "V" according to the diameter of the cylinder.

Drill bit diameters

BIT TYPE	RANGE OF DIA.
Twist	1/64 to 1 in.
Spade	1/4 to 1 1/2 in.
Brad-point	1/8 to 5/8 in.
Masonry (3/8-in. drill)	1/8 to 1 in.
Masonry (1/2-in. drill)	1/8 to 1 1/2 in.
Forstner	1/4 to 2 1/8 in.

Drill perfect pilots on the fly

Take the guesswork out of drilling pilot holes for finish nails by chucking one of the nails into your drill and using it as a drill bit.

Special-purpose drills & accessories offer solutions

Hammer drill for concrete

The hammer drill (available in ⅜ and ½ in. models) uses percussion to help drill bits cut into stubborn concrete. Be sure to use a masonry bit (See page 48) and wear hand, ear and eye protection.

Fly cutter for circular cutouts

The fly cutter is an adjustable drill press accessory that will make smooth circular cutouts up to 6 in. dia. Use the lowest drill press speed setting and be sure to clamp your workpiece to the drill press table.

Bit extension for deep holes

Ever wondered how to drill a cord hole in a lamp base, or how to drill through an 8 in. timber with a 6 in. long bit? By chucking a bit extension into your drill you can add 12 to 24 in. of drilling capacity.

How to drill clean holes in ceramic tile

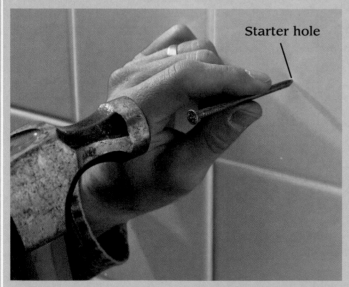

Starter hole

Masonry bit

1 Before drilling into glazed tile, break the slick surface by lightly tapping the tile with a center punch or nail at the centerpoint of your drilling mark. This will create a starting point for the drill bit (without a starter hole, the bit will wander across the surface of the tile, scratching and gouging as it travels).

2 Use a masonry bit to drill through the tile. If you have a variable speed drill, set the tool on its slowest setting. Don't force the bit or you risk cracking the tile.

Drilling

How to cut wood plugs with a plug cutter

1 Install the plug cutter into the chuck of your drill press—most cutters will produce ⅜-in.-dia. flat top plugs. Select a piece of scrap stock from your project with similar grain orientation to the wood with the counterbored holes that will be filled (or use a contrasting wood species). Drill at least ⅜ in. deep into the board to create as many plugs as you need. Don't drill all the way through.

2 Resaw the board to ⅜ to ½ in. thickness, using a band saw or table saw. The individual plugs will drop out as you cut. Glue the plugs into the screw counterbores, then trim them flush with the wood surface (inset photo).

Using a hole saw

A hole saw is a popular hole-cutting device that can be fitted onto your portable power drill or your drill press. Frequently used to drill holes in doors for locksets, hole saws are sold in standard sizes on fixed mandrels, or as adjustable tools where hole saws of differing diameter can be fitted and secured onto a single mandrel. The free end of the mandrel is chucked into the drill and the pilot bit on the other end is used to start the hole and keep the hole saw cutting on-center.

Interchangeable hole saw
(exploded view)

Locknut

Hole saw
(other sizes may be used)

Mandrel

Pilot bit

1 When cutting with a hole saw, position the tip of the pilot bit over the drilling point and begin drilling at slow speed until the teeth of the hole saw engage the workpiece. Adjust the drill speed so the saw is cutting productively, but without bogging down or burnishing the edges of the hole. Hold the drill perpendicular to the workpiece.

2 Cut as deeply into the work area as you can, without cutting all the way through. Make sure the pilot bit has cut through, however. Withdraw the hole saw and finish the cut from the other face of the workpiece (this prevents tear-out from the hole saw).

Guide to common drill bits

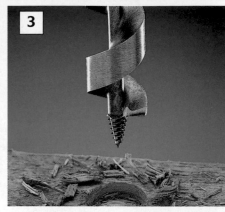

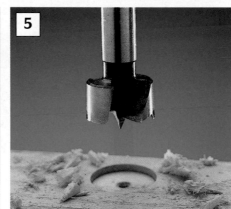

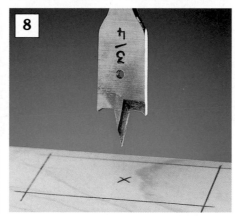
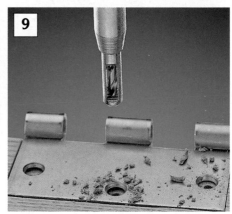

1. Twist bit will bore through angle iron, flat iron or sheet metal and can be used for rough drilling in wood and other materials. Twist bits are available in a wider range of diameters than any other bit type.

2. Brad-point bit looks like a twist bit, but has a center spur and side spurs to keep it from wandering. These bits can make clean cuts in wood and softer materials.

3. Auger bit will bore deep, straight holes into timber or thick softwood. The threaded bit point helps keep the bit cutting true while the spiral cutting head carries wood shavings to the surface. Designed for use with brace-and-bit and other hand-powered drills.

4. Counterboring bit creates a pilot hole and countersink hole to accommodate a screw head and wood plug. Some bits are fully adjustable as to their depth; others are not. Common sizes are for a #5, 6, 8, 10, 12, or 14 wood screw and ¼, ⅜ or ½-in. plugs.

5. Forstner bit will cut very clean holes with flat bottoms. It is especially useful in fine woodworking or when drilling into hardwoods. The bit will produce holes in any grain direction. Anyone with an interest in woodworking should own a full set of these bits.

6. Masonry bit has hard cutting flanges, designed to penetrate concrete and other masonry, including ceramic tile. Best used with a hammer drill.

7. Countersink bit will ream out an existing hole so a screw can be set flush, or recessed, into a surface.

8. Spade bit is useful for boring through wood where precise edging is not critical. It is the bit of choice when boring wiring holes through studs or removing wood before chiseling.

9. Vix bit is designed to drill perfectly centered screw pilot holes through guide holes in hardware plates.

Portable drill guide

This drilling accessory gives a portable power drill the precision of a drill press. You can use it to drill perfectly straight holes on the job site, and many models are scaled to drill at precise angles.

Guide for shelf pin holes

A strip of perforated hardboard (pegboard) makes a handy guide for drilling evenly spaced shelf pin holes in shelf standards. Typically, holes are spaced about 1 in. apart and are drilled with a ¼ in. bit.

Drill press table stopblocks

Straight lengths of scrap wood can be clamped to your drill press table to make stop blocks for drilling uniform holes in multiple workpieces.

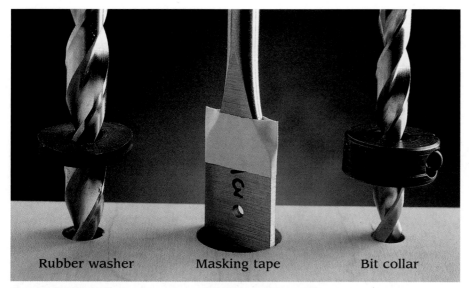

Rubber washer   Masking tape   Bit collar

Do-it-yourself depth stops for portable drills

Drilling depth can be set with a gauge on your drill press, but what about with a portable drill? To take the guesswork out of drilling holes to an exact depth, mark the drill bit at the appropriate depth with a rubber washer or masking tape. You can also use special drill bit collars that are sold at most building centers and hardware stores.

Drilling template

Plot out hole spacing on a paper or hardboard template for woodworking projects. The template will help you drill identical hole patterns on matching workpieces.

Drilling

Shaping is a fairly broad category when it comes to workshop skills. In one sense or another, just about anything you do to a workpiece with a tool alters its shape. But this chapter concerns shaping exercises that don't necessarily change the size of the workpiece, but rather alter its appearance or, in some cases, prepare it to be joined with another workpiece. Routing, planing, filing and shaving or paring are the activities normally done for this purpose.

Shaping is the area of woodworking where hand tools are still used most prevalently. Hand planes, files, drawknives, spokeshaves and other hand-powered tools offer a level of precision and control that's hard to find with power tools. But for their part, power tools (particularly the router) are much faster and, for some types of shaping tasks, more accurate. Making grooves, rabbets, dovetails and other joinery cuts is a perfect chore for the router, provided you use the correct router bit. Shaping complex edge profiles, like ogees and coves, is much easier to do with a router bit than with any hand tool.

Whether you're using hand or power tools, the key to good results when shaping wood is not to try to remove too much material at one time. Make a habit of making several precise, controlled passes with the tool whenever possible. This will yield cleaner, more accurate results, and you're less likely to ruin your workpiece: it's tough to put wood back on once you cut it off.

Invest in a router table

A router is one of the most versatile power tools ever created, but mounted in a router table its usefulness and accuracy become even greater. Commercial models are available, but many handymen prefer to build their own. You can purchase kits for making the mounting plate, fence and even the table surface. The router table shown to the right is made using an inexpensive bathroom vanity as a cabinet, with a piece of post-form countertop for the tabletop. If you plan to use your router table frequently, it's a good idea to buy a dedicated router for it. Look for a fixed-base model with a ½ in. collet. A soft start feature will make the router table safer and easier to manage.

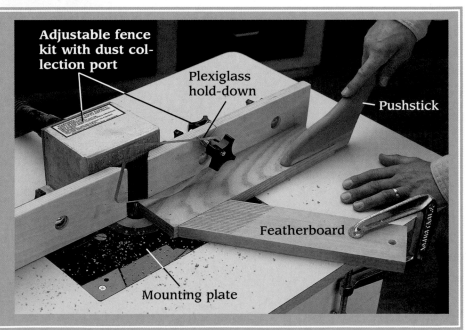

Adjustable fence kit with dust collection port

Plexiglass hold-down

Pushstick

Featherboard

Mounting plate

Three common hand planes for workshop use are the block plane, jack plane and jointer plane. **Block planes** are very handy general purpose tools. They can be used to plane with the grain, but they have shallow blade angles and flat soles so they can also plane end grain effectively. Their small size makes them easy to manage and convenient to store in your tool box. **Jack planes** are medium-sized planes with a slight curve in the sole. Their main purpose is to reduce board thickness by surface planing (see photo above). **Jointer planes** (also called *try planes*) have long soles that can ride a board edge smoothly. Their main use is to smooth board edges, especially in preparation for edge gluing.

Thickness planing with a hand plane

If you don't own a power planer and need to reduce the thickness of a board slightly, a jack plane is the tool you'll want to use. The fastest way to remove stock is by *roughing* with the plane: scraping the plane diagonally to the direction of the grain. To remove smaller amounts of material, and to smooth out after rouging, use a smoothing motion: orient the blade so the blade is diagonal to the wood grain, but follow the grain direction as you push the tool across your workpiece.

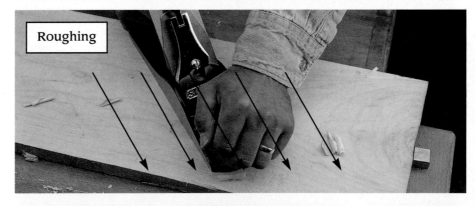

Roughing

Smoothing

Sharpening plane irons

Plane blades (called *irons*) are sharpened in much the same way as wood chisels, typically at an angle of 25° (See page 40). To maintain a steady angle on the irons, you can purchase a *honing guide* through most woodworking catalogs.

Follow the grain as you plane

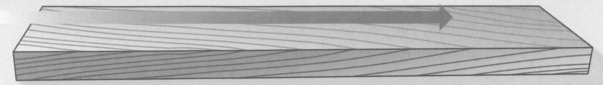

Straight grain: Plane following the upward grain slope

For best results when planing, pay attention to the direction of the wood grain, keeping in mind that the grain is a three-dimensional feature of the wood. In addition to running longitudinally along a board, it also has a general up or down slope on most boards. Inspect the edge of the board to see which direction the grain is running (illustration above) and plane the board to follow the wood grain upward. On some face-sawn boards, the wood grain is wavy or cupped from the side view. On such boards, you'll need to switch planing direction as you work along the board, always planing toward a crest in the wood grain.

Wavy grain: Switch directions to plane toward crests

Shaping

Miniature plane cuts clean grooves for inlays

A special hand plane, called an *inlay plane,* can be used to cut shallow grooves into wood for recessing decorative veneer inlay bands. Clamp a straightedge to the workpiece as a guide.

Overlooked shop tool has multitude of uses

Remove bulges, dips and bumps from contoured cuts by filing them away with a flat or half-round, single cut file. A file or rasp also makes quick work of cutting a roundover or easing a sharp edge.

Drawknife works quickly and cleanly

Once used primarily to strip bark from felled trees, the drawknife can resurface a piece of rough or damaged wood stock as fast as any belt sander, but without the dust and noise. They're also a good choice for chamfering sharp edges on woodworking projects. When left unsanded, the surface marks created by the drawknife can add rough-hewn charm to your project.

Spokeshave makes easy roundovers

You don't need to be a wheelwright to make good use of this time-honored tool. The spokeshave can round over just about any furniture leg or table edge. And many woodworkers enjoy using the spokeshave to make chair spindles and other round parts. Spokeshaves are made in several different sizes with concave blades of varying radii.

Yet another use for the versatile drill/driver

For enlarging holes or reshaping internal cutouts, try installing a rasp bit into your drill/driver. Most tool catalogs and hardware stores carry a nice selection of rasp bits that vary by size and shape. You can also use the rasp bits to strike off bumps and imperfections from contoured cuts.

Here's a sampling of the dozens of rasp bits you can purchase for your drill/driver.

Shaping

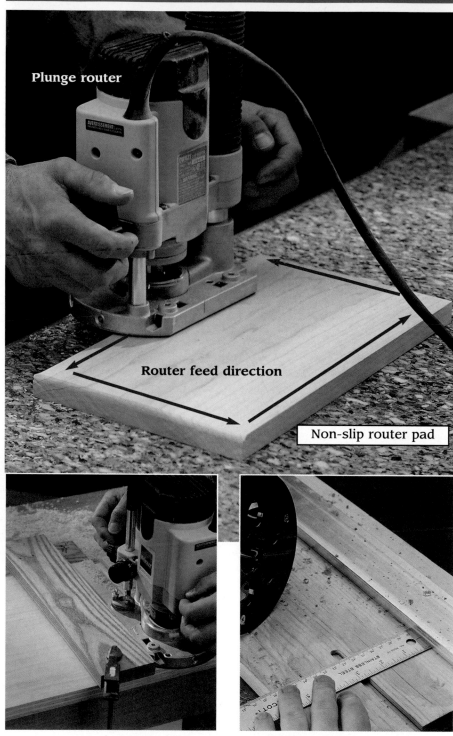

Plunge router

Router feed direction

Non-slip router pad

Shaping

A primer on router usage

It's not unusual for beginning do-it-yourselfers and woodworkers to be a little intimidated by routers. They're loud, aggressive shaping tools and they sometimes seem to have a mind of their own when it comes to following a guide or the edge of a board. But by keeping a few basic points in mind, and with some practice, these extremely versatile tools will amaze you with the variety and quality of work they can produce.

Setup is a very important aspect of correct router usage. Make sure the bit is well secured in the collet and set to an appropriate cutting height. The workpiece must be secured, either with clamps, bench dogs or with a non-slip router pad like the one shown at left. If using a piloted edge-forming bit, you won't need a straightedge or guide for the router base to follow, although you should secure scrap pieces the same thickness as the workpiece at each end if you're only routing one side (this prevents the router from following the corner and cutting into the adjacent sides). With non-piloted groove-forming bits, you'll need to use a straightedge or router guide to keep the tool cutting on line (See photo, left).

Whether you're using a fixed-base router or a plunge router, the bit should be spinning at full speed before you apply it to the workpiece. Wearing hearing and eye protection, engage the bit into the workpiece and draw it toward yourself, keeping your body out of the line of the tool as best you can. To be effective, the bit should cut against the rotation of the bit. In most cases, this means you should feed the router counter-clockwise. Maintain an even cutting pace, and don't set the router down until the bit has stopped spinning. Always practice your cut on scrap wood before cutting the workpiece.

Use a guide when grooving

Guides for making groove cuts can be as simple as a straight piece of scrap wood clamped to the workpiece. You can also use an extruded steel straightedge (See photo, right), or an edge guide that connects to the base.

Find router base setback

To figure out how far from the cutting line to secure your guide. measure the router "setback." Secure a straightedge to scrap and make a practice cut, following the guide. Measure from the closer shoulder of the cut to the guide.

Router bits

Router bits fit into two general categories: *edge-forming bits* and *groove-forming bits.* Edge-forming bits are used to cut decorative profiles on the edges of boards; they are equipped with integral pilots that guide the bit along the edge of the material being cut. Some more inexpensive bits have fixed pilots that are an extension of the bit shank, but most today have ball-bearing pilots that allow the cutter to spin but won't burn the edge of the board as fixed pilots can. Groove-forming bits cut channels of various profiles into the material. Except when carving freehand, they require a cutting guide. Most basic bits are made with either a 1/4 in. or 1/2-in.-dia. shank. Bits with a larger cutting radius can only be used with a router that accepts a 1/2 in. shank. Unless otherwise noted, the sizes listed below refer to cutting radius.

Roundover bit. Piloted bit eliminates sharp edges. Available sizes: 1/16, 1/8, 3/16, 1/4, 3/8, 1/2 in.; 1/2 in. shank only: 5/8, 3/4, 7/8, 1, 1 1/8, 1 1/4 in.

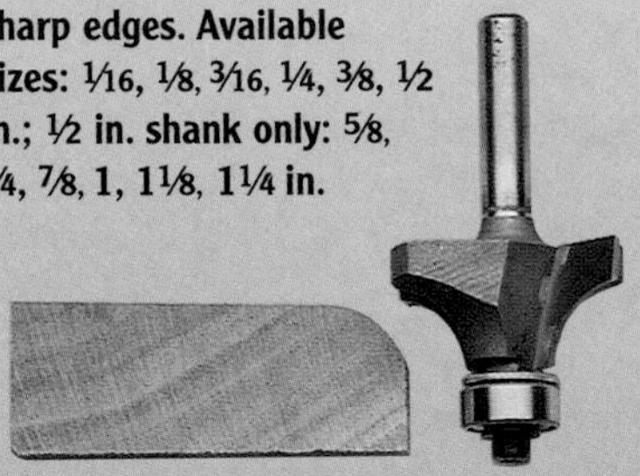

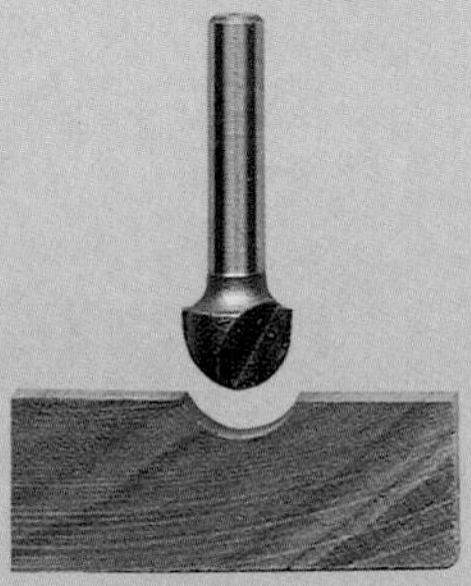

Core box bit. Grooving bit for fluting, veining and carving. Available sizes: 1/4, 3/8, 1/2, 5/8, 3/4 in.; 1/2 in. shank only: 7/8, 15/16, 1 in.

Flush trimming bits. Piloted edge-trimming bits for trimming laminates and pattern routing; 2 or 3 flutes. Available sizes: 1/4, 3/8, 1/2 in.; 1/2 in. shank only: 3/4, 1*, 1 1/8* in.
*top-mounted bearing typical

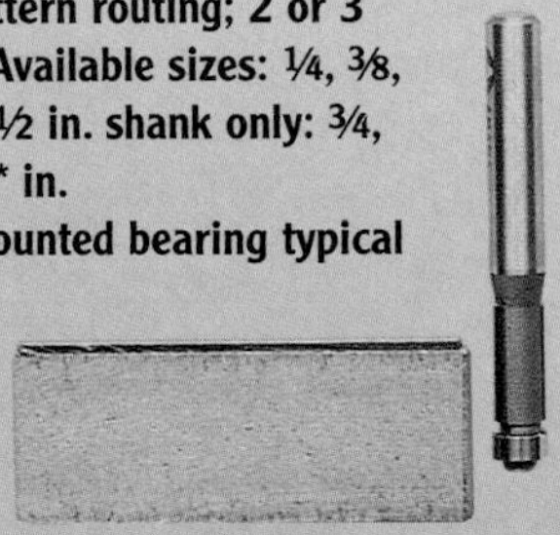

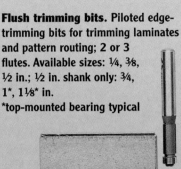

Roman ogee bit. Cut decorative edge profiles and manufacture trim moldings. Available sizes: 5/32, 1/4 in.

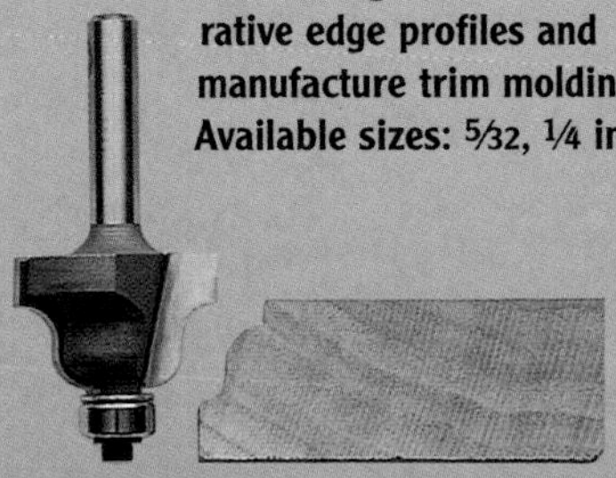

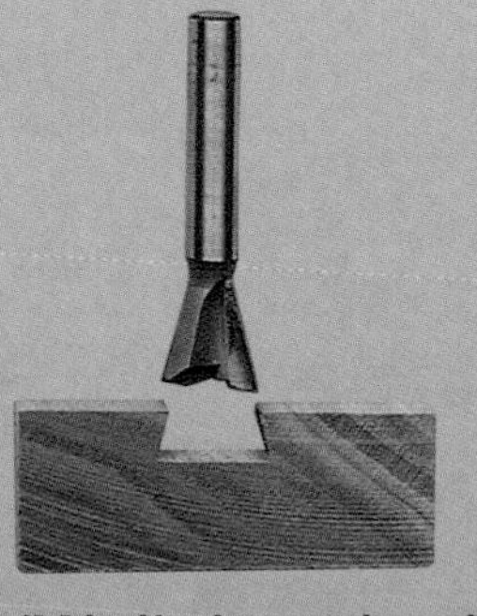

Dovetail bit. Used to cut dovetail joints, generally with a dovetail jig. Angles of flutes vary between 7 and 14°. Available sizes: 1/4, 5/16, 3/8, 1/2, 5/8, 11/16, 3/4 in.; 1/2 in. shank only: 13/16, 1 in.

Chamfer bits. Piloted bit eliminates sharp edges, making smooth, clean angle cut. Vast majority are 45° angle (both 1/4 in. and 1/2 in. shank). Can find bits with 15, 22 1/2 and 30° cutting angles as well.

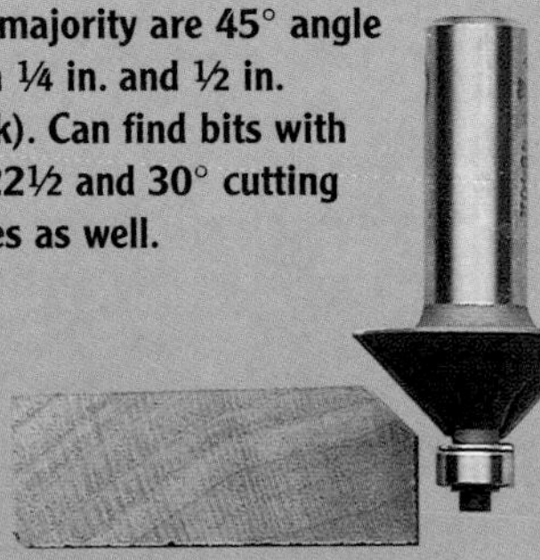

Piloted rabbeting bit. Cut rabbets, tongue-and-grooves and shiplap joints without need for straightedge or other guide. Available sizes (by depth of cut): 1/4, 3/8, 1/2 in.; 1/2 in. shank only: 3/4 in. Can also purchase rabbeting bit with interchangeable bearings varying rabbet depth.

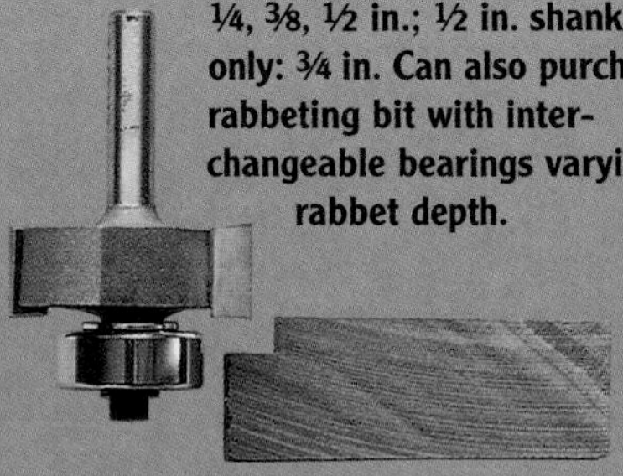

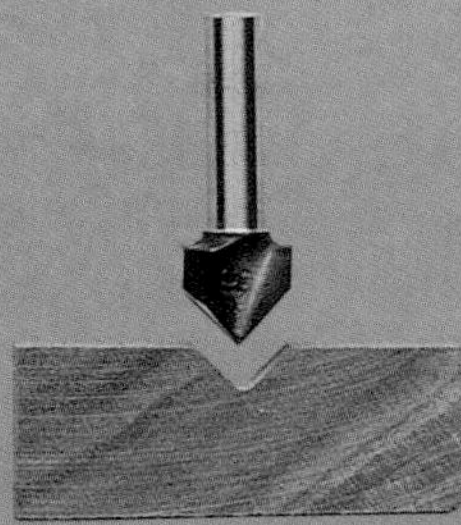

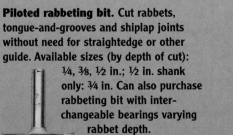

Veining (V-groove) bit. Used for carving, lettering and cutting decorative V-shaped veins. Most are 90° cutting angle, but 45° and 60° bits can be found. Available sizes: 1/4, 3/8, 1/2, 5/8, 3/4 in.; 1/2 in. shank only: 15/16, 1, 1 1/4, 1 1/2, 2 in.

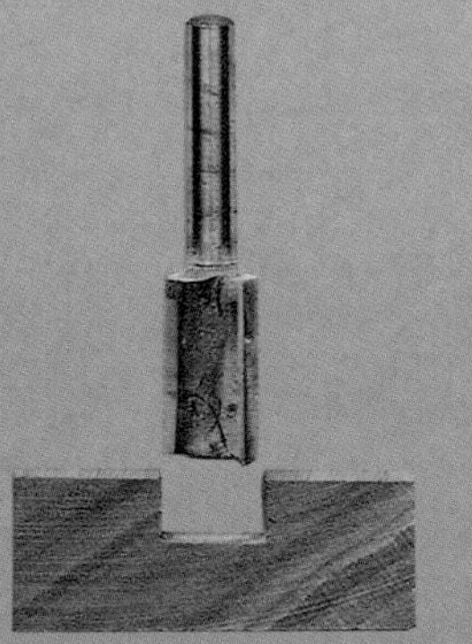

Straight bit. Cleans up edges, cuts grooves, can be used for mortising and carving. Most have 2 flutes. Available sizes: 1/4, 5/16, 3/8, 7/16, 1/2, 9/16, 5/8, 3/4, 7/8, 1 in.; 1/2 in. shank only: 1 3/8, 1 1/4, 2 in.

Rabbeting with a straight bit

Many woodworkers prefer to make rabbet cuts with a straight bit rather than a piloted router bit for a couple of reasons: piloted bits have a tendency to jump and will follow any imperfections in the edge of the board; they also will cut rabbets of only a set depth (even piloted rabbet bits with interchangeable bearings are limited to four set depths). By using a jig like the one shown to the right, you increase the bearing surface, preventing jump-outs, and you can adjust the relationship of the jig to the bit to cut rabbets of any depth up to the maximum cutting capacity of the bit. To make the jig, simply choose a straight piece of scrap about 1 ft. long, make a notch slightly deeper than the bit diameter, and clamp the jig to the router base so the bit protrudes to the depth of the cut.

Shaping

Save money and increase trim options by cutting your own trim molding with a router

Anyone who's done much trim carpentry knows that milled trim moldings can be very expensive, especially if they're made of hardwood. It can also be very difficult to find the size, profile and wood species you're looking for from stock millwork. One good solution to this dilemma is to cut your own trim moldings. Simply choose an edge-forming bit with the profile you like and rout the shape into a piece of stock. You can rout the shape freehand, using a piloted bit, but make sure the stock is wide enough to provide a stable bearing surface for the router base. If you own a router table, use it to make the profile cuts. After the profile is cut, rip-cut the profiled board to the desired trim width on your table saw. If you need more molding, rout the profile into the cut edge of the stock then rip-cut again.

Any edge-forming bit (and some groove-forming bits) will cut a suitable edge. But as you experiment with cutting your own moldings, look into new bit options with more sophisticated profiles, like the double Roman ogee bit shown here. If you're using a router that can accept a ½-in. shank, you'll find a wide selection of interesting bits in just about any woodworking catalog. You can also use two or more bits in combination to form complex and interesting edge treatments.

Double Roman ogee bit

Use a roundover bit to remove sharp edges or renew a beat-up edge

The piloted roundover bit is a quick and reliable tool for easing sharp edges on just about any piece of furniture or trim. In most cases, the best time to roundover the edge is after the furniture is assembled, as with the picnic table that's receiving the roundover treatment in the photo to the right. A roundover bit doesn't have to be used on new furniture projects only. It's also a great device for giving a shot of new life to an older piece of furniture that has damaged, dented or even rotted edges. A bit with a ⅜- or ¼-in. cutting radius is a good general purpose choice.

For information on making circular cutouts with a router, see page 34.

How to trim and shape countertop laminate

One of the most common uses for routers is to trim and profile laminate surfaces on countertops (if you do a lot of this work, look into buying a laminate trimmer, which is essentially a scaled-down router). When you bond the laminate to the countertop surface, make sure to leave ⅛ to ¼ in. overhanging the edge (don't try to align the laminate with the countertop edge—your chances of success are quite low).

1 Install a piloted, flush-trimming bit (the cutting radius doesn't matter) into your router and trim the laminate so the edge is flush with the outside edge of the countertop or countertop trim.

2 Use a piloted edge-forming bit to create a decorative profile on the top edge of the countertop. A chamfer bit, shown above, makes a clean profile that's free from sharp edges.

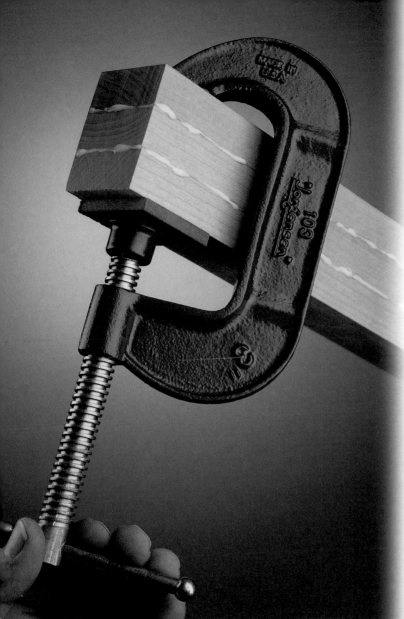

Workshop Tools & Skills
Clamping, gluing & fastening

No matter how carefully you cut project parts and no matter how painstakingly you form the joints, without good clamping, gluing and fastening techniques your project likely will fail.

Clamping serves two fundamental purposes in woodworking: first, it draws parts together tightly and assures that joints that should be square are square; and second, it holds parts together until the glue that will hold them together permanently sets. For non-woodworking shop projects, clamping is also very important. Among its more common jobs are holding workpieces together while fasteners are driven; securing jigs for cutting and drilling; and holding small workpieces so they stay steady while you work on them.

Successful gluing is a matter of choosing the best adhesive for the job, making sure the mating surfaces are properly prepared, and applying the correct amount of glue. From bonding retaining wall blocks together with construction adhesive to applying cabinet veneer, gluing is a skill every handyman should possess.

Fastening is an easy project step to rush through. By the time you're ready to fasten, the last thing you want to do is spend additional time fussing with pilot holes, counterbores and screw patterns. But take the time—there's no more discouraging shop experience than to see a project fail because you neglected to drill a pilot hole and the wood split.

The vise squad

Choosing the best vise for your needs is an important decision. The two types used most frequently in the workshop are the *bench vise* (sometimes called a *machinist's vise*) and the *woodworker's vise*. Lighter-duty *clamp-on vises* can be set up on a sawhorse at your job site, or stored out of the way in your shop and set up on an as-needed basis. If your main interest is woodworking, you should definitely look into a woodworker's vise for your shop. Normally attached to the end of a workbench, the woodworker's vise has smooth jaws designed to be fitted with wood inserts that won't damage wood as the jaws on a bench vise can. Because woodworker's vises are mounted so the tops of the jaws are flush with the worksurface, make sure the jaw width will fit your bench and that the benchscrew will have enough clearance when the jaws are in a closed position.

Jaw insert

Retractable bench dog

Woodworker's vise

Locking pliers

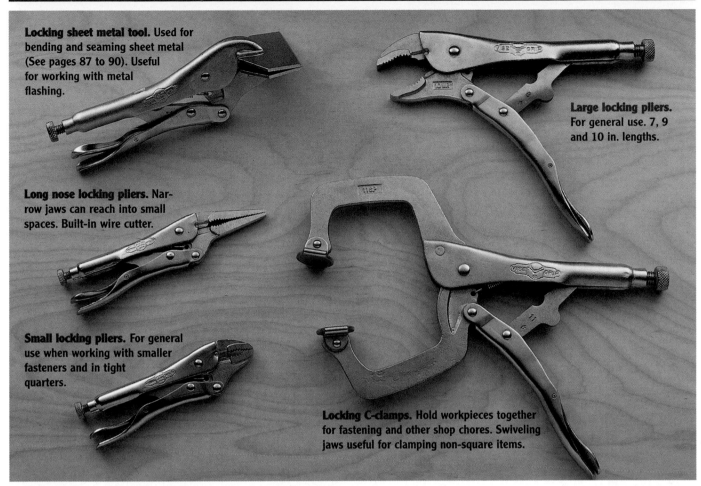

Locking sheet metal tool. Used for bending and seaming sheet metal (See pages 87 to 90). Useful for working with metal flashing.

Long nose locking pliers. Narrow jaws can reach into small spaces. Built-in wire cutter.

Small locking pliers. For general use when working with smaller fasteners and in tight quarters.

Large locking pliers. For general use. 7, 9 and 10 in. lengths.

Locking C-clamps. Hold workpieces together for fastening and other shop chores. Swiveling jaws useful for clamping non-square items.

Locking pliers can do more than just grip nuts and bolts, especially with the assortment of special-purpose tools that are made by most locking pliers manufacturers. The locking technology has been adapted to C-clamps and sheet metal seamers, as well as downsized versions of the standard locking pliers and pliers with specially shaped jaws for tough-to-reach spots.

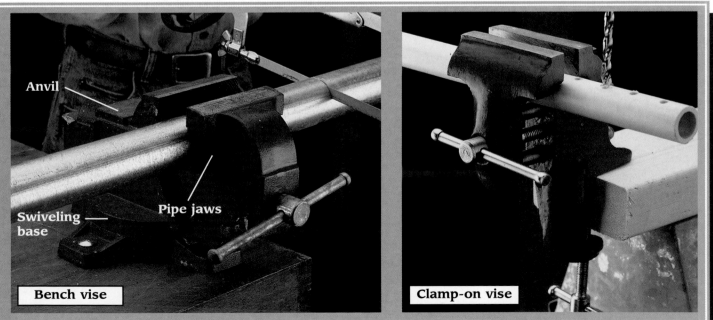

Anvil

Swiveling base

Pipe jaws

Bench vise

Clamp-on vise

Clamping, Gluing & Fastening

Folding worktables

Portable, folding worktables like the Black & Decker Workmate add versatility and efficiency to the workshop—especially the smaller workshop. They're also valuable tools when working on the job site. In addition to their most basic function as a sturdy set-up table that stores out of the way easily, you can use the bench dogs to secure workpieces for machining. The two opposable sections of the worksurface can be clamped together to secure round items like conduit, or one section can be positioned perpendicular to the other and clamped down like a wood caul.

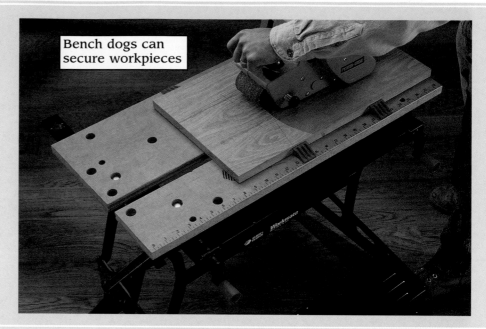

Bench dogs can secure workpieces

Vise grip tip

Pulling old staples out of floor materials has added unplanned hours to countless flooring projects. Staple pullers, screwdrivers, even small prybars are difficult to maneuver under the staple, and often break them or pull only one prong. But a pair of locking pliers will grip even embedded staples, and will pull the staples easily when rocked back.

Trouble gripping small finish nails & brads?

Make handling small fasteners a snap by drilling a small guide hole in a piece of thin wood (like a popsicle stick) to create a nail holder.

Wallboard anchors

LIGHT DUTY:
Plastic sleeve tapped into pilot hole

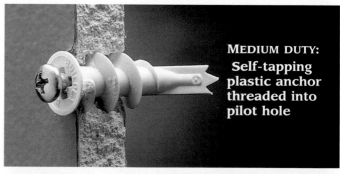

MEDIUM DUTY:
Self-tapping plastic anchor threaded into pilot hole

HEAVY DUTY:
Toggle screw driven through pilot hole

Clamping, Gluing & Fastening

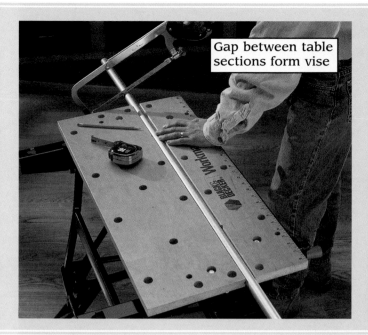
Gap between table sections form vise

Narrow table section forms wood caul

Attaching objects to concrete surfaces

Attaching sole plates for stud walls in the basement or garage and tacking furring strips to your foundation wall when insulating are just two of many do-it-yourself projects that require the use of masonry anchors. Here are a few of the most commonly used systems for screwing or bolting to concrete.

Lead sleeve. Driven into large guide hole before sole plates or furring strips are positioned. Threads of lag screws dig into soft lead as screws are driven. Sleeve expands to create pressure fit in guide hole. Excellent holding power.

Bolt sleeve. Requires same size guide hole for board and for concrete, so can be driven through board and into concrete at same time. Bolt causes sleeve to flare and grip guide hole as nut is tightened. Excellent holding power.

Self-tapping masonry screws. Driven into pilot holes in board and concrete. Hex-head and slotted, countersink versions. Good holding power, fast to install.

Powder-actuated stud driver. Gun powder charge drives masonry nail through sole plate and into concrete floor. Driver can be rented. Good holding power, fast to use, but loud and can split plates.

Concrete nails. Driven with hammer into pilot holes. Poor to good holding power, nails bend easily.

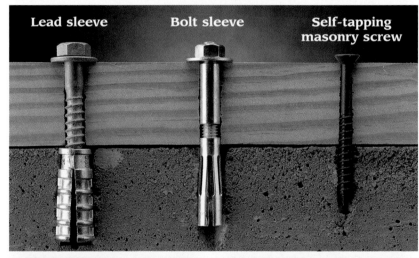
Lead sleeve   Bolt sleeve   Self-tapping masonry screw

Powder-actuated stud driver

Concrete nails

Choosing adhesives

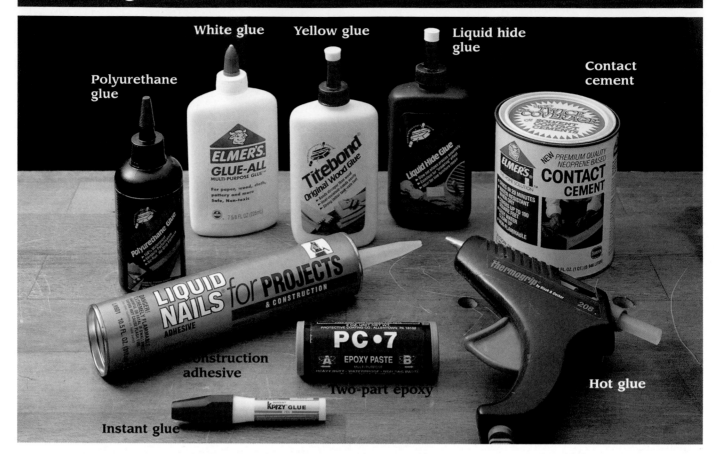

Polyurethane glue

White glue

Yellow glue

Liquid hide glue

Contact cement

Construction adhesive

Two-part epoxy

Hot glue

Instant glue

Selecting the right adhesive for your bonding task

White glue: Used on wood, paper or cloth. Interior use only. Dries in several hours and has a moderately strong bond. Poor resistance to water and heat. Emits no harmful odors. Cleans up with soap and water.

Yellow glue: Used on wood, paper or cloth. Interior use only. Dries faster than white glue and has a slightly stronger bond. Moderate resistance to water and heat. Emits no harmful odors. Cleans up with soap and water.

Liquid hide glue: Ideal for fine wood furniture or musical instruments. Interior use only. Sets slowly. Has good bond and is resistant to solvents and wood finishes. An eye irritant. Will clean up with soap and water.

Polyurethane glue: Used to bond a variety of materials including wood, metal and ceramics. Sets quickly and produces a strong bond. Waterproof. Warning: this glue can cause immediate and residual lung damage. This product should only be used with excellent ventilation. Asthmatics and people with chronic lung conditions should not use this product. Cleans up with acetone or mineral spirits.

Construction adhesive: Used on framing lumber, flooring and roof sheathing, plywood and paneling, wallboard, masonry. Dries within 24 hours and has a very good bond. Cleans up with mineral spirits.

Contact cement: Joins laminates, veneers, cloth, paper, leather, and other materials. Sets instantly and dries in under an hour. Produces a bond that is not suitable for structural applications. Very flammable and an irritant to eyes, skin and lungs (non-flammable contact cement is also available). Cleans up with soap and water.

Hot glue: Joins wood, plastics, glass and other materials. Sets within 60 seconds. Strength is generally low, but depends on type of glue stick. Good resistance to moisture, fair to heat. Heat will loosen bond.

Two-part epoxy: Joins wood, metal, masonry, glass, fiberglass and other materials. Provides the strongest bond of any adhesive. Bond has excellent resistance to moisture and heat. Drying time varies. Warning: fumes are very toxic and flammable. Cleanup sometimes possible with acetone.

Instant (cyanoacrylate) glue: Bonds smooth surfaces such as glass, ceramics, plastics and metal. Has excellent strength, but little flexibility. Dries in just a few seconds. Has excellent resistance to moisture and heat. Warning: toxic and flammable, and the glue can bond skin instantly.

Helpful hints for glue cleanup

Straw scoops wet glue from tight corners

Removing excess glue from corners and edges can be tricky. Often, the best tool for the job is a common plastic drinking straw. The straw can be bent into corners and the sharp edge does a good job of lifting glue. Remember to let the glue set partially before removing it. Otherwise, the excess glue will smear.

Old chisel scrapes away filmed-over glue

Use an old wood chisel to scrape glue squeeze-out from edge-glued joints, or from any flat surface. Keep the beveled edge of the chisel down to avoid marring the wood. Make certain the chisel edge is free of nicks. Wait for the glue to set partially (it should have a light film on the surface) before scraping.

Clamping tips

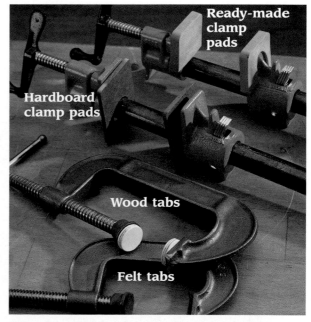

Ready-made clamp pads

Hardboard clamp pads

Wood tabs

Felt tabs

Quick & easy pipe clamp supports

Pipe clamps can be awkward to use when laid flat on a workbench. To remedy the problem, drill a series of 1½ in. diameter holes down the center of a 4-ft.-long 2 × 4, then rip-cut the board in half. The resulting semi-circular cutouts will cradle the pipes, increasing their stability and improving access to the cranks.

Attach pads for hands-free clamping

Eliminate the hassle of trying to slip loose clamping pads between the jaws of your clamps and your workpiece by attaching pads directly to your clamps or clamp jaws. Hot-glue tabs of wood or felt to C-clamp jaws. Slip ready-made clamp pads on the heads of your bar clamps, or make your own bar-clamp pads by drilling 1-in.-dia. holes in pieces of scrap hardboard.

"Wedge-gluing" panels

Applying clamp pressure to the edges of a glue-up panel assures strong, tight joints, but it does little to prevent the panel from buckling. In fact, the side pressure from the clamps can even contribute to buckling problems. To help keep your glue-up panel from looking like corrugated metal, try this simple technique. Alternate the bar clamps on opposite faces of the panel (this is easier to do if you use clamp supports, like those shown on the previous page). Then, cut several hardwood wedges. Drive the wedges between the clamping bars and the panel (don't get too aggressive here). Visually inspect the panel to make sure the pressure is even and it's not buckling. If necessary, adjust the pressure of the wedges.

Wood cauls

Clamping aids come through when duty cauls

Because most clamp jaws are less than 2 in. wide, tightening the clamps directs the clamping pressure to only a small section of the workpiece. As a result, joints (and entire woodworking projects) can be pulled out of square. A good solution to this effect is to use wood cauls when gluing up your projects.

Wood cauls are simply strips of wood that are slipped between clamps and the workpiece to distribute the clamping pressure evenly. Woodworkers have been using them for centuries to help create strong, square joints. You can use any hardwood, or even strips of plywood, to make your own wood cauls. Be sure to have plenty on hand before beginning the glue-up.

Clamping, Gluing & Fastening

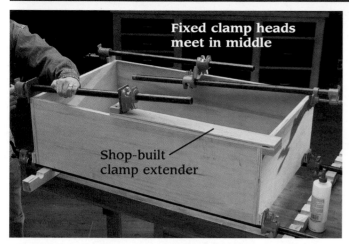

Fixed clamp heads meet in middle

Shop-built clamp extender

Two simple tricks for stretching pipe clamps

For those occasions when you get caught short during glue-up, here are two clever ways to get more reach out of your pipe clamps. If you have two clamps that are both too short, arrange the fixed heads so they meet in the middle: the clamping pressure will hold them together. Or, you can build a clamp extender like the one above from scrap wood.

One way to get around this clamping problem

Clamps aren't designed to work well with round workpieces, such as the tabletop shown above. One way to get even clamping pressure on round workpieces is shown above. Trace the arc of the workpiece onto the edges of two sturdy boards, then cut out the arc with a jig saw to make your clamping aids.

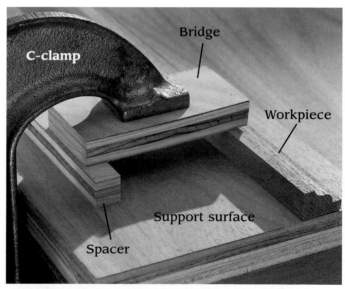

Bridge

C-clamp

Workpiece

Support surface

Spacer

A foolproof system for clamping frames

Build this frame clamp with a few pieces of scrap wood and a woodscrew clamp. It will apply equal pressure on all four corners of a frame. Cut four equal-length wood strips and drill center holes at 1 to 2 in. increments. Cut two shorter strips and drill a hole near each end. Fabricate four L-shaped corner braces out of scrap wood (or an old frame) and drill a hole in the corner of each. Form the strips into two V-shaped assemblies with wing nuts, as shown above. Attach the corner braces, set the frame inside the corners, then use a woodscrew to draw the "V" together.

Wooden bridge extends C-clamp capacity

C-clamps are useful for many tasks, but their relatively shallow throats limit their range. Extend the reach of the clamp by fashioning a clamping bridge with two pieces of scrap wood. One piece (the *spacer*) should be the same thickness as the workpiece being pressed down. The second scrap (the *bridge*) needs to be long enough to span over the spacer and the workpiece. Set the spacer between the workpiece and the edge of the support surface, then lay the bridge across the spacer and over the bridge. Clamping down on the bridge creates clamping pressure on the workpiece.

Clamping, Gluing & Fastening

Gallery of Clamps

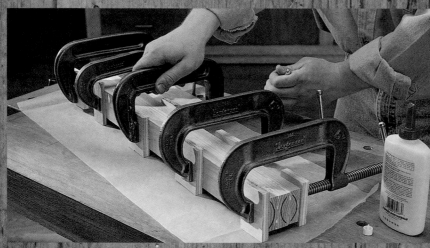

The corner clamp

A corner clamp holds mitered corners firmly in alignment. When fastening frames, glue and clamp opposite corners and let them dry before gluing the remaining two corners.

The strap clamp

Reinforced webbing is wrapped around irregular shapes and tightened with a ratcheting cinch. Perfect for gluing up round tabletops and casework, as well as repairing table legs, lamp bases, and other hard-to-clamp objects. Also called *band clamps* or *web clamps*.

The C-clamp

This classic clamp has nearly unlimited applications in the workshop. Keep a wide assortment of sizes on hand, including a few deep throat C-clamps. No clamp type works better for laminating, as above.

The pipe clamp

Another indispensable weapon in the clamp arsenal, the pipe clamp is the workhorse of wood glue-ups. The clamp heads are purchased separately from the pipes. Typically, ¾ or ½ in. black pipe is used (diameter depends on hole size in clamp heads). One clamp head is fixed in rough position, then the adjustable head is tightened with a hand screw.

The quick clamp

This trigger-activated bar clamp head lets you tighten the clamp with only one hand. They're great for holding work-pieces in rough position for fastening. The bars are sold with the clamps. They range from 6 to 50 in. in length.

The woodscrew

Also called *handscrew clamps* or *Jorgenson's* (after their primary manufacturer), these all-wood clamps have excellent gripping power, wide throat capacity and the wood jaws won't dent or mar most types of wood. Jaw lengths range in size from 4 to 16 in.

The 3-way clamp

The right angle screw in the spine of the clamp is used to apply downward pressure on the edge of a workpiece after the jaws at the top and bottom of the throat are tightened. Perfect for attaching edge trim to sheet goods or for repairing moldings.

Driver shaft

Shown in "X-ray" view, you can see how a wallboard or deck screw is held by the magnetic driver tip inside the telescoping guide sleeve.

Driver shaft slides down in guide column as screw is driven.

Use a magnetic guide for one-handed screw driving

Most woodworkers know that a magnetized drill bit will help hold a screw in place. But a magnetic screw guide will go one better. This simple device will hold a screw firmly to the bit as the metal sleeve guides the screw straight and true when downward pressure is exerted on the driver. With this handy tool you can drive screws straight and without stripping using only one hand, allowing you to hold the workpiece with your free hand.

TIP: Wax your screw threads

Keep a block of beeswax in your shop to lubricate the threads of screws. The wax greatly reduces friction, which makes for less work and fewer stripped screw heads. You can use hand soap for a similar purpose, but it's more likely to discolor the wood.

Drill driver bits

These bits and accessories for drill/drivers (left) will handle just about any fasteners. They are: (A) phillips-head driver; (B) slotted-head driver; (C) magnetic tip holder; (D) hooded slotted-head driver; (E) socket driver; (F) hex driver; (G) finish nail spinner.

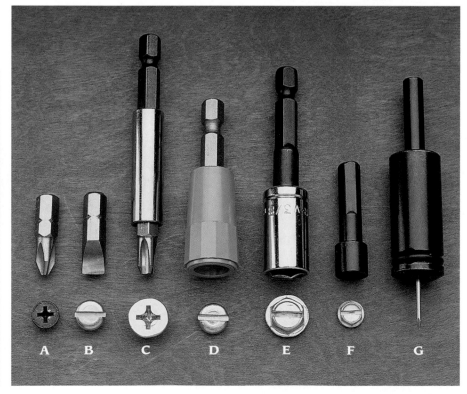

A B C D E F G

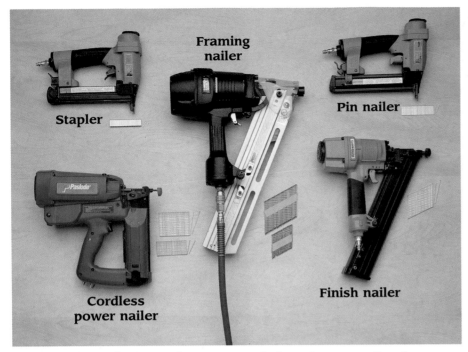

Framing nailer

Stapler

Pin nailer

Cordless power nailer

Finish nailer

Adding air tools can take your workshop to a new level

Compressed-air-powered fasteners can dramatically decrease the amount of time you spend on a project. Many tools will fire fasteners as fast as you can pull the trigger. Most air nailers require a ½ to 1 hp compressor with tank capacity of at least 3 gallons of air. Smaller air nailers and staplers usually run on 2 to 5 cubic feet per minute (cfm) or air volume at a pressure of 70 to 90 pounds per square inch (psi). Larger framing nailers can require as much as 9 cfm and 100 to 120 psi. If you already own a compressor, check to make sure it's able to drive new air tools before purchasing them. When working with air-powered fasteners, it is essential to wear approved safety goggles and ear protection. Familiarize yourself with the operation of the tool before beginning work. A device that can send a nail deep into a 2 × 4 can do a great deal of harm to the human body. NOTE: Recently, a similar tool to air nailers, the cordless power nailer, has become available for home use or for rental (See description below).

Pneumatic staplers: Air-powered staplers can drive crown-style staples from ¼ to ½ in. wide, and up to 2 in. long. Smaller staplers are useful for installing carpeting, roofing felt, floor underlayment and insulation. Larger capacity staplers can attach fence boards, strip flooring and even roof decking (check with your local building codes first).

Framing nailers: The "big boy" of air-powered fasteners, these powerful, high-capacity tools will drive nails up to 3½ in. long for all types of frame construction. The magazine can hold upwards of 100 nails.

Pin nailers: Drive brads up to 1¼ in. long. Used to attach trim, carpet strips and moldings. This lightweight tool allows you to nail one-handed, a real help when aligning trim molding pieces.

Finish nailer: Drives finish nails from ¾ to 2 in. long. Useful for installing siding, flooring, door and window casing and most types of finish carpentry.

Cordless power nailer: Relies on battery power and disposable fuel cells to power-drive nails. Also called *impulse nailers.* Require special fasteners, generally 16 gauge, from 1½ to 3¼ in. long, depending on the model. Each fuel cell will drive from 1200 to 2500 nails, depending on length, and a single battery charge will drive up to 4000 nails.

5-gallon bucket with dividers keeps hardware organized

If you do any amount of taping wallboard seams, your shop or garage is likely cluttered with the leftover 5-gallon buckets used to package premixed joint compound. They seem so useful, it's hard for most of us to throw them away. Here's one good way to put these leftover buckets to use: make them into hardware/fastener organizers. Use a jig saw with an edge guide to trim off the bottom 3 in. or so of several buckets, then cut pieces of scrap plywood so they're 2½ in. wide and the same length as the inside diameter of the bucket. Fasten the strips to the buckets by driving wallboard screws up through the bucket bottom. To divide the bucket bottom into quadrants, simply add shorter scrap strips. Because the buckets are wider at the top than the bottom, several bucket bottoms can be stacked inside one bucket, creating a totable hardware store.

Nail types

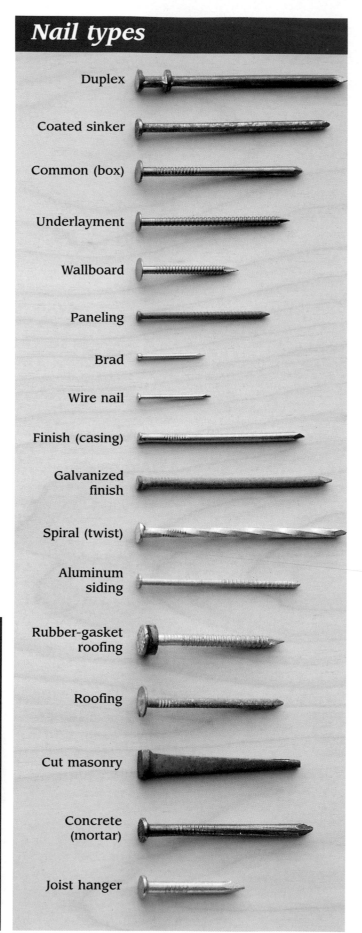

Duplex

Coated sinker

Common (box)

Underlayment

Wallboard

Paneling

Brad

Wire nail

Finish (casing)

Galvanized finish

Spiral (twist)

Aluminum siding

Rubber-gasket roofing

Roofing

Cut masonry

Concrete (mortar)

Joist hanger

Screw types

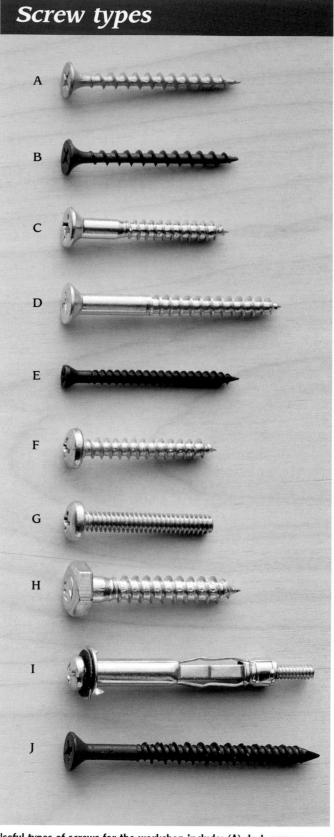

A

B

C

D

E

F

G

H

I

J

Useful types of screws for the workshop include: (A) deck screws; (B) wallboard screws; (C) wood screws; (D) brass-plated wood screws; (E) trim head screws; (F) sheet metal screws; (G) machine screws; (H) lag screws; (I) wall anchor screws; (J) high-low thread screws.

Wood Screw Sizes

GAUGE NO.	NOMINAL DIA. (in.)	(mm)	LENGTH (in.)	(mm)
0	0.060	1.52	3/16	4.8
1	0.070	1.78	1/4	6.4
2	0.082	2.08	5/16	7.9
3	0.094	2.39	3/8	9.5
4	0.108	2.74	7/16	11.1
5	0.122	3.10	1/2	12.7
6	0.136	3.45	5/8	15.9
7	0.150	3.81	3/4	19.1
8	0.164	4.17	7/8	22.2
9	0.178	4.52	1	25.4
10	0.192	4.88	1 1/4	31.8
12	0.220	5.59	1 1/2	38.1

Nail Sizes

PENNYWEIGHT	LENGTH (in.)	(cm)	DIAMETER (in.)	(cm)
2d	1	2.5	.068	.17
3d	1 1/4	3.2	.102	.26
4d	1 1/2	3.8	.102	.26
5d	1 3/4	4.4	.102	.26
6d	2	5.1	.115	.29
7d	2 1/4	5.7	.115	.29
8d	2 1/2	6.4	.131	.33
9d	2 3/4	7.0	.131	.33
10d	3	7.6	.148	.38
12d	3 1/4	8.3	.148	.38
16d	3 1/2	8.9	.148	.38
20d	4	10.2	.203	.51

Screw head styles

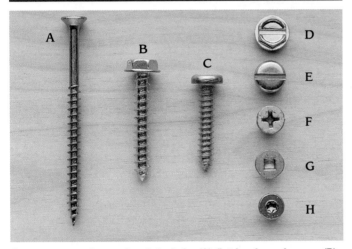

Common types of screw heads include: (A) flat-head wood screw; (B) hex head; (C) pan head. Slot styles include: (D) hex/slot; (E) straight; (F) phillips head; (G) square drive; (H) torx.

Nuts, bolts & washers

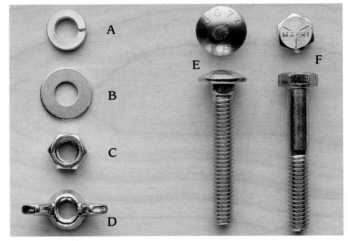

Nuts, bolts and washer types include: (A) lock washer; (B) flat washer; (C) hex nut; (D) wing nut; (E) hex-head bolt; (F) carriage bolt.

Standard staple sizes

1/4 in.   3/8 in.   1/2 in.

Choosing Caulk

TYPE	EASE OF USE	DURABILITY
Acrylic latex	Easy	Very Good
Butyl	Difficult	Good
Latex	Easy	Poor
Oil	Easy	Poor
Paintable silicone	Moderate	Very Good
Polyurethane	Moderate	Excellent
Silicone	Moderate	Excellent
Synthetic rubber	Difficult	Good

Clamping, Gluing & Fastening

After spending hours, days or even months of labor on a workshop project, don't let an incorrectly or hastily applied finish spoil all your hard work. Take the time to prepare the wood for the finish by sanding thoroughly with a sequence of finer-grit sandpapers. Make sure all screw plugs are securely in their counterbores and flush with the wood surface. Don't let the project sit for more than 48 hours between final sanding and finish application so that it has time to attract dust. Then, choose the finishing products that best meet your needs: both in terms of protection and appearance. And once the finish is applied, patch up any dents, nail holes or small cracks with tinted wood putty.

Choosing the best finishing products can be very daunting. There are dozens upon dozens of paints, stains, dyes, varnishes, penetrating oils, lacquers and countless other finishing products on the shelves of most building centers. Deciding which to use is a matter of learning a little bit about the products. Don't rely too much on the claims you'll see on the labels—look for basic information on the composition of the product and see how it fits into finish selection charts, like the ones on pages 80 and 81. But with today's labeling practices it's sometimes difficult to determine exactly what kind of product you're examining even after reading the label top to bottom. In such cases, don't be shy about asking the store clerk for information. And whenever you decide to try a product you've never used before, always test it out first on some scrap

Highlight surface flaws

Sanding marks, small scratches and dents and other minor surface flaws can be very difficult to detect—until you apply your wood finish, when they show up with glaring clarity. To spot these surface imperfections before applying your finish, use a desk lamp or other low lamp source (a 60-watt bulb is about right). Set the lamp next to the surface so the light hits it at a low angle. From the opposite side of the workpiece, view the surface. Even slight scratches and flaws will be highlighted by the shadows created by the light. Mark flawed areas with a light pencil mark, sand them away, then check again.

Sanding strategies

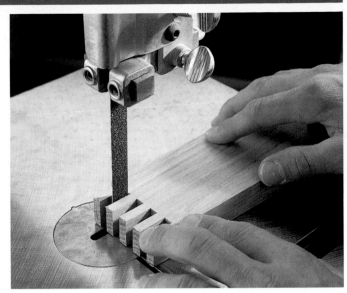

Prolong life of sandpaper and sanding belts

Sandpaper, sanding pads and sanding belts will gum up quickly when sanding, losing most of their tooth. But don't throw them away. Belts, pads and papers can be cleaned with a sanding stick (shown above) or just about any clean, uncolored rubber (an old tennis shoe sole, for example). With power sanders, simply turn on the tool and apply the sanding stick to the paper until the residue disappears.

Turn a band saw into a band sander

Stationary belt and disc sanders are powerful tools that remove a lot of material quickly. This characteristic is great for many sanding tasks, but if you're doing more delicate work more power isn't what you're looking for. The band saw can provide a solution for delicate sanding projects. Simply replace the band saw blade with an abrasive band to create a sanding tool that lets you remove very small amounts of wood.

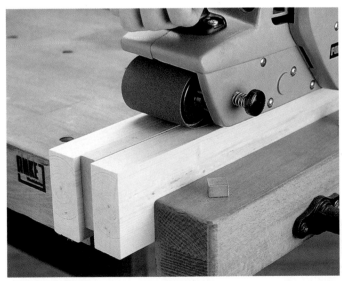

Keep belt sanders on track

To impart a smooth, crisp edge on a board, use a belt sander. To prevent the sander from rocking and causing roundovers along the edge, sandwich the workpiece between two pieces of scrap wood, making sure all three edges are flush. Clamp the "sandwich" into the vise in your workbench.

Smooth rough cuts with a cabinet scraper

A lot of experienced woodworkers view sanding as a last resort. It's messy, noisy, time-consuming and it creates sanding marks. A cabinet scraper is a better tool for smoothing out rough cuts. It works equally well on curved surfaces, as above, or on broad, flat surfaces. See page 77 for more information on using cabinet scrapers.

Sanding & Finishing

Emery cloth for metal and plastics

40-grit aluminum oxide

100-grit aluminum oxide

220-grit aluminum oxide

400-grit wet/dry

Sandpaper Grit Chart

Grit Number	Description	Use
12 16 20 24	Very Coarse	Very rough work requiring high speed, heavy machinery. Used for unplaned woods, uneven wood floors and rough-cut lumber.
30 36 40 50	Coarse	Rough carpentry.
60 80 100	Medium	General carpentry.
120 150 180	Fine	Preparation of hardwoods and final smoothing of softwoods.
220 240 280	Very Fine	Final and between-coat sanding. Used to remove sanding marks left by coarser grits.
320 360 400	Extra Fine	Sanding between finish coats and wet sanding paints and varnishes.
500 600	Super Fine	Sanding metal, plastics, ceramics and wet sanding.

Slick trick for a rough customer

Sandpaper is difficult to tear in a straight line, and cutting it with scissors or a utility knife will dull blades very quickly. Build yourself a sandpaper cutter by attaching a hacksaw blade to a piece of scrap wood, with the sharp edge of the blade facing toward the edge of the board. Attach a strip of wood parallel to the blade. Position the strip so it's the same distance from the cutting edge of the blade as the most common dimension you'll need to fit your pad sander. Slip a piece of sandpaper underneath the blade and up against the strip. Pull upward against the blade for a neat cut.

Keep sandpaper scraps on file

An expanding, accordion-style file holder makes a great storage center for sandpaper scraps. Assign a grit number to each storage compartment and file your sandpaper sheets in the appropriate compartment so they're be easy to find when needed.

Sanders & sanding blocks

PORTABLE POWER SANDERS

3 × 24 belt sander

Random-orbit sander

Detail sander

Finishing sander (¼ sheet)

A sander for any sanding task

Assemble a team of sanders for your woodworking and carpentry projects. The most versatile sander is the *random-orbit sander.* The irregular sanding action of this tool keeps sanding marks to a minimum, and is suitable for both rough sanding and fine finish sanding. *Belt sanders* can remove a lot of material in a hurry, making them useful for resurfacing as well as smoothing very rough stock. A *detail sander* has a small, triangular pad that can get into those hard-to-reach spots. A ¼ or ⅓ sheet *finishing sander* does a fine job preparing surfaces for a finish, and is cheaper than a random-orbit sander.

HAND SANDERS & SANDING BLOCKS

Commercial sanding block

Sanding sponges

"Tear-drop" sanding blocks

A sampling of sanders and sanding blocks

Fabricated sanding blocks have soft pads and are designed to be easy and comfortable to grip. *"Tear-drop" sanding blocks* are made to fit the most common molding profiles. *Sanding sponges* can remove surprising amounts of material quickly and will conform to irregular surfaces.

How to make custom sanding blocks for molding & trim

1 Cut a 4- to 6-in. strip of the molding or trim you need to sand. Tack a small piece of scrap wood to each end of the molding strip to create "forms." Fill or cover the molding with auto body filler, smoothing the filler so it's level with the tops of the forms. Let the filler dry according to the manufacturer's recommendations.

2 Remove the molded auto body filler and hot-glue a block of wood to the flat face to give the sanding block greater rigidity and durability. Wrap a piece of sandpaper around the shaped face and start sanding. NOTE: This techniques also works with convex sanding profiles.

Sanding tips

Sanding wallboard

Use a wallboard sanding block fitted with metal sanding mesh to smooth out dried wallboard compound on taped wallboard seams. The sanding mesh removes compound smoothly, without creating fine dust.

Try detail sanders

New power sanders are hitting the market all the time. Many of the more recent innovations are in the detail sander area. These compact tools have triangular sanding pads that let them fit into areas that otherwise could only be hand-sanded.

Build a drum sander dust-collection box

Drum sander attachments for the drill press are terrific for smoothing curves and sanding interior cutouts, but they can make quite a mess. Keep sanding dust in check by building a dust collection box that's clamped to your drill press table. Make a cutout in the side of the box for a vacuum hose port, and another cutout on the top for the sanding drums to fit into. The top of the box also comes in handy as a sanding table.

Flex blade to bow toward the direction of the scraping motion

To use a cabinet scraper, hold the ends and press in with your thumbs to cause a slight flex. Hold the scraper at a fairly steep angle and push it away from yourself, applying downward pressure as you push (you can also flex the scraper inward and draw it toward yourself).

Cabinet scrapers

The cabinet scraper isn't just a tool for cabinetmakers. This simple metal blade can do away with almost all of the need for sanding in woodworking shops. As long as the cutting burr is sharp, the cabinet scraper will shave off paper-thin wisps of wood, leaving behind a glass-smooth surface that has no sanding marks. If you've never used a cabinet scraper, it's well worth investing a few dollars to try out this valuable tool. You may never go back to sanding again.

How to make sharp burrs on cabinet scraper edges

1 File down any traces of the old burrs on all edges of the cabinet scraper, using a fine single-cut metal file. Don't get too aggressive with the file—it doesn't take much power to remove a fine burr.

2 With the cabinet scraper held firmly in a vertical position, file the edges flat at an exact 90° angle, using the metal file. Take care not to overwork the edge.

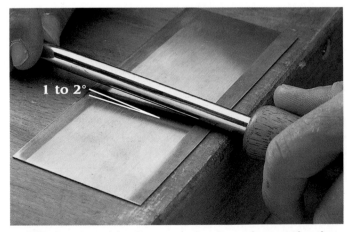

3 With the scraper lying flat on a worksurface, rub across the edges of the scraper with a burnishing tool held at a very slight angle. If you don't have a burnishing tool, any piece of round hardened steel (like the top of a chisel shank) will do. The edge of the scraper should be set back just slightly from the edge of the worksurface to prevent you from burnishing at an angle that's too steep.

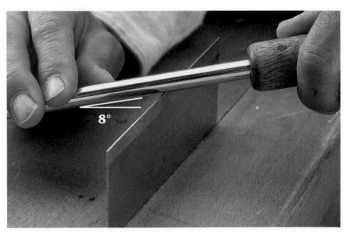

4 Scrape across the edge of the scraper with the burnishing tool, holding the tool at an angle of about 8°. This will create a slight burr that accomplishes the cutting action of the scraper. Create burrs on all four edges of the scraper, flipping the tool as each edge becomes dull.

Plugging screw counterbores

Screw hole counterbores can be plugged with matching wood plugs or with contrasting plugs that give the project decorative flair, as above.

Screw Counterbore Sizes

Gauge	Head bore	Shank bore	Pilot hole
2	11/64	3/32	1/16
3	13/64	7/64	1/16
4	15/64	7/64	5/64
5	1/4	1/8	5/64
6	9/32	9/64	3/32
7	5/16	5/32	7/64
8	11/32	5/32	7/64
9	23/64	11/64	1/8
10	25/64	3/16	1/8
12	7/16	7/32	9/64
14	1/2	1/4	5/32

How to counterbore and plug for wood screws

1 Drill a counterbored pilot hole using a counterboring bit (See page 48) or by drilling a pilot hole, then counterboring for the screw shank and the screw head, according to the dimensions in the chart above.

2 After the screw is driven, apply wood glue to the end of a screw plug (either a readymade plug or one you've cut yourself). Set the plug into the counterbore hole with a wood mallet.

3 After the glue has dried, trim the plug flush with the wood surface using a flush-cutting saw (See photo, above left). Take care not to mar the surrounding wood surface. Sand the plug smooth.

Tinted or untinted wood putty?

Untinted wood putty stained with rest of project

Tinted wood putty applied to project after staining

Debate over the best method to conceal nail and screw heads with wood putty has raged for generations. We've had the best success filling holes with putty tinted to match the finished color of the surrounding wood, rather than applying untinted putty and staining it at the same time as the rest of the project.

For information on how to cut your own screw counterbore plugs, see page 47.

Steel Wool Types and Uses

Type	Description	Suggested uses
#3	Coarse	Remove old paint and varnish
#2	Med. coarse	Clean rough metal, concrete or brick. Clean garden tools, remove paint from molding
#1	Medium	Clean resilient floors, copper pipe and fittings
#0	Med. fine	Clean grills, pots, pans. Remove rust from metal tools (use oil)
#00	Fine	Buff painted finish. Clean screens and frames. Remove old finish from antiques
#000	Very fine	Polish aluminum, copper, brass and zinc. Remove minor burns from wood and leather
#0000	Super fine	Buff woodwork, shellac and varnish. Smooth clear finishes. Clean delicate tools.

Steel wool and abrasive pads (synthetic steel wool) have many uses in the shop, from general cleanup to buffing to stripping old finishes.

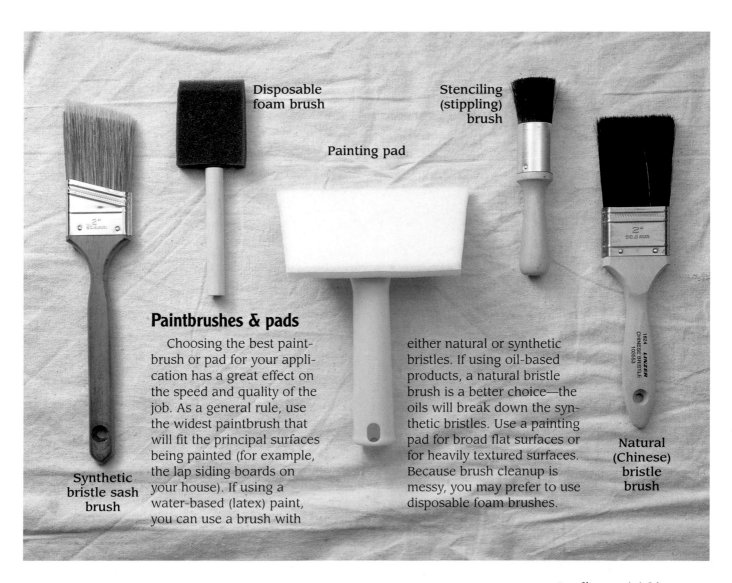

Paintbrushes & pads

Choosing the best paint-brush or pad for your application has a great effect on the speed and quality of the job. As a general rule, use the widest paintbrush that will fit the principal surfaces being painted (for example, the lap siding boards on your house). If using a water-based (latex) paint, you can use a brush with either natural or synthetic bristles. If using oil-based products, a natural bristle brush is a better choice—the oils will break down the synthetic bristles. Use a painting pad for broad flat surfaces or for heavily textured surfaces. Because brush cleanup is messy, you may prefer to use disposable foam brushes.

Synthetic bristle sash brush · Disposable foam brush · Painting pad · Stenciling (stippling) brush · Natural (Chinese) bristle brush

Wood Coloring Agents

TYPE	STRENGTHS	WEAKNESSES	RECOMMENDED FOR:
Liquid stain	Can be built up to control color. Both conditions and seals the wood. Spray-on application can speed up and simplify application process.	Difficult cleanup. Application can be messy. Slow curing time allows dust to settle in the finish. May show brush marks.	Previously stained wood. Touching up wood finish.
Gel stain	Neat and easy to apply, with no running. Even drying. Color can be deepened with layering. Buffing will result in a hard surface.	High cost, difficult clean-up and limited color selection. Requires buffing between coats. Does not penetrate wood. Vulnerable to streaking.	Woodwork with vertical surfaces. Furniture with spindles and other rounded parts.
Aniline dyes	Color can be lightened or changed with a solvent long after initial application. Wide range of colors available. Greater control of tone.	Granular dyes must first be mixed with a solvent. Do not penetrate or bond well with pores of open-grain woods like oak or ash, requiring application of wood filler in spots.	Touch-up and repairs. Coloring or tinting a topcoat made of a similar solvent.

Do-it-yourself tack cloths

Make your own tack cloths for wood finishing by dampening cheesecloth with equal amounts of boiled linseed oil and varnish. Store them in a covered jar.

Sand lightly between coats of finish

After each coat of finish dries, sand it lightly with 400 to 600 grit sandpaper to knock down bubbles and surface defects. Wipe with a tack cloth when done.

Store finishing materials in a metal cabinet

Finishing materials and other potentially flammable or dangerous chemicals should be stored in a sturdy, lockable metal cabinet. Used office furnishing stores are an excellent source for this kind of cabinet.

Water-based vs. oil-based finishing products

Wood coloring agents and topcoating products are available in both water-based and oil-based varieties. Each has its own advantages and drawbacks.

1960s' clean-air legislation prompted manufacturers to produce water-based finishes, and recent health concerns have bolstered their popularity. They are nontoxic and nonflammable. They also have weaker odors than oil-based varieties and can be cleaned up with soap and water. However, the transparent nature of water-based products produces a flatter finish than the oil-based versions, which tend to carry a more vivid sheen. It is easier to achieve an even application when finishing with oil-based products than with water-based.

Another characteristic of oil-based products is their enhanced workability, due to their slower drying times and weaker penetration of the wood. Water-based versions are absorbed deeper into the wood, drying quickly and producing an extremely hard finish. They also have a tendency to raise the wood grain.

Although technology for creating non-petroleum-based finishing materials is advancing quickly, the majority of tradespeople still prefer the oil-based products. But when deciding between the two finish types, be sure to consider the available ventilation and whether or not there are youngsters present. If ventilation is poor or kids may be in the area, water-based products may be a better idea.

Topcoat Types and Characteristics

TYPE	USES	CHARACTERISTICS
Oil-based polyurethane	High-use furniture and outdoor projects.	A durable, hard finish that resists water and alcohol.
Water-based polyurethane	Floors, interior wood-work (especially eating surfaces and toys).	Dries fast and cleans up easily while resisting water and alcohol. Nontoxic and nonflammable.
Lacquer	Low-use furniture.	Medium durability in a rich-looking finish that is easily buffed to a luster.
Paste wax	Floors, antiques and fine furniture.	Provides a natural appearance that is easily renewed, but wears away quickly and must be reapplied with some regularity.
Shellac	Initial sealer coat and repairing blemishes in other finishes.	Highly resistant to humidity. Nontoxic and long lasting.
Tung oil	Uneven surfaces (e.g., chairs with spindles) and wood with highly figured grain.	A durable, moisture-resistant and nondarkening finish. It gives a low-luster, natural appearance while being easily applied or renewed.
Danish oil	Low-use furniture and antique restoration.	A durable, easily repaired finish that gives a warm, natural-looking tone with higher sheen than tung oil.
Linseed oil	Antique restoration.	Provides a low-luster, hand-rubbed look, but lacks durability and longevity.

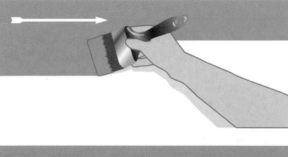

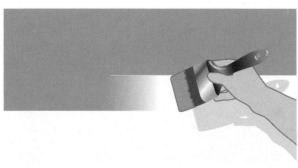

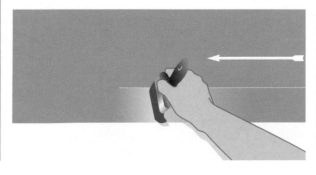

Feather paint for a smooth finish

Painting large, broad surfaces with a brush can produce streaking and brush strokes that remain visible after the paint has dried. Using the proper feathering technique is the best way to ensure that painted surfaces are smooth and even. Start by applying a fully loaded brush (paint should be ⅓ to ½ way up the bristles) across the surface from left to right—always begin at the top of the project area. As soon as the paint coverage begins to thin out, lift the brush slowly. Then, reload the brush and apply paint from right to left, in line with the previous stroke. Slowly lift the brush as you approach the endpoint of the previous stroke. Partially load the brush with paint and sweep it back and forth in the area between the two strokes to blend them together.

How to revitalize hardened paint brushes

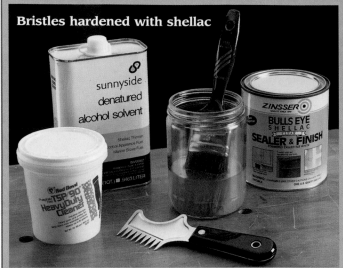

Bristles hardened with shellac

Bristles hardened with other finishing products

Most of us have a few old crusty paint brushes that have been lying around the basement for months or even years. Whether they were cleaned improperly or not cleaned at all, we can't bring ourselves to admit that they're ruined. Well, they may not be. Try one of these tricks for softening bristles and giving new life to old hardened brushes. If the brush was used to apply shellac, simply soak it in alcohol overnight, then rinse and wash in a trisodium phosphate (tsp) solution. Use a brush comb to help clean and condition the bristles. For brushes that are crusted with other materials, try soaking them in paint and varnish stripper to dissolve the gunk, then rinse with tsp and comb. If you know the exact type of solvent used for the product that has dried, try soaking the brush in that product (for example, lacquer thinner) before opting to use stripper.

A one-two punch for cleaning oily hands

You should always wear rubber gloves when working with finishing materials, but just in case some product does get on your hands, here's an effective trick for cleaning it off. Wash your hands in ordinary vegetable oil to dissolve the oily mess. Then, rinse your hands with grease-dissolving dish detergent and warm water. You'll be amazed at the effectiveness of this one-two punch.

Suspend discarded oily rags in water

There is perhaps no greater fire hazard in the workshop than oily rags. Left crumpled in a corner or, worse yet, in a pile, rags containing petroleum distillate are highly flammable, and have been known to spontaneously combust. Don't take any chances. When you're through with an oily rag, drop it into a bucket of water until it can be properly disposed of at a hazardous waste collection site.

Storing hazardous finishing materials

All oil-based products, most solvents and paint removers, and even some water-based products fall into the hazardous waste classification. Leftovers should be handled and stored with care until they can be disposed of properly at a hazardous waste disposal site. Here are a few tips to note:

- Store in a cool, dark location, away from direct sunlight and heat sources.
- Do not set metal cans on damp concrete floors.
- Leave the product in the original container so you know exactly what it is and how to handle it.
- Do not store products in old food or beverage containers.
- Dispose of all products in a timely fashion. Most local waste management centers operate hazardous waste collection programs.

Evaporate unused paint before disposing of cans

Containers for water-based paints and finishes that are not considered hazardous wastes (See Tip, left) can be disposed of in your normal trash collection if they are completely empty and dry. Before disposal, set open cans in a well-ventilated area and allow the old product to evaporate until only a dry residue remains.

Using chemical strippers

Get the facts on chemical strippers before making your choice

Chemical strippers are very controversial these days. Most of the traditional strippers contain dangerous solvents that can cause health issues if proper protection isn't taken. Methylene chloride, acetone, tuolene and xylene are some of the active ingredients in chemical strippers that are considered dangerous. Because of these hazards, "safer" paint and varnish strippers have been introduced. Some have organic active ingredients that are less caustic, others simply evaporate more slowly, reducing the exposure. Many people who have tried these newer strippers have found them to be less effective than the older types (although frequently the problem is a failure to follow the directions properly). The best advice is to try a few different products, taking care to follow the manufacturer's directions, and decide which one you prefer. Perhaps even better advice is to avoid using chemical strippers altogether. A good sharp scraper will remove most finishes quickly and safely.

Save those planer shavings

The messiest part of using chemical strippers is scraping off and disposing of the goo and residue that's created by the stripping process. To make this step a little neater, scatter shavings from your power planer (sawdust is ineffective) onto the stripper after it has done its job, and allow the chemicals to soak into the shavings. Then, simply wipe up the shavings and dispose of them properly.

Many handymen who are right at home working with wood and other common building materials balk at the thought of working with metal. But in many regards, metal is actually easier to work and more forgiving than wood. All it takes is the right tools, a little know-how and some practice. Light-gauge sheet metal is a very versatile, easy-to-handle workshop material. It is worked mostly by cutting, bending and joining with mechanical fasteners. Light-gauge metals, such as aluminum, copper and brass are also easy to cut and shape. Heavier-gauge steel requires more patience and, eventually, will require you to develop welding skills.

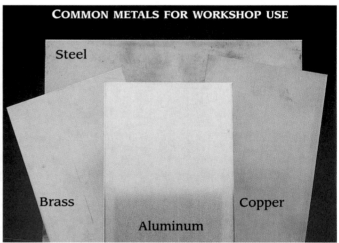

COMMON METALS FOR WORKSHOP USE

Steel

Brass

Copper

Aluminum

Common Metal Properties and Uses

METAL OR ALLOY	PROPERTIES	USES
Stainless steel	Tough but difficult to work. Will not rust or corrode.	Kitchenware, furniture, picture frames and sinks.
Aluminum	Light, soft and malleable. Easy to work or cast.	Siding, roofing, gutters, flashing and auto parts.
Copper	Soft and easily worked. A good electrical conductor.	Plumbing and wiring. Also a major component of brass and bronze.
Brass	Soft. Can be worked either hot or cold. Casts and polishes well.	Marine fittings, architectural trim and bearings.
Tin	Soft, malleable, resists corrosion.	Galvanizing and alloys.
Cast iron	Hard and brittle. Slow rusting.	Engine blocks, machine bases, fireplace equipment and bathtubs.
Medium-carbon steel	Hard and strong. Fast rusting.	Nuts, bolts, axles and pins.

Fabricated metal types & data

Sheet Steel Gauges

Gauge	lbs./sq. ft.	Thickness (in.)
#6	8.12	0.2031
#7	7.50	0.1875
#8	6.87	0.1719
#10	5.62	0.1406
#12	4.37	0.1094
#14	3.12	0.0781
#16	2.50	0.0625
#18	2.00	0.0500
#20	1.50	0.0375
#22	1.25	0.0312
#24	1.00	0.0250
#26	0.750	0.0187
#28	0.625	0.0156
#30	0.500	0.0125

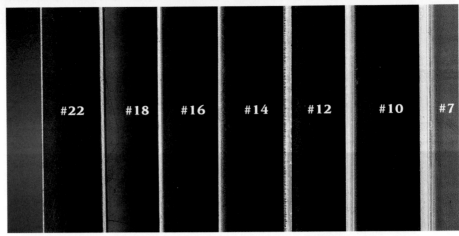

Sheet steel is manufactured in a variety of thicknesses or gauges. Lower gauge numbers indicate thicker metal (See chart, left). Thin galvanized sheet metal (#28 and #30), used commonly for bending projects, flashing and ductwork, is sold at most building centers, usually in the ductwork section. Thicker rolled steel sheets are usually sold only through metal distributors.

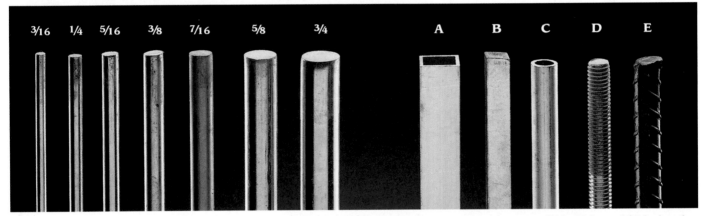

Metal rods. Steel, brass and aluminum rods are sold in many building centers in the stock diameters above, usually in 24-in. and 36-in. lengths. You can also purchase square metal tubes (A), square rods (B), round tubes (C), threaded rod (D) and rebar (E) to use as raw materials for your metalworking projects.

Corrugated sheet metal. Used mainly as cladding or roofing material for outbuildings, corrugated sheet metal is typically sold in 4 × 8 sheets with a variety of profiles and finishes. Overlapping seams are sealed with foam tape and secured with self-tapping screws fitted with rubber washers.

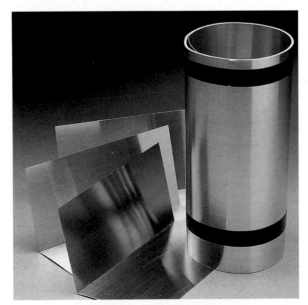

Flashing. Even if you haven't attempted much metalworking in the past, you've probably worked with metal flashing. The most common types are step flashing (left) and roll flashing (right). Both can be purchased in aluminum or galvanized steel.

Gallery of Metalworking Tools

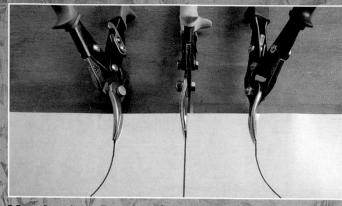

Metal snips: Pay attention to handle color

Aviator snips for cutting metal are coded by handle color. Green-handled snips are used to cut curves to the right, yellow-handled snips are best used to make straight cuts, and red-handled snips cut left curves.

Hacksaw

This everyday workshop tool can be used to cut metal up to ⅓ as wide as length of the hacksaw blade (10 or 12 in. for most saws). Hacksaw blades are made of hardened, tempered steel, featuring 14, 18 or 24 teeth per inch (tpi)—use higher tpi blades for denser metal. Carbide chip blades are available for cutting milder metal.

Center punch

Used primarily to punch starter indentations for drilling metal.

Cold chisel

The wedge-shaped cold chisel is used to shape edges, score metal and shear off bolt heads.

Reciprocating saw

Fitted with a metal-cutting blade, this versatile saw will cut through rebar, metal posts and just about any other tough-to-cut metal.

Hook-nose aviator snips

The broad, flat jaw rides on the metal surface for greater stability when cutting delicate curves.

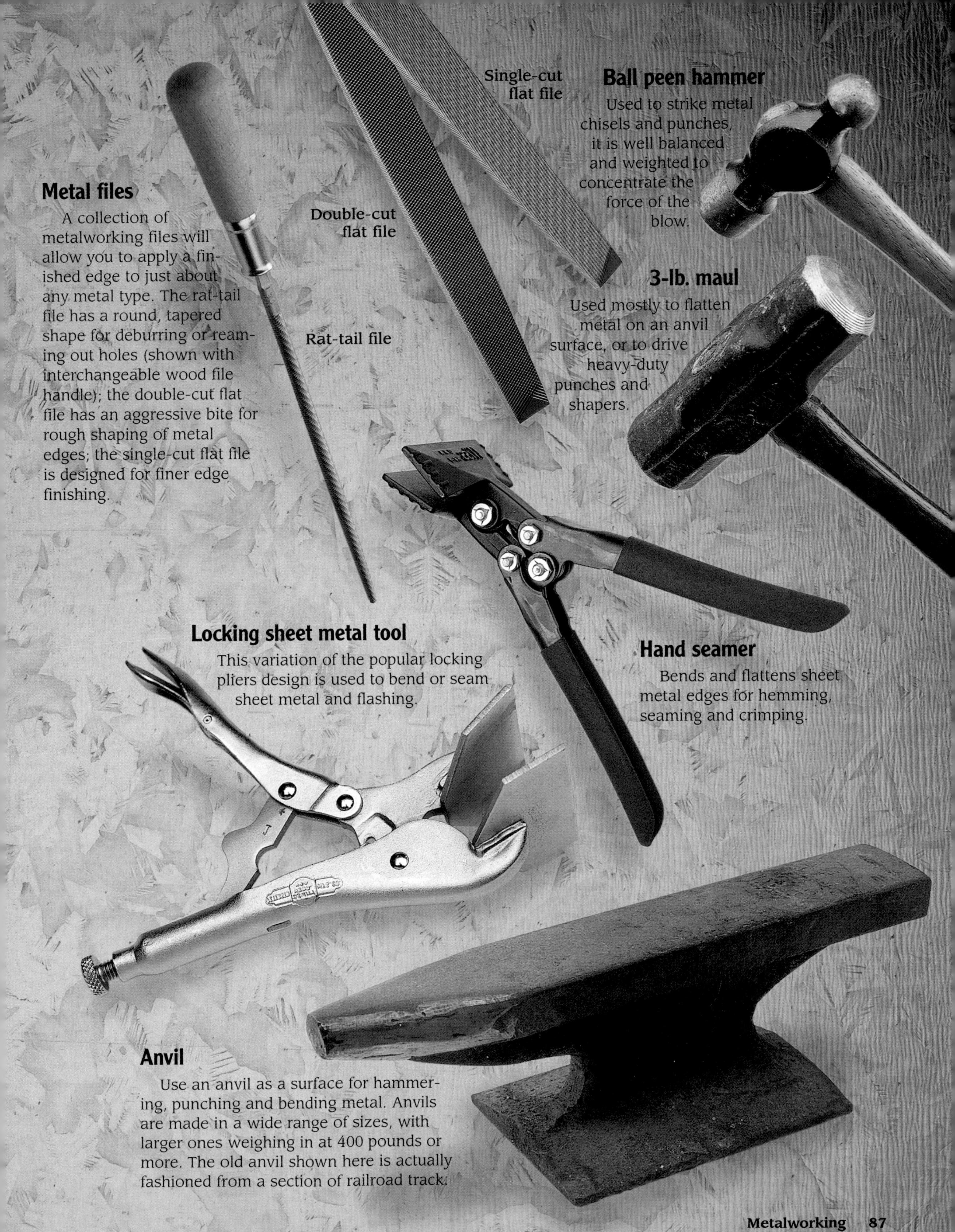

Metal files

A collection of metalworking files will allow you to apply a finished edge to just about any metal type. The rat-tail file has a round, tapered shape for deburring or reaming out holes (shown with interchangeable wood file handle); the double-cut flat file has an aggressive bite for rough shaping of metal edges; the single-cut flat file is designed for finer edge finishing.

Single-cut flat file

Double-cut flat file

Rat-tail file

Ball peen hammer

Used to strike metal chisels and punches, it is well balanced and weighted to concentrate the force of the blow.

3-lb. maul

Used mostly to flatten metal on an anvil surface, or to drive heavy-duty punches and shapers.

Locking sheet metal tool

This variation of the popular locking pliers design is used to bend or seam sheet metal and flashing.

Hand seamer

Bends and flattens sheet metal edges for hemming, seaming and crimping.

Anvil

Use an anvil as a surface for hammering, punching and bending metal. Anvils are made in a wide range of sizes, with larger ones weighing in at 400 pounds or more. The old anvil shown here is actually fashioned from a section of railroad track.

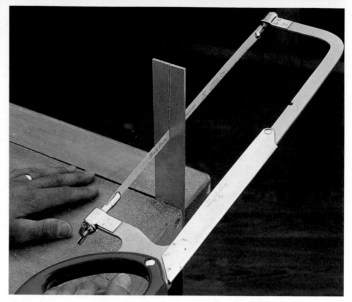

Use two hands for better hacksaw control

For best results when cutting with a hacksaw, first clamp the workpiece securely in a vise, with the cutting line close to the jaws of the vise (if cutting metal strips, scribe the cutting line with a punch or diamond-point chisel). Make a light forward stroke to score the cutting line, then steady the front of the blade with your free hand and proceed with the cut. Cut with light pressure when moving the blade forward, and do not apply any pressure on the return stroke.

Turn blade 90° to make vertical cuts

The thick spine of the hacksaw provides rigidity when cutting, but it does limit the depth of cut you make. One way around this problem, when making a lengthwise cut on a narrow strip of metal, is to install the hacksaw blade so it's in a vertical position when the saw is held flat. Make sure the blade is secure in the blade holders, then proceed with the cut.

Make a metal sandwich when cutting soft, thin sheet metal

Many mild metals used for decorative purposes can be cut easily with power saws and a metal cutting or jeweler's blade. But there's just one problem: these delicate materials rip easily from the force of the saw blade. An effective solution to the dilemma is to sandwich the material (light-gauge copper sheeting is shown here) between two pieces of thin plywood or hardboard. Secure the "metal sandwich" with masking tape, then draw your cutting lines and make your cuts through the wood and the metal at once (you can also gang-cut several sheets of metal at one time using this method).

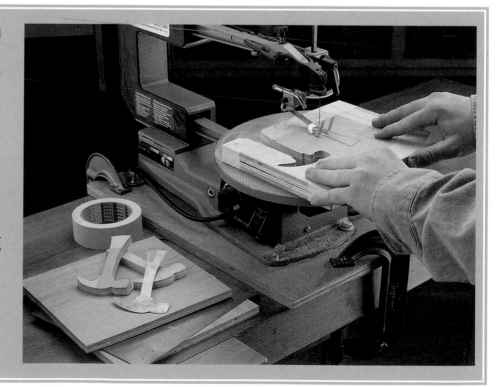

Use a tough saw to cut tough metal

A reciprocating saw with a metal cutting blade is one of the few tools that can cut rebar and other stubborn steel materials. Be sure to secure the metal object in a vise or with clamps as close to the cutting line as possible (this will help dampen vibrations). Cut with the foot of the saw up against the rebar, and do not force the cut—the weight of the saw provides more than enough downward pressure.

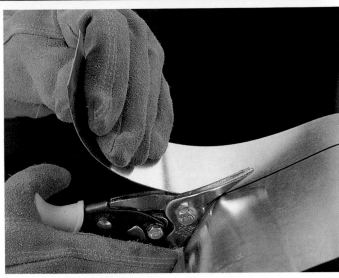

Keep waste out of the way with aviator snips

Practically everyone has cut flashing or other light-gauge metal with aviator snips or tin snips, but few people have done it correctly. If you're making a straight cut, be sure to use the yellow-handled snips designed for straight cutting (See page 86). Start your cut, holding the waste section with your free hand. Peel the waste away as you cut, preventing it from causing the snips to bind in the saw kerf. To keep the cut from kinking, never close the jaws of the snips all the way.

Keep cool when drilling metal

Use light machine oil for lubrication when drilling holes in metal. Create a depression for the bit to follow with a metal punch first. Select hardened metal twist bits to drill holes in metal, and set your drill press or portable drill at its slowest drilling speed (See page 45).

Grind away rust with an angle grinder

For fast removal of rust from heavy metal items, use an angle grinder fitted with a flap-style abrasive grinding disc. Always wear eye protection and gloves when operating this or any other metalworking tool to protect your eyes from flying sparks or bits of metal.

Two ways to bend flashing and light sheet metal

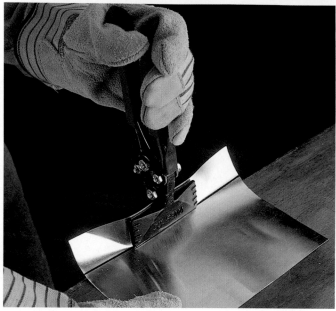

Use a hand seamer or locking sheet metal tool (See page 87) to crease and bend seams in small pieces of roll flashing or step flashing. The hand seamer is also an effective tool for hemming and seaming sheet metal (See page 92). Start bending or creasing in the middle of the workpiece, and work your way toward the ends, alternating from side to side.

Use a straightedge, like the top of a sawhorse, as a guide for hand-bending roll flashing (for example, to make hip or valley flashing when roofing). Clamp or attach a stop block to set the distance of the crease from the edge of the flashing. Wearing gloves, simply press down on the flashing along the bending line until a neat crease is formed in the metal.

Three ways to deburr cut metal

Use a rotary grinding tool with a grinding wheel to smooth away burrs from the inside edges of metal tubing or conduit.

Use a metalworking file (See page 87) to smooth out rough edges from rolled steel and plate steel. Use a double-cut file for roughing and a single-cut file for final smoothing.

Use a bench grinder to smooth out burrs on metal used for rough construction, like the conduit shown above. The grinding wheel does fast, neat work but has a limited range of angles from which to apply the workpiece.

Tool rest

Rounding corners with a bench grinder

Create a roundover on strap steel and other metal types with your bench grinder. Use the tool rest as a guide to keep the edge of the roundover perpendicular. Cool the metal by dabbing it with a damp sponge.

How to twist metal straps

Metal strap steel can be twisted into a regular spiral shape with this simple trick. Clamp one end of the strap in your machinist's vise and grasp the free end with a pipe wrench. Tighten another pipe wrench an inch or two in from the end of the strap, then slowly spin the wrenches as if you were turning the steering wheel of a car. The metal will develop even twists for a spiral effect. Protect the end of the strap with masking tape before attaching the pipe wrenches. You can use the twisted strap or straps for many metalworking projects, including plant hangers and stair rail balusters.

How to bend metal strap

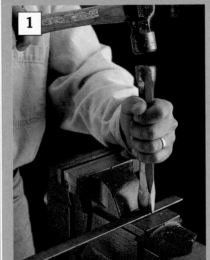

1 Measure and lay out the desired location of the bend. Lay the strap on an anvil or on the anvil portion of a bench vise and score along the bending line by rapping a cold chisel with a hammer.

2 Secure the strap in the jaws of your vise so the scored bending line projects above the jaws of the vise slightly. Slip a piece of metal conduit over the free end of the strap. Gently pull down on the conduit so the direction of the force is in line with the flat face of the strap. This will cause the strap to bend at its weakest point: the scored line. Pull down until the desired angle is achieved.

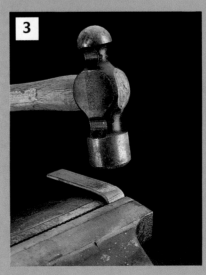

3 If making a 90° bend, use a hammer or maul to flatten the corner of strap at the bending line. For a very crisp, 90° bend, remove the strap and hammer both legs of the corner on an anvil until they're as smooth and crisp as possible.

Metalworking

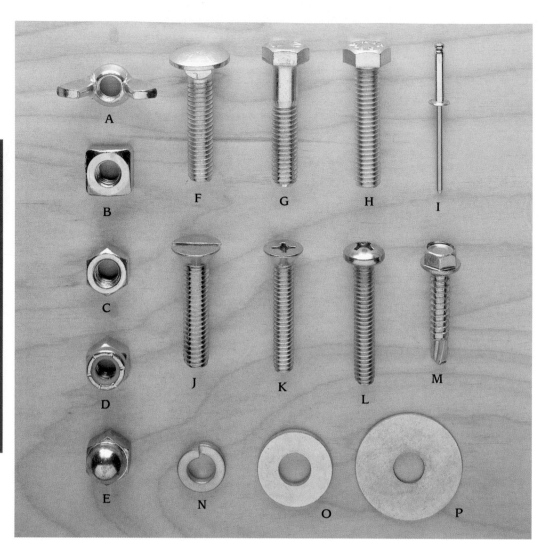

Fasteners for metal

Joining metal with mechanical fasteners is much the same as joining wood. The trick lies in doing careful layout and preparation work, drilling pilot and guide holes accurately, and selecting the right fastener for the job. Whenever possible, select hardware made from the same type of metal as the parts being joined.

Common nuts used in metalworking include: (A) wing nut; (B) square nut; (C) hex nut; (D) stop nut (locks down when tightened); (E) cap nut (conceals bolt heads).
Common fasteners used in metalworking include: (F) carriage bolt; (G) machine bolt; (H) tap bolt; (I) pop rivet; (J) stove bolt; (K) flathead machine screw; (L) roundhead machine screw; (M) self-tapping metal screw. Common washers used in metalworking include: (N) lock washer; (O) flat washer; (P) fender washer.

Folded seams and hems for sheet metal

Standing seam: used for rectangular or square ductwork. Mating parts are folded, then hooked together. Seams can be up to 1 in. high.

Folded seam: used mostly for installing metal roofing and siding. Mating parts are folded then hooked together. Typically ¼ in. wide.

Grooved seam: used mostly for long joints and cylinders. Prefolded and hooked, then final side is hammered flush. Typically ¼ in. wide.

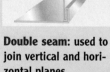

Double seam: used to join vertical and horizontal planes. Prefolded, then folded again after sheets are hooked together. Typically ¼ in. wide.

Single fold hem (left) and double fold hem (right).

Seams and hems are keys to strength in fabricated sheet metal projects

Many useful and decorative items can be built by fabricating sheet metal: tool boxes, drawers, roofing fixtures, workshop jigs, and birdhouses, just to name a few. When building with sheet metal, draw patterns for the project parts directly onto the metal with a wax crayon. At joints between parts, use folded seams for strong construction that's free of sharp edges. The folded seams and hems illustrated here are bent using a hand seamer (See page 87). Be sure to allow for the width of seams and hems when laying out your patterns.

How to use a pop rivet gun

Pop rivets are easy-to-use fasteners that join two or more pieces of light-gauge metal. They're especially useful for repairing sheet metal objects, like file cabinets, that have come apart at the seams.

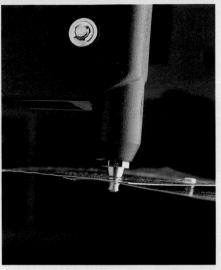

1 Start by positioning the parts to be joined and drill a guide hole through the seam for each pop rivet. The guide hole should be the same diameter as the pop rivet mandrel (shaft).

2 Insert the mandrel of a pop rivet into the hole in the nosepiece of the pop rivet gun. Squeeze the gun handles together to hold the rivet and insert the end of the rivet into the guide hole. The head of the rivet should be flush on the surface of the metal. Avoid rocking the gun.

3 Squeeze the gun handles together repeatedly until they resist squeezing. Check to make sure the head of the rivet is still flush on the metal surface. Squeeze the handles together again (this can take some effort) until the pressure from the gun causes the mandrel to snap off from the head of the pop rivet. Check the fit of the rivet: you may need to drive the top of the mandrel stump down into the rivet head with a punch.

Coatings & treatments used with metal

Most metals are well suited for painting, but you should use special paints and coatings designed for use with metal. Among the more common of these are:

(A) enamel spray paint; (B) high-temperature spray paint for grills, stoves, etc.; (C) spray version anti-rust primer; (D) rust-inhibiting metal paint; (E) chain link fence paint; (F) rust-inhibiting metal primer; (G) naval jelly for dissolving rust; (H) rust stop solution for preparing rusted metal surfaces for paint.

Penetrating machine oil: A general lubricant used for drilling, cleaning and removing rust from metal.

Spray silicon: A multi-use lubricant that won't attract dirt. Non-corrosive, lubricates, waterproofs and insulates metals and other materials.

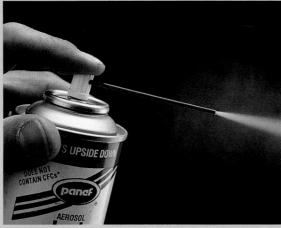

Spray graphite: An exceptionally slick lubricant used for locks, bearings and other precise mechanical parts.

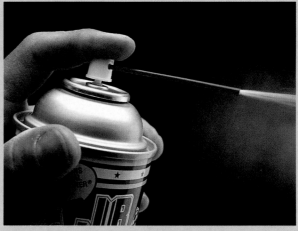

Penetrating lubricants: Lubricate and condition metal, dissolve rust and loosen rusted hardware. Protects metal from corrosion. Brand names include WD40 and others.

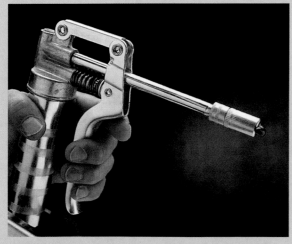

Lithium grease: Mechanical joint lubricant that's cleaner, longer lasting and more heat resistant than standard petroleum-based grease lubricants.

Paste wax: When buffed onto metal surfaces creates a smooth, resistance-free finish and protective barrier. Used on stationary tool tables.

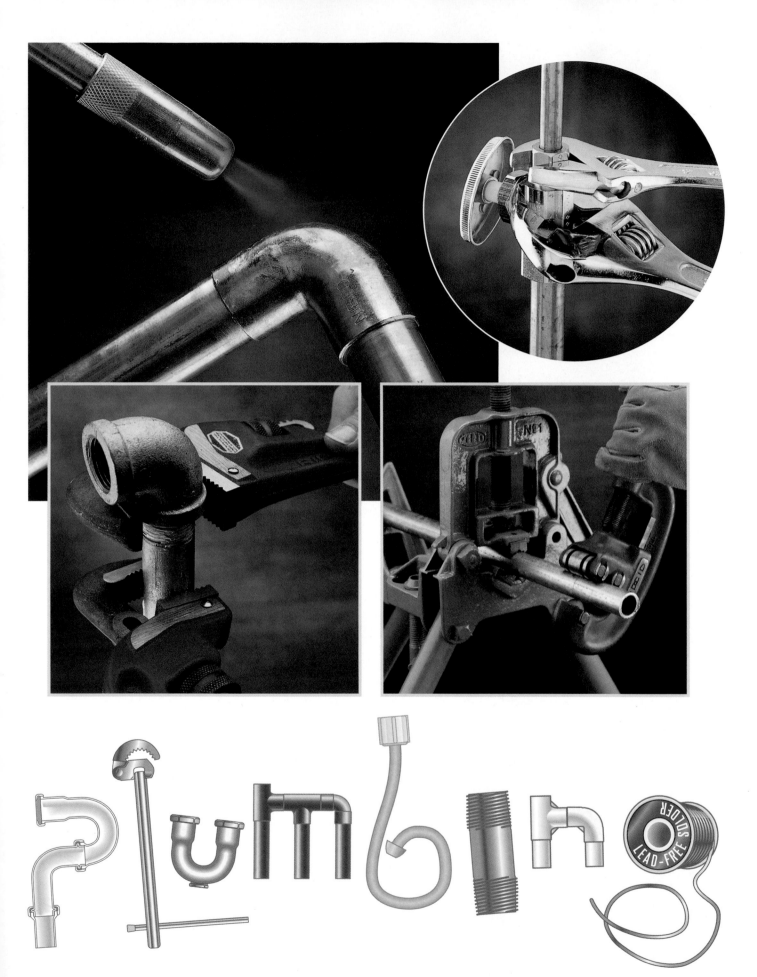

Plumbing

Once you understand the basic theories behind moving water through a home and get to know the basic materials and materials handling techniques, you'll be able to tackle just about any plumbing repair or project with confidence.

In a nutshell, here's how plumbing works: Water is brought into the home under pressure through a metered water main. The main is connected to supply pipes, usually ¾-in.-dia. copper. The supply pipes run in parallel pairs throughout your home. One takes a detour at the water heater, then rejoins the cold water supply pipe to carry hot water to sinks, bathtubs and showers. The supply pipes typically run through joist and wall cavities, passing through floors or walls near plumbing fixtures, where they're connected to the fixtures with water supply lines, usually ½-in. copper or plastic. Usually, several plumbing fixtures are serviced by one loop of the supply pipes. Throughout the network of pipes, and at each plumbing fixture, shut-off valves are inserted into the supply lines so the water flow can be stopped if needed.

The water leaves your home through a network of drains that form the drain/waste/vent (DWV) system. Individual fixtures are connected to a vertical main drain stack via branch drains that run at a slight downward slope through floor and wall cavities. The main stack connects directly to the sewer or septic line outside the home. To prevent pressure and gas buildup, the entire DWV system is connected to a network of vent pipes that also work their way back to the main stack, which rises all the way through your home and exits through the roof in the form of a roof vent.

Plumbing codes

Because of the potential for disastrous water damage and the high cost of repairing a plumbing system once it's up and running, plumbing is a closely regulated practice. The Uniform Plumbing Code (UPC) is a national set of codes that's updated every three years. It forms the foundation of most local plumbing codes. But for a number of reasons, including climate, local codes often vary from the UPC standards—usually on the more restrictive side. Use the UPC as a general guide when planning a plumbing project or repair, but make sure to consult with your local building inspection department before beginning any work. For new installations, a permit is normally required.

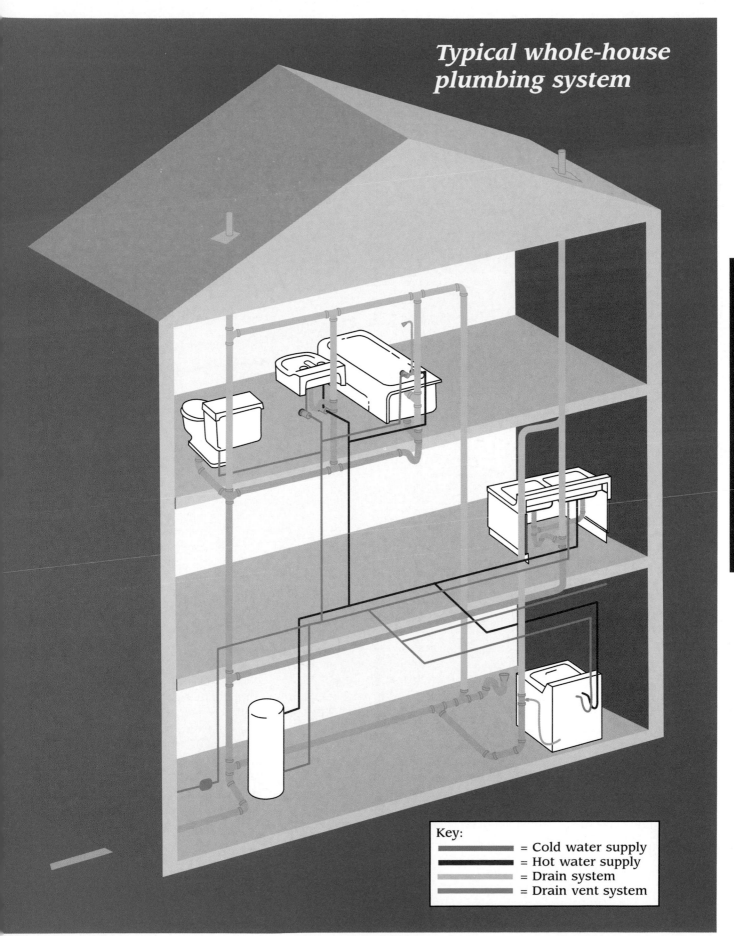

Typical whole-house plumbing system

Key:
- ═══ = Cold water supply
- ═══ = Hot water supply
- ═══ = Drain system
- ═══ = Drain vent system

Typical DWV system

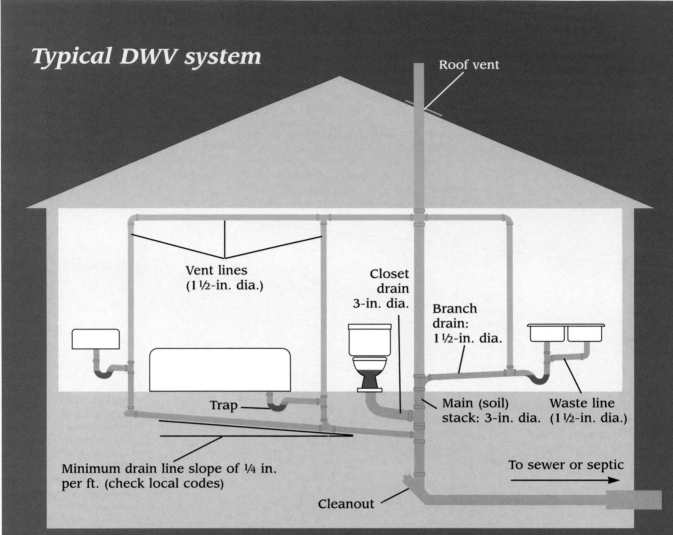

Roof vent

Vent lines
(1½-in. dia.)

Closet
drain
3-in. dia.

Branch
drain:
1½-in. dia.

Trap

Main (soil)
stack: 3-in. dia.

Waste line
(1½-in. dia.)

Minimum drain line slope of ¼ in.
per ft. (check local codes)

To sewer or septic

Cleanout

DWV system basics

Waste and sewage are removed from the home through a system of drains and branch drains that are vented through the roof via a network of vent pipes. A large-diameter drain pipe, called the soil stack or main stack, runs vertically through the house. All other branch drains tie into this stack, the bottom of which terminates at a large drain pipe leading directly to the sewer or septic system. The vent system also ties into the main stack, although it's not uncommon to have a secondary vent stack that also exits through the roof. The branch drains that tie into the main stack are connected to individual plumbing fixtures with waste lines. Each waste line contains a trap that is always filled with water to prevent sewer gases

from escaping through the drain system and into the house.

Both the branch drain and the waste pipes must slope toward the main stack at a rate of at least ¼ in. per ft. to ensure steady flow. Vent lines should slope upward slightly to keep water and condensation from accumulating and weakening the pipes.

Today, drain and vent systems almost always are constructed with PVC pipe. But many houses still contain DWV systems with a cast iron main stack and galvanized steel branch and waste lines. Consult your local building inspection office for specific information on drain and vent pipe size, slope and spacing requirements in your area.

Plumbing Systems

The water supply system

Required supply pipe diameters for common plumbing fixtures

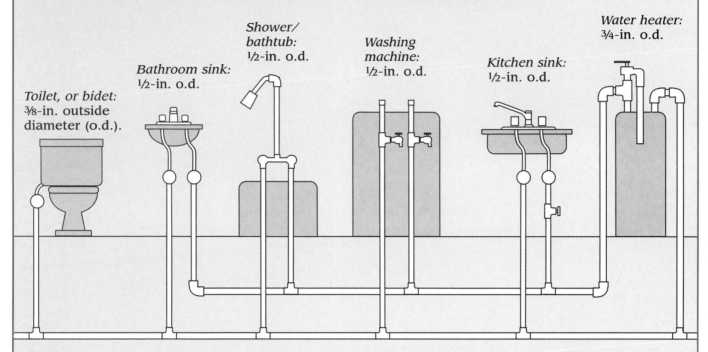

Water heater: 3/4-in. o.d.

Shower/ bathtub: 1/2-in. o.d.

Washing machine: 1/2-in. o.d.

Bathroom sink: 1/2-in. o.d.

Kitchen sink: 1/2-in. o.d.

Toilet, or bidet: 3/8-in. outside diameter (o.d.).

Not shown: dishwasher, laundry tub and hose bib (exterior faucet) all require 1/2-in. supply pipe.

Add air chambers to supply lines to eliminate rattling pipes

If your water supply pipes knock or rattle inside the walls, your plumbing system has a condition known as *water hammering*. The hammering is caused by the force of the rushing water within the pipes. When a valve is suddenly closed, the momentum of the rushing water "hammers" against the pipes. The way to alleviate the hammering is to install air chambers, which provide a small cushion of air to relieve the pressure of the rushing water. Air chambers eventually lose their effectiveness as the air is slowly absorbed into the water. The chambers can be recharged by draining your plumbing system.

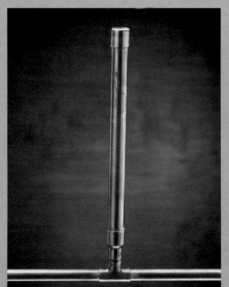

Option 1: Do-it-yourself air chamber. An air chamber can be made from a length of capped copper tubing. Simply install a short length of vertical tubing on a horizontal run of piping and cap the end. The vertical tube will hold air and provide a cushion against water hammer.

Option 2: Ready-made air chamber. Air chambers can also be purchased from plumbing supply stores. These devices can be installed at an angle or upside down.

Plumbing Systems

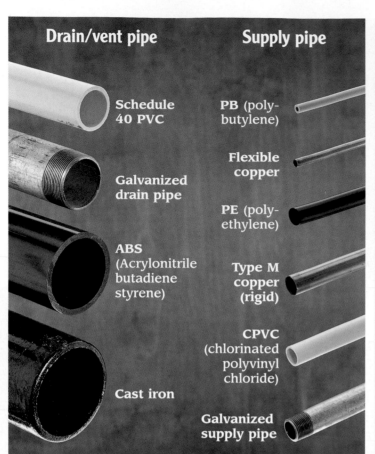

Drain/vent pipe

Schedule
40 PVC

Galvanized
drain pipe

ABS
(Acrylonitrile
butadiene
styrene)

Cast iron

Supply pipe

PB (poly-
butylene)

Flexible
copper

PE (poly-
ethylene)

Type M
copper
(rigid)

CPVC
(chlorinated
polyvinyl
chloride)

Galvanized
supply pipe

Standard pipe diameters

Material	Inside dia.	Outside dia.	Circumf.
Copper	1/4	3/8	1 1/8
	3/8	1/2	1 1/2
	1/2	5/8	2
	3/4	7/8	2 3/4
	1	1 1/8	3 1/2
	1 1/4	1 3/8	4 5/16
	1 1/2	1 5/8	5 1/8
Galvanized steel	3/8	5/8	2
	1/2	7/8	2 3/8
	3/4	1	3 1/8
	1	1 1/4	4
	1 1/4	1 1/2	4 3/4
	1 1/2	1 3/4	5 1/2
	2	2 1/4	7
Plastic (PVC)	1/2	7/8	2 3/4
	3/4	1 1/8	3 1/2
	1	1 3/8	4 5/16
	1 1/4	1 5/8	5 1/8
	1 1/2	1 7/8	6
	2	2 3/8	7 1/2
	3	3 3/8	10 1/2
	4	4 3/8	14
Cast iron	2	2 1/4	7
	3	3 1/4	10 1/8
	4	4 1/4	13 3/8

Pipe hangers

Using the correct type of pipe hanger is necessary to preserve your pipes. Pipes that bang or rub against other materials could eventually burst. Unsupported pipes are likely to sustain joint failure. Pipes that are supported by a hanger of a different metal type can corrode. Do not exceed maximum spacing requirements for hangers (see chart below).

Allowable distance between pipe hangers

MATERIAL	SUPPORT SPACING
ABS	4 ft.
Galvanized	12 ft.
Copper	6 ft.
CPVC	3 ft.
Cast iron	5 ft.
PVC	4 ft.
PB pipe	32 in.

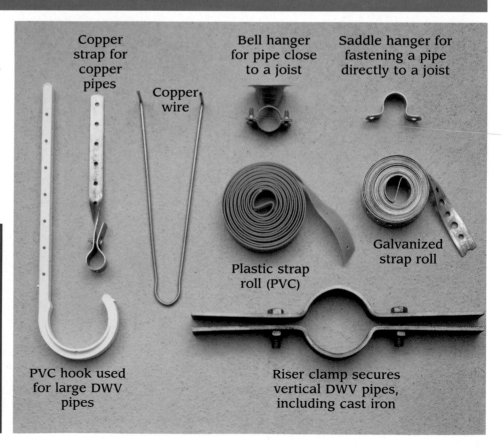

Copper strap for copper pipes

Copper wire

Bell hanger for pipe close to a joist

Saddle hanger for fastening a pipe directly to a joist

Galvanized strap roll

Plastic strap roll (PVC)

PVC hook used for large DWV pipes

Riser clamp secures vertical DWV pipes, including cast iron

Tools you'll use for plumbing projects

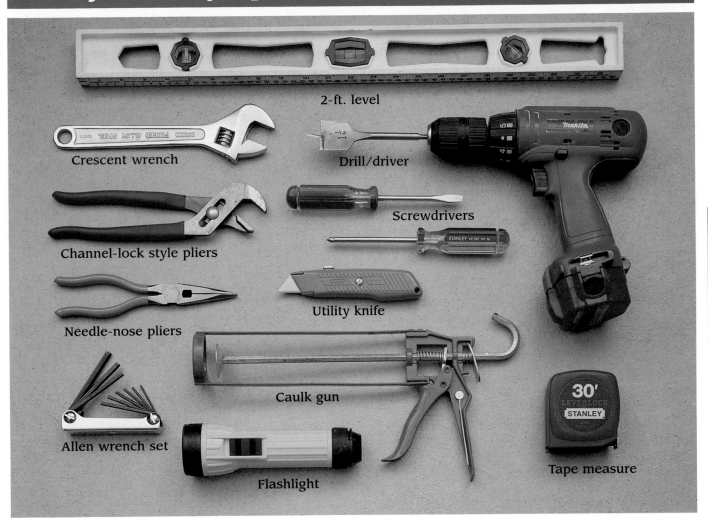

2-ft. level

Crescent wrench

Drill/driver

Channel-lock style pliers

Screwdrivers

Needle-nose pliers

Utility knife

Caulk gun

Allen wrench set

Flashlight

Tape measure

Everyday shop tools. Before starting a plumbing project, make certain your workshop has the right stuff. These tools are common to many repair projects, but don't get stuck in the middle of a plumbing job when you discover you are missing an obvious tool.

Cutting tools. When parts of your plumbing system need repair or replacement, it's likely you're going to be doing some cutting. Choose the right tool. Your results will be better, and you'll work more safely.

Power miter box (A) is great for cutting pipe; **reamer (B)** is necessary when threading galvanized pipe; **galvanized pipe cutter (C)** makes the neat, even cuts you need when joining galvanized pipe; **plastic tubing cutter (D)** works like pruning shears to cut plastic pipe quickly; **hacksaw (E)** is the simple workhorse of many plumbers; **plastic pipe saw (F)** slices quickly through plastic pipe, especially large-diameter pipe; **reciprocating saw (G)** will cut through pipe, studs, nails or just about anything that needs removal; **pipe threader (H)** will cut threads on galvanized pipe; **copper tubing cutter** (also called a thumb-cutter) **(H)** cuts copper tubing neatly, even in tight areas.

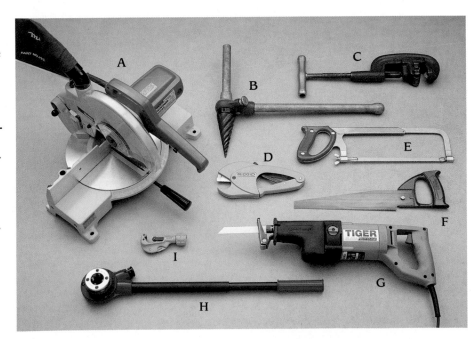

Specialty plumbing tools

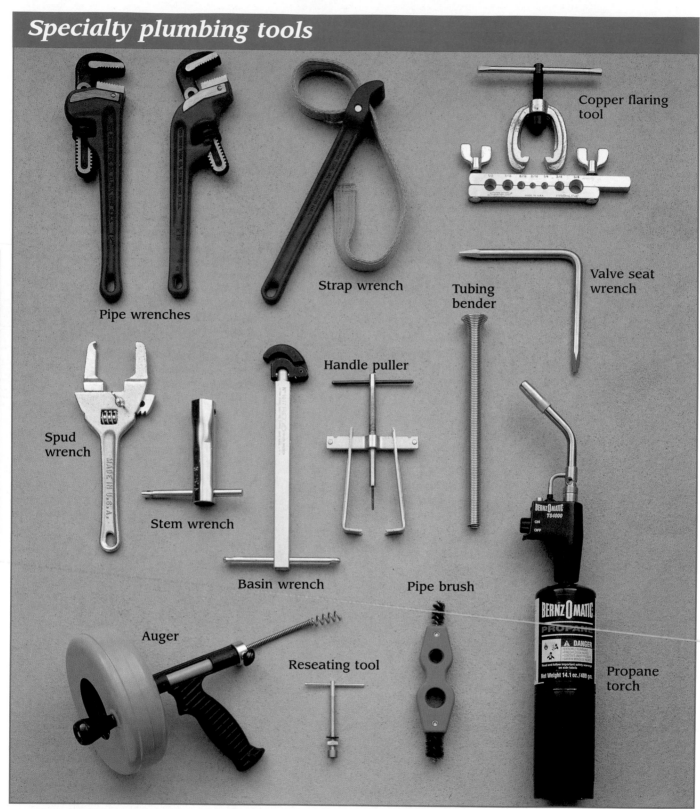

Copper flaring tool

Strap wrench

Tubing bender

Valve seat wrench

Pipe wrenches

Spud wrench

Handle puller

Stem wrench

Basin wrench

Pipe brush

Auger

Reseating tool

Propane torch

Specialty plumbing tools will help you do the job right. The investment is not great, especially when you compare the cost of new tools to the hourly rates of your local plumber. Many of these tools are shown in use on the following page and throughout this chapter: **Pipe wrenches** for turning galvanized pipe—you'll need two for most jobs; **strap (or cloth) wrench** for removing easily-marred chrome pipes; **copper flaring tool** shapes the ends of copper tubing for flare fittings; **valve seat wrench** removes the small valve seats from worn

faucets; **spud wrench** tightens large nuts that are 2 to 4 in. in diameter; **stem wrench** removes faucet stems hidden in recessed holes; **basin wrench** twists off hard-to-reach nuts on plumbing fixtures; **handle puller** will free faucet handles from corrosion bonds; **tubing bender** ensures neat, kink-free copper tubing bends; **auger** clears drain lines of debris; **reseating tool** will grind a smooth faucet seat; **pipe brush** cleans pipes prior to gluing or soldering; auto-igniting **propane torch** provides heat for soldering copper and other plumbing projects.

Specialty plumbing tools in use

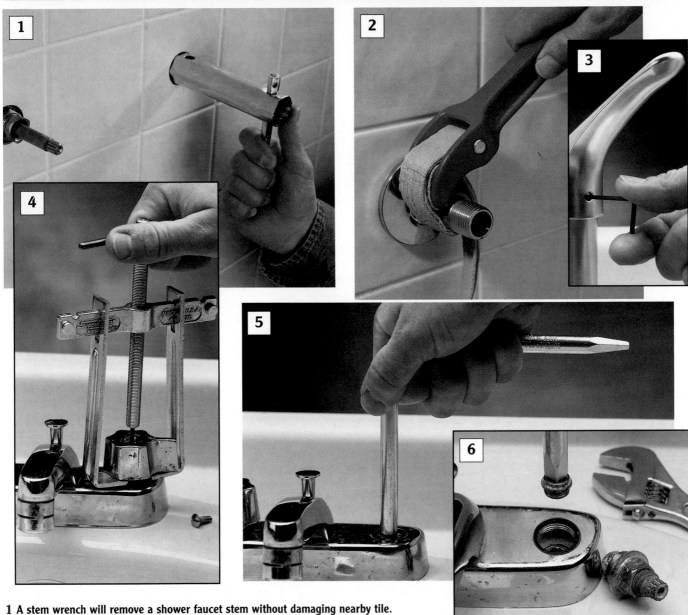

1 A stem wrench will remove a shower faucet stem without damaging nearby tile.

2 A strap wrench, also called a cloth wrench, will grasp and turn pipes and fixtures that are chromed-plated or made from other delicate materials without damaging them.

3 Allen wrenches are necessary to repair some modern plumbing fixtures. Many kitchen faucets and some tub spouts are secured with an Allen screw.

4 With older compression faucets, it's not uncommon for corrosion to lock the faucet handle onto the faucet stem. You'll need a faucet puller to break this corrosion bond. Simply place the bottom jaws of the puller under the handle and align the puller onto the stem. Then draw the handle off the stem by rotating the screw.

5 To remove a worn valve seat from a faucet, you'll need a valve seat wrench. Make certain to use the correct end of the puller: either the square end or the hexagonal end. Push the wrench down firmly, and turn the tool counterclockwise. Carefully lift out the valve seat with the valve wrench (Photo 6).

7 A spud wrench allows you remove large nuts, such as the nut securing a kitchen sink drain. The hooked jaws on the ends of the wrench latch onto the lugs of large nuts. An adjustable spud wrench, shown here, will remove nuts of many sizes.

Valves used in home plumbing

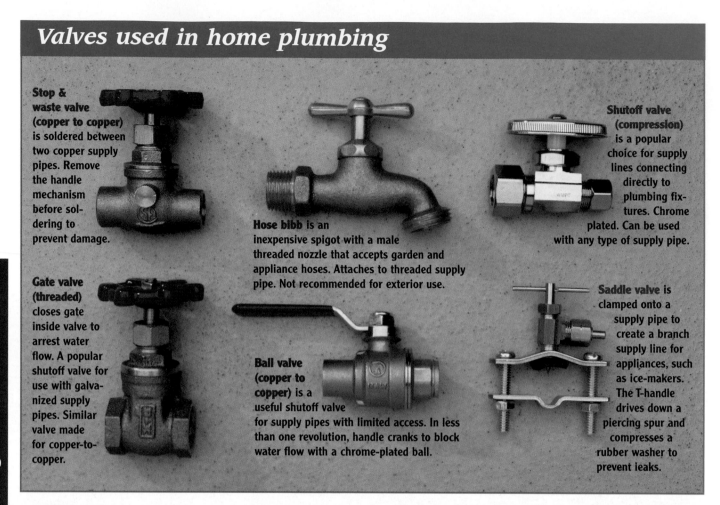

Stop & waste valve (copper to copper) is soldered between two copper supply pipes. Remove the handle mechanism before soldering to prevent damage.

Gate valve (threaded) closes gate inside valve to arrest water flow. A popular shutoff valve for use with galvanized supply pipes. Similar valve made for copper-to-copper.

Hose bibb is an inexpensive spigot with a male threaded nozzle that accepts garden and appliance hoses. Attaches to threaded supply pipe. Not recommended for exterior use.

Ball valve (copper to copper) is a useful shutoff valve for supply pipes with limited access. In less than one revolution, handle cranks to block water flow with a chrome-plated ball.

Shutoff valve (compression) is a popular choice for supply lines connecting directly to plumbing fixtures. Chrome plated. Can be used with any type of supply pipe.

Saddle valve is clamped onto a supply pipe to create a branch supply line for appliances, such as ice-makers. The T-handle drives down a piercing spur and compresses a rubber washer to prevent leaks.

How to fix a leaky valve with a valve seat grinder

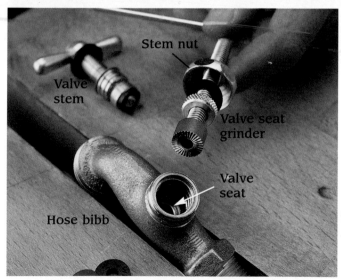

Stem nut

Valve stem

Valve seat grinder

Valve seat

Hose bibb

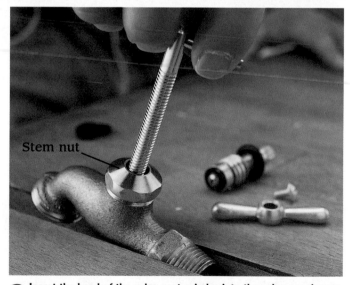

Stem nut

1 If a faucet valve seat is not smooth, the washer or diaphragm that fits against the seat will not provide a good seal, making a leak likely. To regrind a seat, you'll need a tool called, straightforwardly, a valve seat grinder. You can perform this repair without disconnecting the hose bibb if you shut off the water supply. With the leaky hose bibb held securely, remove the valve stem and any washers or diaphragms covering the valve seat.

2 Insert the head of the valve seat grinder into the valve opening so it presses against the valve seat. Slip the stem nut from the valve stem over the free end of the grinder, then screw it onto the male-threaded valve opening. Turn the seat grinder handle three rotations (you don't need to press down—the pressure from the stem nut is sufficient). Remove the grinder and inspect the valve seat with a flashlight. Repeat if necessary, then reassemble the valve.

Copper supply fittings

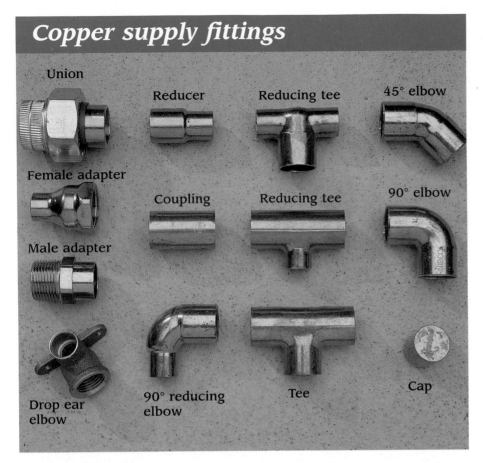

Union

Female adapter

Male adapter

Drop ear elbow

Reducer

Coupling

90° reducing elbow

Reducing tee

Reducing tee

Tee

45° elbow

90° elbow

Cap

Copper tubing & fittings

Copper supply pipe has become the industry standard, replacing galvanized pipe and fencing off a challenge from PVC supply pipe. The reasons for its popularity are simple: it's lightweight, easy to cut, corrosion-resistant and the joints formed by soldering two pieces of copper are extremely strong and durable when made correctly.

Copper supply in residential installations is generally either ½- or ¾-in. There are two basic types of copper tubing: rigid and flexible. Rigid pipe is used for most of the water supply system. It comes in three grades, ranked according to the thickness of the pipe walls. Type M is the thinnest and cheapest copper pipe. It's suitable for most household plumbing uses. Type L is generally used for commercial applications, and Type K is the thickest rigid copper and is not used in residential plumbing. Flexible copper tubing can be used for water supply lines in some cases, but is used most commonly for gas lines. Connections can be made with compression or flare fittings, as well as soldered.

Materials for soldering copper

Before starting any soldering job, check to see that you have the right materials. Solder, flux and a flux brush are mandatory. Flux cleans and prepares the copper surface for the solder that's melted into the joint. Some background information: Decades-old solder hiding in your workshop can contain lead, which can leach into your water supply. Solder and flux produced today are lead-free, which means you won't have trace amounts of lead leaching into your drinking water. The drawback is that lead-free solder melts at a higher temperature and therefore requires a little more time to apply correctly.

Flux

Solder

Flux brush

The propane torch

An auto-igniting propane torch can help you solder more quickly and efficiently. The torch produces a flame with the push of a button, saving you fuel and allowing you to work faster. A propane torch with an auto-igniting starter is also safer than a manually-lighted torch. There is less chance of a flare-up when starting and the flame is eliminated when you release the button.

Two ways to protect walls from torch flames

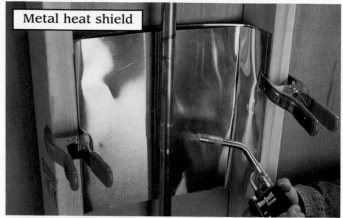

Metal heat shield

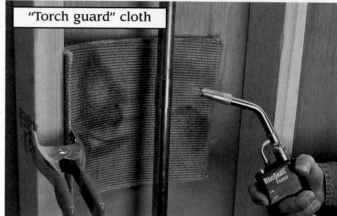

"Torch guard" cloth

A propane torch can easily ignite nearby flammable materials when soldering. If you are working on pipes near anything flammable, use a heat block. An effective block can be fashioned out of sheet metal (at least 26-gauge). Clamp the metal to nearby studs. Be warned, however, that the metal can become very hot. Another option is to use specially designed "torch guard" cloth behind pipes you are soldering.

Tubing bender puts a smooth curve in copper

When bending flexible copper tubing, kinks can occur unless you use a coil-spring tubing bender. Use a bender that matches the outside diameter of the tubing. Bend the tubing slowly, and never bend it more than 90°. Do not attempt to bend copper pipe after joints have been soldered—the pressure can weaken or break the joints.

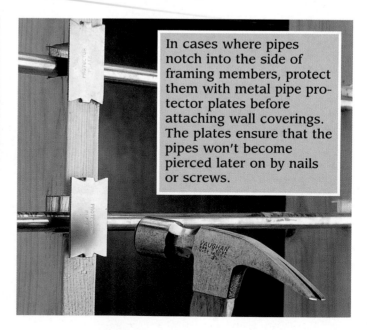

In cases where pipes notch into the side of framing members, protect them with metal pipe protector plates before attaching wall coverings. The plates ensure that the pipes won't become pierced later on by nails or screws.

How to cut copper pipe with a tubing cutter

While copper tubing can be cut with a hacksaw, a tubing cutter produces a much smoother, more even cut, which helps ensure a tight solder joint. Because it doesn't stress the pipes as a saw does, it can be used on pipes that have been soldered. And its small profile allows it to fit into tight areas where other tools can't be used.

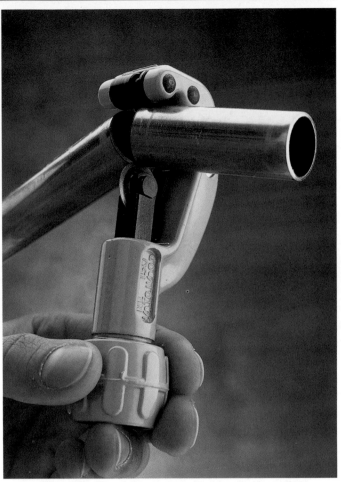

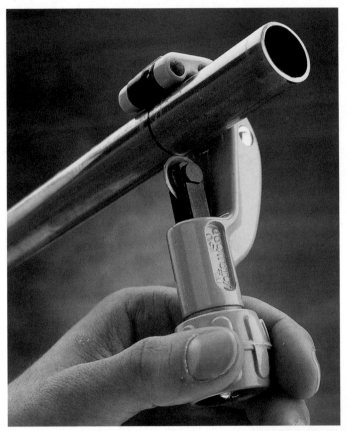

1 Mark the length you want to cut with a black magic marker. Then place the tubing cutter over the pipe and tighten the handle. The cutting wheel should be aligned with the cutting line and both rollers on the tubing cutter should be making contact with the pipe. Turn the tubing cutter one complete rotation, scoring a continuous straight line around the pipe.

2 Rotate the cutter in opposite directions, tightening the handle slightly after every two rotations until the cut is complete and the waste piece of pipe drops free.

3 Remove burrs from the inside lip of the pipe with the reaming blade found on the back of the tubing cutter, or use a rattail file. Removing all the burrs and creating a perfectly smooth edge is critical to successful soldering. It also ensures good water flow and fewer deposits over time.

Making a sweated joint

A well-soldered copper joint will be watertight and durable. When soldering, enough heat must be applied to the pipe to draw the solder into the gap between the pipe and the fitting. Too much heat, or uneven heating, can result in a faulty joint. In addition, pipes and fittings must be clean and dry before and during soldering. If you're sweating a brass or bronze fitting, such as a shutoff valve, be aware that it takes these metals a little longer to reach the melting point of the solder. Be patient, and resist the temptation to force the solder into the joint before the metal is sufficiently heated. Also, first remove any rubber or plastic parts from the fittings like valve stems or washers to keep them from melting or distorting as you solder. Reinstall these parts after the solder joints have completely cooled.

1 Clean the pipe. Copper pipes must be clean and burr-free before soldering. A brush tool allows you to clean both the inside and outside of pipes, and to scuff the copper slightly, creating a bonding surface for the solder.

2 Clean the fitting. Here, a brush tool is used to clean the inside of an elbow fitting. Avoid touching the mating areas of the pipes and fittings—the oil residue from your skin can interfere with the bond. For best protection, wear rubber gloves.

3 After a pipe is clean and dry, apply a thin layer of soldering flux (sometimes called soldering paste) to the ends of the pipe. The flux cleans and prepares the copper surface for the solder. It should cover about 1 in. of the pipe end.

4 Apply flux to the inside, mating surface of the fitting, using the flux brush.

5 After assembling the joint so it fits together snugly, heat the fitting—not the pipe—with a propane torch for several seconds. The flux should begin to sizzle. Heat all sides of the fitting.

Soldering copper

6 Before heating the joint, prepare the wire solder by unwinding about 1 ft. of wire and bending the first two in. into a right angle. Then, when the joint is hot, touch the solder to the pipe. If the solder melts, the pipe is ready. Remove the torch and quickly push ½ to ¾ in. of solder wire into the joint. You don't need to move the solder around the pipe, capillary action will draw melted solder into the joint. A thin bead of solder should form all the way around the lip.

7 With a dry rag, wipe away any excess solder from the joint. Take care: the pipes will be extremely hot. When the pipe has cooled, turn on the water and check for leaks. If water does seep from a joint, drain the pipes, resist the urge to reapply additional soldering paste to the rim of the joint and reapply solder. This fix usually fails.

How to break a soldered joint

1 If a soldered joint fails, the best solution is to break the joint, clean up the pipes, and try again with a new fitting. First, turn off the water supply in the house and drain the pipes by opening the highest and lowest faucets. Then, heat the fitting using a propane torch. Hold the flame to the fitting until the solder begins to melt.

2 Using channel-lock style pliers, grip the pipe and pull it free from the fitting before the solder resets. Be careful to avoid any steam trapped inside the pipe.

3 Allow the pipe to cool (you can speed cooling by wrapping the pipe in a damp rag). Clean the old solder residue from the pipes using emery paper and a pipe brush.

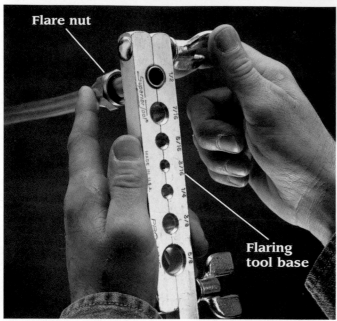

Flare nut

Flaring tool base

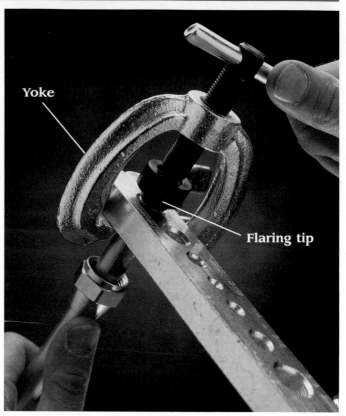

Yoke

Flaring tip

1 Flare fittings are used in situations where the pipe may need to be disconnected (such as at a shutoff valve before a fixture), or where soldering is unsafe or difficult. Flare fittings are also often used for flexible copper gas lines. When flare fittings are used on water supply lines, the connections must not be concealed by walls. To flare copper, you'll need a two-piece flaring kit and brass flare fittings. Slide the flare nut over the tubing, then clamp the tubing into the flaring tool. The tubing end must be flush with the face of the flaring tool base. Note: Do not attempt to use a flare fitting with rigid copper; flare fittings should be used with flexible copper only.

2 Slip the yoke part of the flaring tool around the base. Center the flaring tip of the yoke over the pipe. Turn the handle until it stops against the face of the flaring tool base, resulting in a flared end on the tubing. Tip: Oiling the flaring tip will produce a smoother flare.

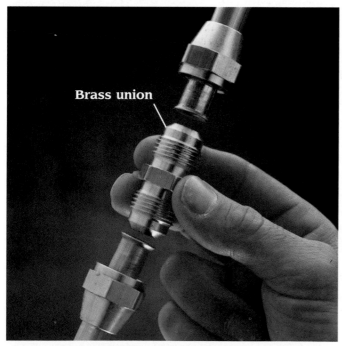

Brass union

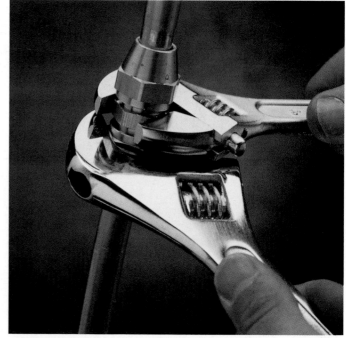

3 Flare the end of the other tube, then place the brass union between the flared ends.

4 Tighten the flare nuts onto the union using two pliers or wrenches and turning in opposite directions. Joint compound is not necessary. Check for leaks. If the fitting leaks, tighten the nuts slightly.

Plastic pipe & fittings

Buoyed by growing acceptance in the plumbing codes, PVC and other types of plastic pipe are more popular today than ever before. As a building material, PVC pipe is inexpensive, easy to work, light-weight and relatively forgiving. PVC and ABS are rigid forms of plastic pipe that are used almost exclusively for drain and vent systems. CPVC is a rigid plastic that's used for water supply systems—it resists heat better than ordinary PVC. Other types of plastic pipe include PE, used mostly for exterior, underground installations, and PB, a flexible plastic that's also used for supply pipe (PB fell out of favor for a period of time due to some problems with PB fittings, but those problems have been dealt with and its use is increasing, particularly in warmer climates). See page 100 for examples of these plastic types.

PVC drain & vent fittings

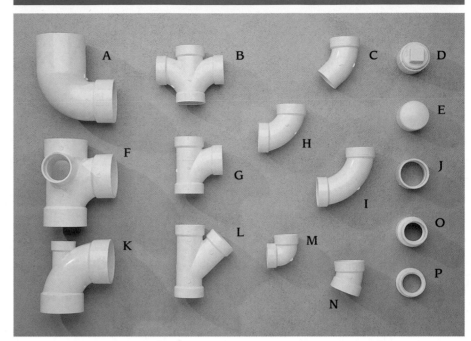

(A) closet bend; (B) waste cross; (C) 45° reducing elbow; (D) cleanout plug; (E) cap; (F) waste tee with side inlet; (G) waste/sanitary tee; (H) 90° elbow; (I) long-sweep 90° elbow; (J) coupling; (K) 90° elbow with side inlet; (L) wye fitting; (M) vent elbow; (N) 22° elbow; (O) reducer; (P) reducing bushing.

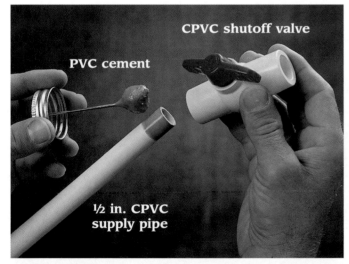

CPVC supply pipe growing in code acceptance

Until recently, most water supply pipe used to hook up plumbing fixtures has been copper or stainless steel. CPVC (chlorinated polyvinyl chloride) supply pipe has been around for some time, but many local codemakers have been reluctant to accept it. That's changing. CPVC has been found to be a reliable supply pipe material that's easy to work and also has better insulating power than other materials. It's installed using the same solvent welding process as PVC (See page 113). Check with your local building inspection department to find out if CPVC supply pipe is allowed in your area.

Materials for chemically welding PVC

When working with PVC pipe, make certain you use the correct materials. Solvent and primer should be labeled for PVC pipe. Colored solvent and primer allow you to inspect more easily to make sure all parts are coated. Sandcloth or emery paper is used to smooth rough edges. Primer helps degloss the pipe's slick surface, ensuring a good seal. Solvents and primers are toxic and flammable. Provide good ventilation and keep these products away from heat.

Options for cutting plastic pipe

Plastic tubing cutters

A PVC ratchet cutter will make short work of smaller PVC pipes. This tool is especially useful if you have a large variety of plastic pipes to cut.

Power miter saw

If you have a lot of plastic pipe to cut—and you want to make neat cuts very quickly—use a power miter saw fitted with a blade that has a high number of teeth per inch (See pages 30 to 31).

PVC pipe saw

To cut PVC pipe by hand, a PVC pipe saw will give you better results than an ordinary hacksaw. Make certain to hold the pipe securely in a vise and keep the saw blade straight while cutting.

Preparing plastic pipe for solvent-gluing

Trim away burrs created by cutting

PVC pipe must be smooth and free of burrs to ensure a watertight connection. Use a utility knife to slice off burrs from the edges of cuts.

Scuff and degloss mating surfaces of pipes

It's a good idea to lightly sand the outside of the pipe and the inside of the connection hub using sandcloth or emery paper before applying primer. Surfaces that are to be glued together should have a dull finish.

How to solvent-glue plastic pipe

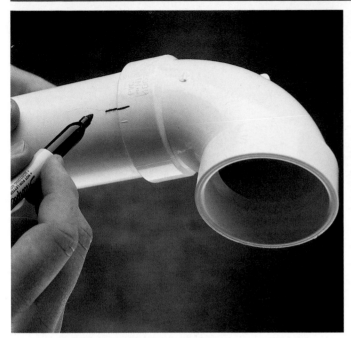

1 Cut the pipes to length and prepare the mating surfaces (see previous page). Fit the pipes and fittings together in the desired layout. Draw an alignment mark across each joint with a permanent marker.

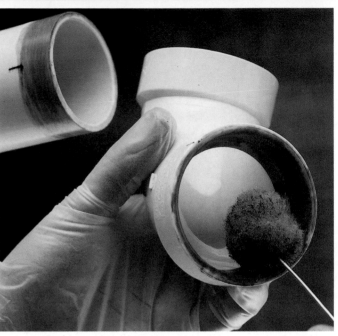

2 Apply PVC primer to the outside of the pipe and the inside of the connection hub or fitting. The primer is colored so you can see when full coverage has been achieved. Wear disposable gloves, and make sure the work area is adequately ventilated. Also be sure to read the directions and safety precautions on the labels of all products you'll be using.

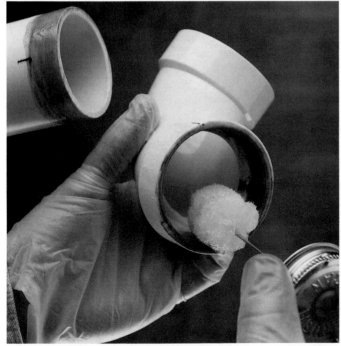

3 Apply a thick coat of solvent glue to the outside of the pipe and a thin coat on the inside of the connection hub.

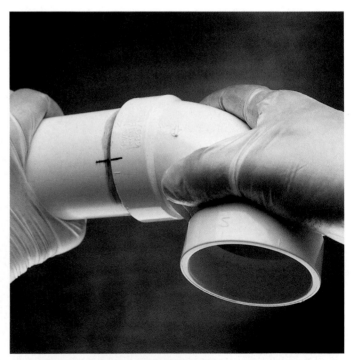

4 Quickly slip the pipes and fittings together so the alignment mark you drew across the joint is about 2 in. off center, then twist the pipes into alignment. This will ensure the solvent is spread evenly. The solvent will set in about 30 seconds, so don't waste time. Hold the pipes steady for another 20 seconds, then wipe away excess solvent with a rag. Don't disturb the joint for 30 minutes.

Galvanized pipe fittings

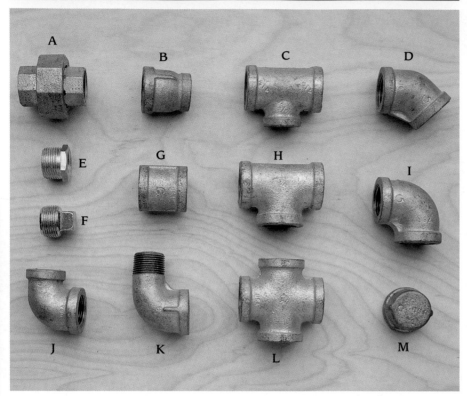

(A) union; (B) reducing coupling; (C) reducing tee; (D) 45° elbow; (E) hex bushing; (F) square head plug; (G) coupling; (H) tee; (I) 90° elbow; (J) 90° reducing elbow; (K) 90° street elbow; (L) cross connector; (M) cap.

Lubing and sealing mechanical joints

Pipe joint compound and Teflon tape are each used to lubricate, seal and protect the joints on pipe threads. Pipe joint compound comes in tubes, cans or sticks. Some pipe joint compound contains Teflon, which can be used on PVC and other plastic pipe. Often, the choice comes down to convenience. Tape is considered easier for a do-it-yourselfer, while pipe joint compound usually costs less.

Pipe joint compound

Teflon tape

Galvanized pipe & fittings

Galvanized pipe is rarely installed in new construction today for one main reason: it's time-consuming to install. Compared to soldering copper tubing, or solvent-welding plastic pipe, putting together galvanized pipe is slow work. However, replacing a section of old galvanized pipe with new galvanized pipe is a reasonable project for the do-it-yourselfer.

Galvanized pipe is connected with threaded joints. You'll need to rent a pipe vise, a reamer and a threader to thread your own galvanized pipes at home. Get a threader with a head that is the same nominal diameter as the pipe you are planning to thread. You'll also need a bottle of cutting oil.

Like all metal pipe, galvanized iron will eventually corrode and need replacing. But replacing an entire system of galvanized pipe is a big, time-consuming job. Remember that with galvanized iron, you cannot simply unscrew a middle section of piping without first disassembling the entire run.

Occasionally, however, galvanized pipe will corrode in just a small area. How do you replace the damaged section without removing a whole run of piping? Simple. Use a three-piece union. The union will allow you to sidestep the laborious job of disassembling an entire run of pipe.

When shopping for replacement pipe, specify the interior diameter (ID) of the pipe you need. Pre-threaded pipes, called nipples, are available in lengths up to 1 ft. or longer. For longer runs, have the store cut and thread the pipe to your dimensions. You can also thread your own by following the steps outlined on the next page.

One warning: Galvanized iron pipe, which has a silver color, is sometimes confused with "black iron" pipe. Black iron pipe is used only for gas lines and will corrode shut very quickly if used to carry water.

How to thread galvanized pipe

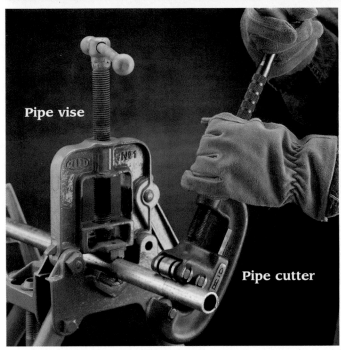

Pipe vise

Pipe cutter

Reamer

1 Before cutting, mark the length you want. Then, secure the pipe in the pipe vise (pipe fitting tools can be rented at most rental centers). Tighten a pipe cutter on the mark and rotate the cutter first one direction, then the other. Tighten the cutter every two rotations until the pipe is cut all the way through.

2 A reamer will remove burrs and jagged edges inside the pipe. Simply insert the nose of the reamer into the pipe, push and turn clockwise. Put a catch basin under the work area to collect pipe shavings and oil as you work.

Threader

3 To thread the pipe, slip the head of the threader over the end of the pipe. Push down on the threader and tighten it until the threader's head, also called the die, bites into the pipe. At that point stop tightening the tool and turn it clockwise around the pipe. Apply lots of cutting oil while turning. Keep turning the threader until the cutting head has cleared the pipe by at least one full turn. If the threader sticks, metal chips are probably blocking progress. In that case, rotate the tool backwards slightly and blow the chips away.

4 When done threading, remove the threader and clean the newly cut threads with a stiff wire brush.

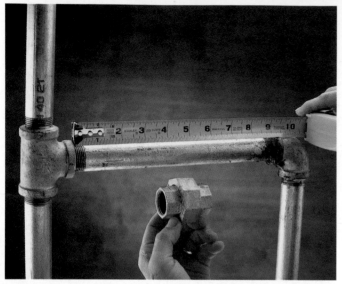

1 Measure the length of replacement pipe you will need. Make certain to include ½ in. for each threaded end that inserts into a fitting. However, subtract the width of the union from the measurements. When assembled, the union and replacement pipe must equal the length of the section being removed.

2 Cut through the old galvanized pipe with a hacksaw or reciprocating saw fitted with a metal-cutting blade.

3 Remove the corroded pipe with a pipe wrench. If the fitting is stubborn, grasp the fitting with a second pipe wrench. If the joint still won't loosen, heat it with a propane torch for five to ten seconds, making certain not to ignite any nearby materials. Once the fitting is removed, clean the pipe threads with a wire brush.

4 To remove corroded fittings, use two wrenches. Face the jaws in opposite directions and use one wrench to remove the fitting while the other wrench holds the pipe in place.

5 To attach a new fitting, apply pipe joint compound on the threaded ends of all pipes and nipples. Screw the new fitting onto the pipe and tighten with two pipe wrenches. Leave the fitting about ⅛-turn out of alignment to permit installation of the union.

Nipple

6 Attach a new pipe, or nipple, to the fitting. Apply pipe joint compound or strips of teflon tape to all threads. Tighten with a pipe wrench. Wrap the tape counterclockwise to keep it from unwinding as you thread the pipe into the fitting.

Ring nut

Hubbed union nut

7 Slide a ring nut onto the installed nipple. Then screw a hubbed union nut onto the nipple. Tighten with a pipe wrench.

Threaded union nut

8 Attach the second nipple to the opposite fitting. Tighten with a pipe wrench. Then screw the threaded union nut onto this nipple. Hold the nipple with a second wrench while attaching the union nut.

Threaded union nut

Hubbed union nut

Ring nut

9 Align the pipes so the lip of the hubbed union nut fits inside the threaded union nut. Tighten the connection by screwing the ring nut onto the threaded union nut.

Galvanized Pipe & Fittings

Making transitions between different pipe types

Transitions & Unions

PVC to copper

When attaching PVC (here, CPVC) to copper tubing, a four-piece union is needed. First, solder the brass union to the copper tubing. Let the brass cool before inserting the rubber seal. Then attach the plastic adapter to the PVC pipe with solvent glue. Make certain the slip nut is in place before gluing. After the glue has set (at least 30 minutes), tighten.

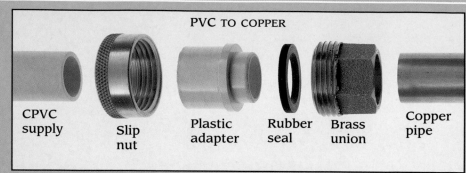

PVC TO COPPER

CPVC supply | Slip nut | Plastic adapter | Rubber seal | Brass union | Copper pipe

PVC to galvanized

Connect galvanized pipe to PVC pipe with male and the female threaded adapters. The plastic adapter is attached to the PVC pipe with solvent glue. Threads of metal pipe should have a coating of pipe joint compound or teflon tape. The metal pipe is then screwed directly to the adapter.

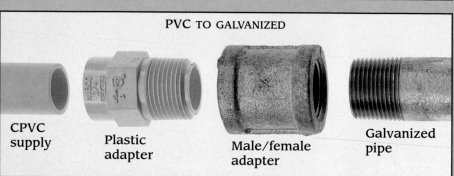

PVC TO GALVANIZED

CPVC supply | Plastic adapter | Male/female adapter | Galvanized pipe

Galvanized to copper

A dielectric union is needed to connect copper to galvanized iron. The union is soldered to the copper and threaded onto the iron. The dielectric union has a plastic spacer that prevents corrosion caused by an electro-chemical reaction between the different metals. See sequence, next page.

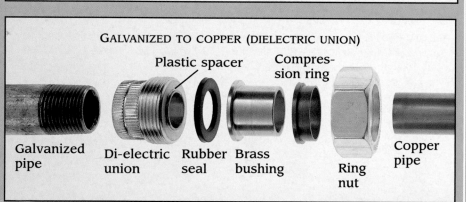

GALVANIZED TO COPPER (DIELECTRIC UNION)

Plastic spacer | Compression ring

Galvanized pipe | Di-electric union | Rubber seal | Brass bushing | Ring nut | Copper pipe

Polyethylene connections

Polyethylene (PE) is soft, synthetic rubber tubing that's used primarily for light-duty outdoor plumbing projects, such as installing an underground sprinkler system. The sections of PE tubing are joined using rigid plastic connectors with flared grip rings at the ends. The connectors are simply slipped into the ends of the PE tubes (See photo 1), then secured with a small hose clamp (See photo 2).

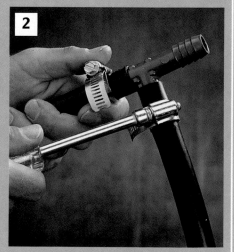

How to make a copper-to-galvanized dielectric union

When connecting copper pipe to galvanized iron pipe, you need to install a *dielectric union* between the two materials. That's because if copper and iron come in contact with each other, a chemical reaction between the metals will create increased corrosion. The dielectric union will prevent this corrosion from occurring.

Step 1: Solder the copper or brass bushing from the dielectric union onto the copper pipe using normal soldering techniques: apply flux, insert the fitting, heat the pipe for several seconds until the flux begins to sizzle, then quickly push the solder wire into each joint. The soldered joint should have a thin bead of solder around the lip of the fitting. Make certain not to damage the plastic spacer with the heat from the torch.

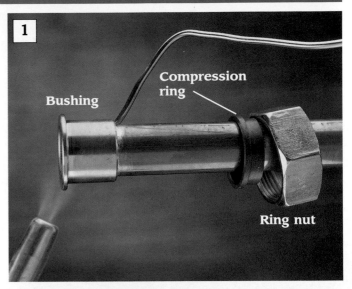

Bushing — Compression ring — Ring nut

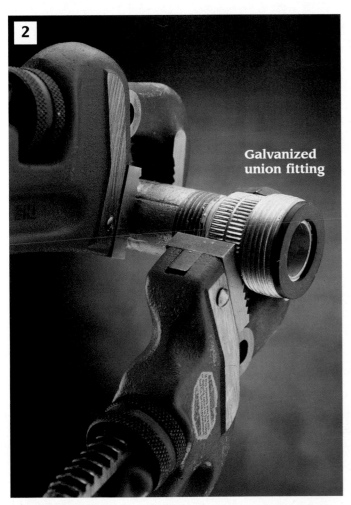

Galvanized union fitting

Step 2: Screw the galvanized portion of the union onto the galvanized pipe. First apply a bead of pipe joint compound on the threaded end of the pipe. Use two wrenches to apply the fitting: one to hold the galvanized iron pipe steady and the other to turn the union fitting.

Step 3: Connect the parts of the dielectric union. Make certain the spacer is properly aligned, and then tighten the ring nut that draws the dielectric union together, using two wrenches.

Shutoff Valves

According to the Uniform Plumbing Code, every water supply line leading into a plumbing fixture should have a working shut-off valve. If you're repairing a toilet, you need to turn off the water supply without affecting the rest of the house. And if a fixture should somehow spring a leak, you'll need to turn off the water immediately before your house suffers from water damage. Here you'll see how to attach a shut-off valve featuring a compression fitting to a fixture supply tube.

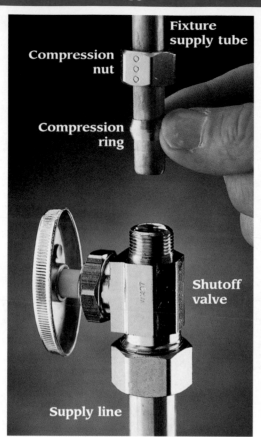

1 Solder the shutoff valve to the incoming supply line, then cut the fixture supply tube to length, allowing ½ in. for the portion that will fit inside the shutoff valve. Slip a compression ring and compression nut (usually included with valve) onto the end of the fixture supply pipe.

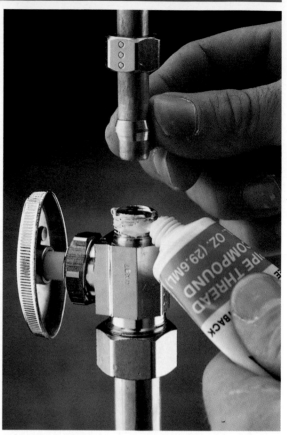

2 Apply pipe joint compound to the threads of the valve opening. The compound will serve as a lubricant during compression.

3 Insert the fixture supply tube into the valve and hand-tighten the compression nut over the compression ring.

4 Tighten the compression nut with two wrenches. Turn on the water supply. If the fitting leaks, try gently tightening the nuts.

How to insert a PVC connector into a cast iron stack

2 × 4 cleat

Riser clamp

Most older houses, and even some newer ones, have a main stack made out of cast iron. Cutting into the stack to add an auxiliary drain or vent line can be difficult and dangerous. This sequence shows the correct way to support the main stack, cut out a section, and insert a drain or vent connector fitting. Cast iron cutters can be rented at most rental centers.

1 Cast iron drain stacks must be braced with a riser clamp at each floor the stack passes through. Make sure the bracing exists, then mark the location for the new connector—the cutout should be sized to the height of the connector, plus 4 to 6 in. of pipe that should be solvent-welded to each end of the connector so it's the same diameter as the stack. Install a riser clamp about 6 in. above the top of the cutout area. Attach cleats to the wall studs to support the riser clamp.

2 Cut out the section of the main stack with a cast iron cutter (sometimes called a pipe breaker). The tool, equipped with cutting wheels on a heavy-linked chain, wraps around the pipe. Ratcheting the cutter wrench handle up and down tightens the chain until the pipe snaps. For safety, it's not a bad idea to support the section to be removed with a riser clamp before cutting it. Make the upper cut first. Remove the waste section carefully.

Banded coupling

Neoprene sleeve

3 Slip a banded coupling onto each end of the stack. Slip a neoprene sleeve over the pipe ends. Fold the sleeve out of the way.

PVC connector

4 Insert the connector into the opening, making sure the inlets are oriented exactly as you want them to be.

5 Fold the sleeves over the connector, making sure the ridge inside each sleeve is flush with the joint. Tighten the screw clamps.

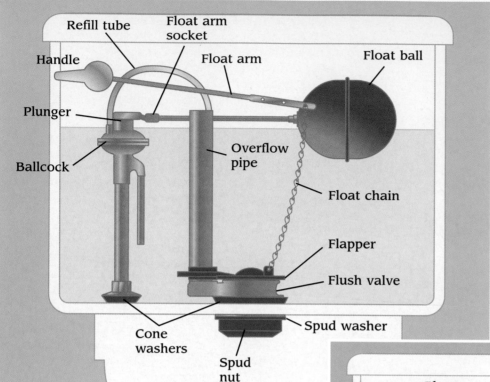

Float ball flush & fill mechanism

Most older toilets in use today employ this familiar system for flushing and filling the toilet tank. A float ball is connected to a plunger with a metal arm. When the toilet is flushed, the float ball sinks down to the lower water level, then gradually returns upward as the water level rises. When the tank is full, the float arm depresses a plunger on top of the ballcock, causing the inlet valve to close when the tank is full of water.

Float cup flush & fill mechanism

This variation of the float ball mechanism is becoming increasingly popular because it's more reliable than the float ball system. The basic principle is the same, but instead of a detached float, a plastic float cup mounted on the shank of the ballcock moves up and down with the tank water level. A pull rod connected directly to the plunger controls the flow of water into the tank. It also comes with an anti-siphon valve, which is now required by code for new construction toilet installations.

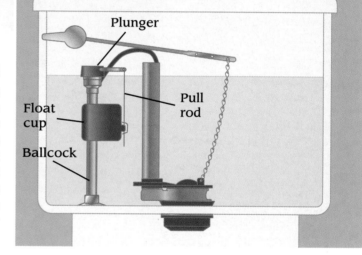

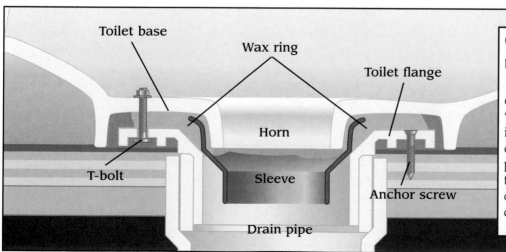

Cross-section of toilet mounting system

The toilet is bolted down to the floor so the "horn" where waste exits is directly over the floor drain opening. A compressible wax ring seals the joint between the base of the toilet and the floor drain opening.

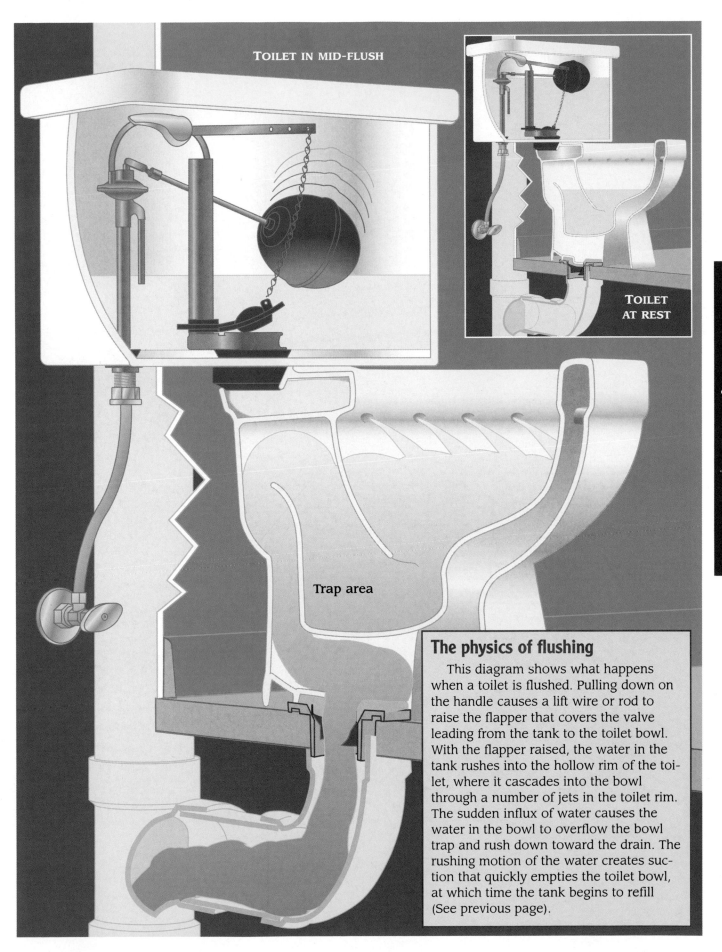

TOILET IN MID-FLUSH

TOILET AT REST

Trap area

The physics of flushing

This diagram shows what happens when a toilet is flushed. Pulling down on the handle causes a lift wire or rod to raise the flapper that covers the valve leading from the tank to the toilet bowl. With the flapper raised, the water in the tank rushes into the hollow rim of the toilet, where it cascades into the bowl through a number of jets in the toilet rim. The sudden influx of water causes the water in the bowl to overflow the bowl trap and rush down toward the drain. The rushing motion of the water creates suction that quickly empties the toilet bowl, at which time the tank begins to refill (See previous page).

Hook-up Illustrations

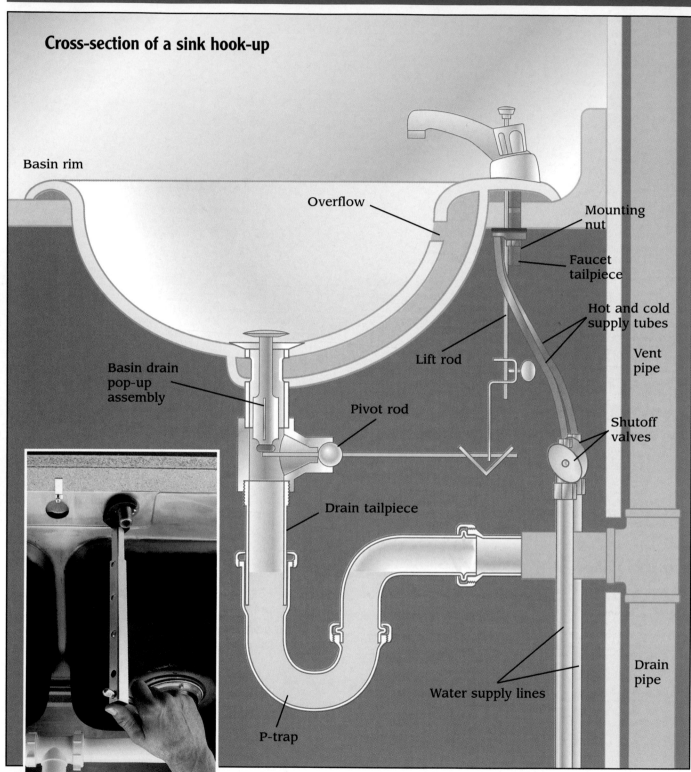

Cross-section of a sink hook-up

Basin rim

Overflow

Mounting nut

Faucet tailpiece

Hot and cold supply tubes

Vent pipe

Lift rod

Basin drain pop-up assembly

Pivot rod

Shutoff valves

Drain tailpiece

Water supply lines

Drain pipe

P-trap

Use a basin wrench

A basin wrench will simplify removing hard-to-reach nuts, such as the mounting nuts that thread onto faucet tailpieces.

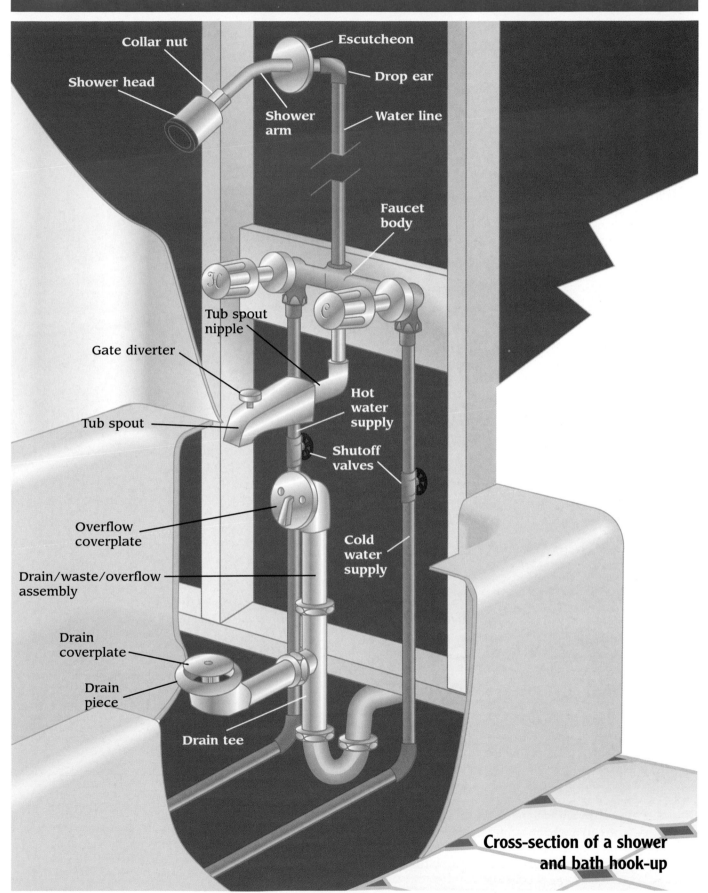

Collar nut

Escutcheon

Shower head

Drop ear

Shower arm

Water line

Faucet body

Tub spout nipple

Gate diverter

Hot water supply

Tub spout

Shutoff valves

Overflow coverplate

Cold water supply

Drain/waste/overflow assembly

Drain coverplate

Drain piece

Drain tee

Cross-section of a shower and bath hook-up

Hook-up Illustrations

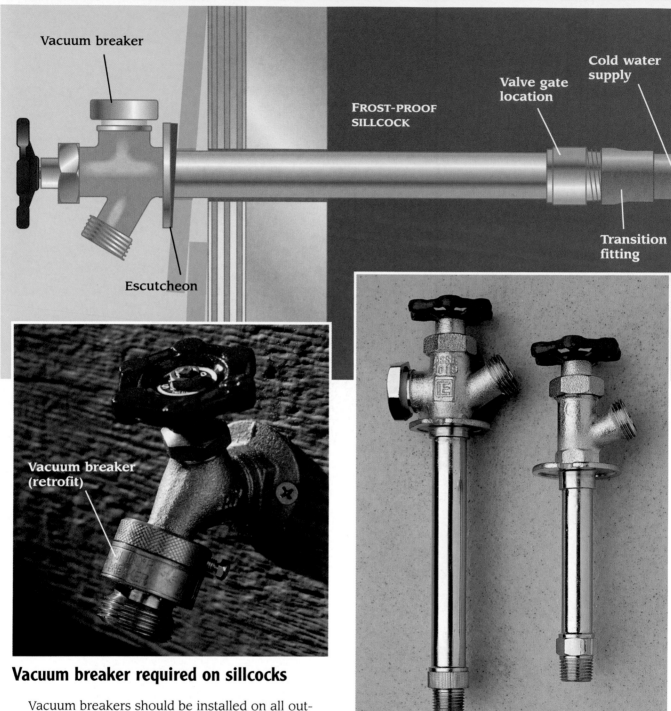

Vacuum breaker

Vacuum breaker (retrofit)

Escutcheon

FROST-PROOF SILLCOCK

Valve gate location

Cold water supply

Transition fitting

Vacuum breaker required on sillcocks

Vacuum breakers should be installed on all outdoor hose bibs to prevent cross-contamination of your home drinking supply. Cross-contamination can occur if the water pressure drops suddenly, creating negative pressure. A broken water main, for example, can sometimes produce backflow. If an outdoor hose is turned on and submerged into a muddy pool, the backflow can suck the contaminated water into your home plumbing system. A vacuum breaker prevents backflows. Most building codes now require vacuum breakers in new construction.

Frost-proof sillcocks

To prevent the water supply leads for sillcocks from freezing and bursting, homeowners in colder climates should install a frost-proof sillcock. These devices are equipped with shutoff gates that are located far enough back into the supply lead that they stop the water flow inside the house. Some are equipped with vacuum breakers.

wiring

Wiring

Installing wiring is not difficult. If you can use a tape measure, swing a hammer and operate a portable drill, you're halfway there. But there are professional techniques for working with wiring tools and materials that will simplify your work. It also is important to know proper installation requirements so your wiring project meets electrical code requirements.

The tools and skills information in this section shows you techniques and installation requirements for working with wiring materials used in the most common wiring projects. You see which types of electrical boxes to use and where to place them. Then you see how to install plastic sheathed cable, metal or plastic conduit, or armored cable. The best methods for connecting wires to switches, receptacles and fixtures also are demonstrated.

Tips are shown for installing wiring within existing rooms. You learn how to use a fishtape and run cable within a finished wall. You see how to create a wiring path behind baseboard and other trim. A basic ceiling fixture installation is shown, as well as how to replace a ceiling unit within a recessed fixture. Installing a vent fan and the special requirements for installing a ceiling fan also are shown. Plus, see how to work with three-way switches, GFCI receptacles, and how to install a new circuit breaker in the main service panel.

This information will help you do wiring projects that keep your home comfortable and functional. And you will save money doing the the work yourself.

Electrical codes

The information found on these pages conforms to the National Electrical Code requirements. These requirements ensure safe, durable wiring installations that will best serve your needs. But your wiring project may have additional requirements not covered by the Code. Also, the Code requirements in your community may differ from those in the National Code. Local Code always takes precedence in these situations. Always check with your local electrical inspector to make certain your project will comply with local standards. If your wiring project is part of a larger remodeling or building project that includes plumbing work, remember that plumbing has the right-of-way. Always do the plumbing installation before beginning any wiring work in that area.

Electrical equations & data

- Wattage divided by voltage = Amperage
- Kilowatts × 1000 = Wattage

- *Here is a sample calculation of circuit load:*
Circuit #3 (non-dedicated)
Circuit Information: Voltage = 120, Amperage = 20

Appliance	Wattage/Voltage	Amperage
Microwave	800/120	= 6.7
Toaster	1050/120	= 8.75
Exhaust Fan	100/120	= .83
Total Load on Circuit #3		**= 16.28 Amps**

- Typical **watt/amp** ratings for household appliances:
  Toaster: 1050/8.75   **Microwave: 800/6.7**
  Refrigerator: 600/5   **Dishwasher:1500/12.5**
  Air conditioner: 2000/8.3   **Computer: 600/6**
  Circular saw: 1200/10   **Table saw : 2160/18**

How to test for electrical current

At a receptacle: Turn off power at the main panel. Insert the circuit tester probes into the receptacle slots. Check both halves of the receptacle. If the tester glows, power is still present. Turn off the appropriate circuit and test again.

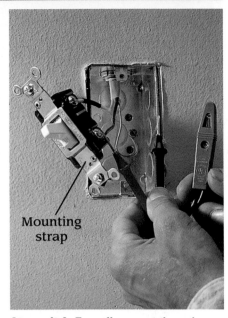

Mounting strap

At a switch: Turn off power at the main panel. Carefully pull the switch out of the box, touching only the mounting strap. Touch one circuit tester probe to the grounded metal box or bare copper grounding wire. Touch the other probe to each screw terminal. If tester glows, power is present. Turn off another circuit and test again.

Is a receptacle wired correctly?

Use a receptacle tester to check that a receptacle is correctly wired. Insert the tester prongs into each half of the receptacle. Glowing lights indicate whether the receptacle is properly grounded and if the hot and neutral wires are attached to the correct terminals.

Neutral bus bar

At the main panel: Turn off the main breaker but leave all other breakers on. Touch one circuit tester probe to the neutral bus bar. Touch the other probe to each terminal on a double-pole breaker (but not the main breaker). If tester glows, power is still present. Make sure main breaker is off and test again. NOTE: Wires to the main breaker terminal are always "hot", even when the main breaker is shut off. Use care when working near them.

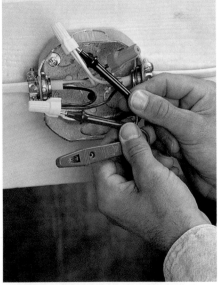

At wire connections: Turn off power at the main panel. Remember that more than one circuit may pass through a box. Remove the box cover. Insert one circuit tester probe into the wire connector for the black wires and the other probe into the wire connector for the white wires. If the tester glows, power is still present. Turn off the appropriate circuit and test again.

At a light fixture: Turn off power at the main panel. Remove the globe, light bulb and fixture mounting screws and pull the fixture away from the box. Touch one circuit tester probe to the green grounding screw or bare copper grounding wire. Insert the other probe into each fixture wire connector. If the tester glows, power is still present. Turn off the appropriate circuit and test again.

Wiring Basics 129

Wiring Basics

Code specifications for room wiring

Code for general living areas

Always check with your local electrical inspector for regulations applying to your work.

One 15-amp or 20-amp basic lighting and receptacle circuit should supply every 600 sq. ft. of living space. Every room should have at least one light fixture controlled by a switch located at the entryway. Receptacles should be spaced no more than 12 ft. apart, though closer spacing may be more useful. Any separate wall surface more than 24 in. wide, such as a wall between doorways, must have a receptacle.

Receptacle boxes should be installed 12 in. above the finished floor surface, and switch boxes are typically at 48 in. Special situations, such as making switches wheelchair accessible, are allowed; check with your inspector. Route cable to the receptacles at 20 in.

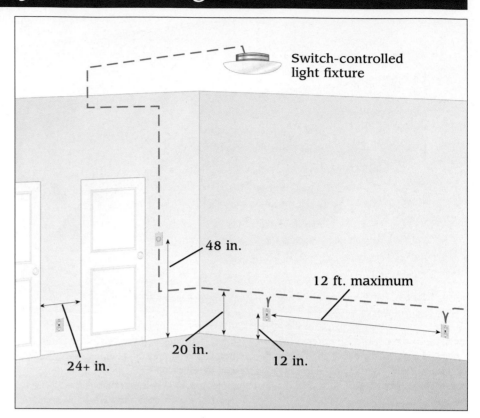

Switch-controlled light fixture

48 in.

12 ft. maximum

20 in.

12 in.

24+ in.

Code for kitchens & baths

Basic Code requirements for general living areas (above) apply to the kitchen and bath, but these rooms also have special requirements. Check with your local inspector regarding regulations applying to your work.

The switch-controlled light fixture must be ceiling-mounted. The switch should be on the latch side of the entryway. In the bathroom, no switch should be within 3 ft. of a bathtub or shower.

All accessible receptacles must be GFCI-protected. Receptacles installed above countertops should be no more than 4 ft. apart, though closer spacing in high-use areas may be helpful. Any separate countertop space more than 24 in. wide, such as countertop between a stove and refrigerator, must have a receptacle.

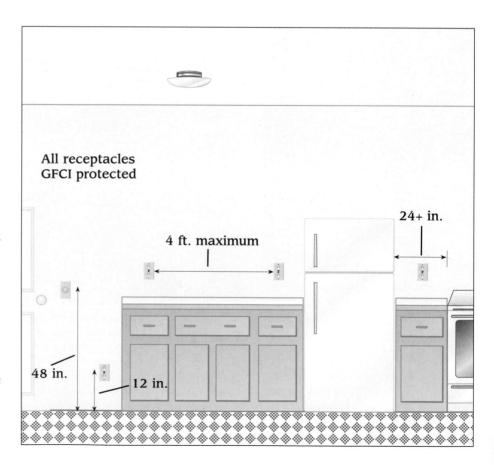

All receptacles GFCI protected

4 ft. maximum

24+ in.

48 in.

12 in.

Electrical boxes

Types of boxes: (A) plastic boxes with preattached mounting nails for indoor construction installations, (B) weatherproof cast aluminum and plastic boxes for exterior installations, (C) brace and fixture box for fixture installation between framing members, (D) heavy-duty brace and box for ceiling fan or heavy light fixture installation, (E) metal boxes for conduit or interior cable installations, (F) plastic remodeling boxes, also called retrofit boxes, for installations in existing ceiling and wall surfaces (metal remodeling boxes also are available).

Electrical box wire capacities

Outlet Box		Max. no. of wires			
Box size	Box shape	#14	#12	#10	#8
4 × 1¼	Round/oct.	6	5	5	4
4 × 1½	Round/oct.	7	6	6	5
4 × 2⅛	Round/oct.	10	9	8	7
4 × 1¼	Square	9	8	7	6
4 × 1½	Square	10	9	8	7
4 × 2⅛	Square	15	13	12	10
4¹¹⁄₁₆ × 1¼	Square	12	11	10	8
4¹¹⁄₁₆ × 1½	Square	14	13	11	9
4¹¹⁄₁₆ × 2⅛	Square	21	18	16	14
Switch Box					
3 × 2 × 1½		3	3	3	2
3 × 2 × 2		5	4	4	3
3 × 2 × 2¼		5	4	4	3
3 × 2 × 2½		6	5	5	4
3 × 2 × 2¾		7	6	5	4
3 × 2 × 3½		9	8	7	6

How to make cutouts for boxes in lath & plaster walls

1 Drill a ½-in. hole near the center of the planned new electrical box location. Cut an opening roughly 1 in. square, using a portable jig saw.

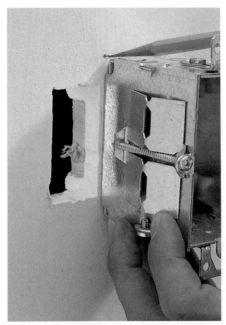

2 Place the box next to the opening. Adjust the height of the box after determining the position of the lath strips in the opening. Only the lath piece in the center should be completely cut through when the box opening is finished. Position the box over the opening and mark its outline.

3 Complete the box opening. The small semi-circles cut at the top and bottom of the opening allow for the switch or receptacle mounting screws. They are easily cut with a drill, using the side of a ⅜-in. bit.

Choosing electrical cable

CABLE TYPE	APPLICATIONS
NM (nonmetallic)	The primary type of cable used for most non-exposed interior installations. It features two or three vinyl insulated wires as well as a bare ground wire. Modern NM features vinyl outer sheathing, which provides better durability than the previously rubberized fabric sheathed version.
UF (underground feeder)	Designed for underground use, the vinyl sheathing of this cable is molded directly to the insulated wires as well as a bare ground.
Armored cable	Generally used for short exposed runs in interior situations such as basements. There is no separate ground wire because the flexible metal sheathing not only protects the wires but also acts as the ground. A bonding strip ensures a good grounding path.
Metal conduit	Provides excellent protection in exposed wiring situations. Conduit must be cut, bent and connected with specific fittings before the wiring is pulled through.

Select the proper type of cable for the task

Vinyl-sheathed cable is classified as either NM (nonmetallic) or UF (underground feeder). NM cable can be used only for indoor projects in dry locations. UF cable is intended for damp or wet locations and can be buried directly in the ground. Both types of cable are identified by the gauge (size) and number of insulated wires they contain. The bare copper grounding wire is not counted, but is included in the labeling as "with ground", or "G". For example, a cable labeled 14/3 G contains three insulated 14-gauge wires plus the bare grounding wire. The gauge indicates what level of current (ampacity) the wire can safely carry, which determines its use in a wiring project.

How to strip NM (nonmetallic) cable

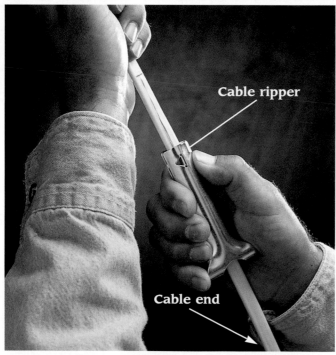

Cable ripper

Cable end

1 Use a cable ripper to cut through the cable sheathing without damaging the wires inside. This works best on cable containing two wires with ground. Insert the cable through the ripper, then firmly press the arms together, forcing the cutting tip into the sheathing. Pull the ripper to the end of the cable to cut through the sheathing.

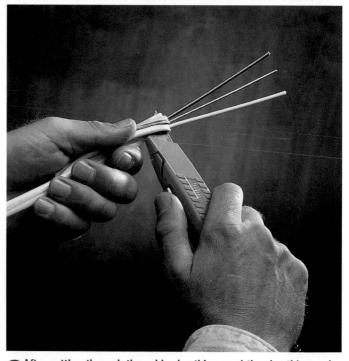

2 After cutting through the cable sheathing, peel the sheathing and the paper wrapper back, then cut them off with a utility knife or wire cutters. Be careful that you don't nick the wire insulation as you do this.

Working with Cable

Working with 3-wire cable

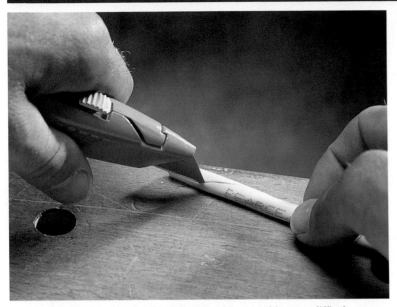

Cutting through sheathing on 3-wire cable with ground is more difficult because the wires spiral inside the sheathing. A utility knife may work better than a cable ripper to do this. You must follow the twist of the wires carefully with the knife so you don't damage the insulation on the individual wires. Once the sheathing is ripped, peel it and the paper wrappers back, then cut them off with a utility knife.

Three-wire cable, because it's heavier and stiffer, can be more difficult to install than 2-wire cable, particularly if it contains wires larger than 14-gauge. A helper will make pulling the cable over longer distances much easier. Where possible, drill larger holes in the framing members, but only as large as necessary. For example, a ¾-in. hole is adequate for 12-gauge, 3-wire with ground cable.

One 3-wire cable can carry two circuits from a double-pole breaker in the main service panel to a location some distance from the panel, such as a basement, attic or detached garage. This saves the time and cost of running two 2-wire cables to accomplish the same thing. At the first electrical box in this location the circuits can branch out from the 3-wire cable, using 2-wire cable.

Three-wire cable is used when creating two circuits with alternating receptacles. Use 3-wire cable between three-way switches to make connections to the three terminals found on each switch. Three-wire cable also is used for installation of 120/240 volt circuits.

How to strip UF (underground feeder) cable

1 Use a utility knife to cut away about ½ in. of the solid sheathing from the wires at the cable tip. Don't worry if you cut into the insulation on the individual wires since these wire ends will be cut off later.

2 Grip one wire tip with a needlenose pliers and use another pliers to firmly hold the cable. Pull the pliers apart to rip the individual wire out of the solid sheathing until you have about 10 in. exposed. Repeat this action for the other individual wires. Cut off the empty sheathing with a utility knife or wire cutters.

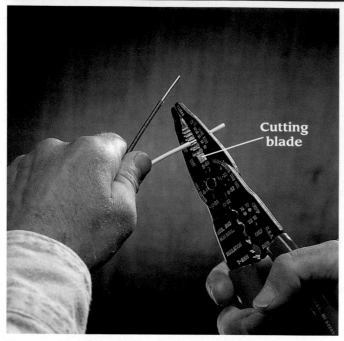

Cutting blade

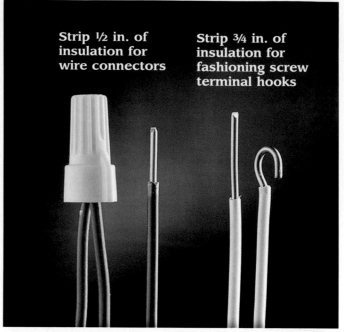

Strip ½ in. of insulation for wire connectors

Strip ¾ in. of insulation for fashioning screw terminal hooks

Use a combination tool to cut individual wires to length and strip off the insulation. After using the tool's cutting blade to cut a wire to correct length, open the combination tool jaws and place the end of the wire into the opening in the tool that matches the wire gauge. Close the jaws and pull the tool to the end of the wire to remove the insulation. Take care not to nick the wire.

When stripping individual wires, remove ½ in. of insulation if using a wire connector (left) or ¾ in. of insulation when you will make a hook to attach to a screw terminal (right). No bare wire should show beyond the bottom of the wire connector, and insulation should end at the screw terminal.

An internal cable clamp (A), shown on a metal remodeling box, makes connecting cable to a box in an existing wall surface much easier. External clamps are simple to use in new construction. Types available include a threaded metal clamp (B) and a plastic snap-fitting clamp (C). (Wires are shown cut short for photo clarity.)

Cable clamps secure cables to box

A cable clamp must be used to attach a cable to a metal electrical box. Any type may be used, as long as it is the correct size to fit the knockout opening in the box. Typically, one clamp is used for each cable entering the box. It is important to tighten the clamp so the cable is held securely, but not so the sheathing or wires are crushed or crimped.

Clamps for single-gang plastic boxes aren't necessary since the cable can be stapled within 8 in. of the box. Plastic boxes larger than 2 × 4 in. and all remodeling boxes, both metal and plastic, must contain internal cable clamps.

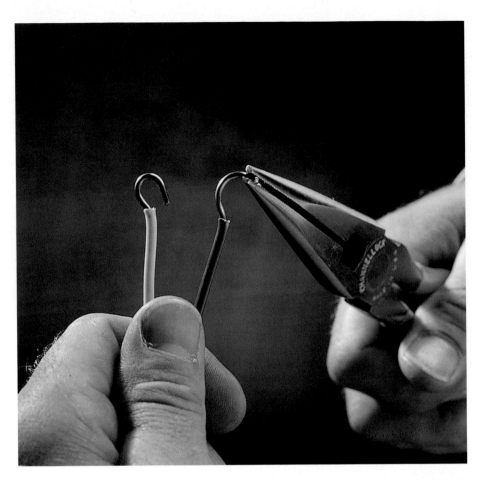

How to fashion screw terminal hooks

When attaching a wire to a screw terminal, it is important to have a hook that properly fits under the terminal. If the hook is too large, the screw will touch only part of the wire, creating a poor connection. This connection can loosen with use and become a safety hazard. If the hook is too small, it won't wrap around the terminal enough to form a secure connection, again posing a safety hazard.

Use the rectangular tip of a combination tool to create a wire hook that is the correct size and shape to fit under a screw terminal. Grasp the end of the wire in the serrated portion of the tool's jaws. Bend the wire tightly around the rectangular tip of one arm of the jaw to create the hook. A needle-nose pliers can be used to make the hook, but you need to determine where to grasp the wire in the pliers to shape the hook properly.

Color-coding helps you choose wire connectors at a glance

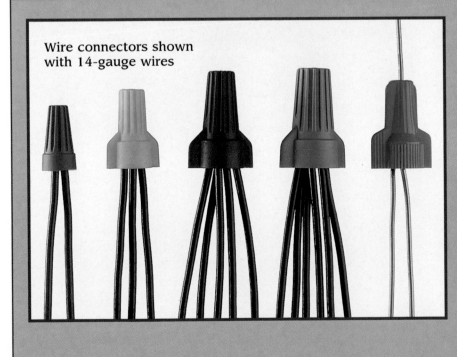

Wire connectors shown with 14-gauge wires

Use the correct connector

Wire connectors are color-coded to indicate the number of wires of various gauges they can connect. An orange connector handles up to two 14-gauge wires. Yellow accepts three 14-gauge or two to three 12-gauge wires. Red connects four to five 14-gauge or four 12-gauge wires. Gray connects six 14-gauge or five 12-gauge wires. Green wire connectors are used with grounding wires. They can handle two to four 14-gauge or 12-gauge wires. Some green connectors have a hole in the tip allowing one grounding wire to pass through and connect to a grounding screw terminal, so an extra pigtail isn't needed. Wire connector packages should list the maximum number of all wire gauge sizes and combinations they can safely connect.

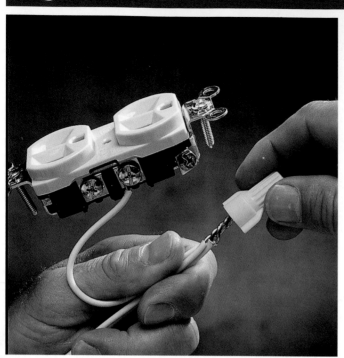

Pigtails connect multiple wires to a single screw terminal

A *pigtail* is used to connect two or more wires to one screw terminal, since only one wire may be attached to a terminal. Cut a short length of wire of the same color as the wires that need connecting. (Keep excess cable pieces for this purpose.) Strip ½ in. of insulation off of one end, then strip ¾ in. off the other end and make a hook (See pages 134 to 135). Attach the hook end to the terminal, then connect the other end to the wires.

Use a wire connector when connecting wires together. Strip ½ in. of sheathing from the end of each wire. Hold the wires so the stripped ends are parallel, with their ends aligned. Place the wire connector over the wire ends and twist it onto the ends in a clockwise direction. Continue turning the connector until the sheathed portions of the wires begin to twist together. The photo at left illustrates how the wire connector twists the bare ends of the individual wires tightly together. No bare wire should extend past the bottom of the connector.

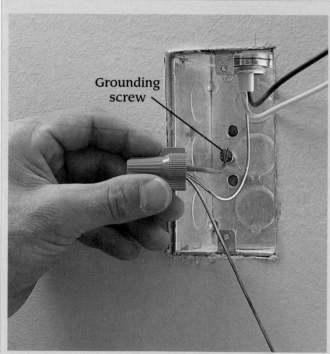

Grounding screw

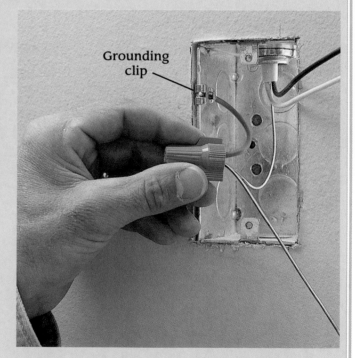

Grounding clip

How to ground metal boxes

Metal boxes must be connected to the circuit grounding system so they are safely grounded. A green wire connector should connect one end of a green insulated pigtail to the cable grounding wires and to the fixture grounding wires or to the grounding terminal on a receptacle or switch. The other end of the insulated pigtail is attached to a green grounding screw (photo left) or to a grounding clip (photo right) if the box doesn't have a grounding screw. In a conduit installation, Code allows the conduit to be the grounding conductor, but most electricians use the grounding pigtail to ensure that the system is properly grounded.

Working with armored cable

Armored cable can be an easy-to-install substitute for conduit

Armored cable is a flexible galvanized metal tubing containing wires. It can be installed in the same dry, interior locations as plastic-sheathed cable. It is installed in locations where wires need greater protection than sheathed cable can provide.

Because of its flexibility armored cable is easier to install than conduit (See page 139). Installation methods are similar to those used with sheathed cable. Use galvanized metal staples and cable connectors (See photo, below right) designated for use with armored cable. Another advantage armored cable has over conduit is that no wire-pulling is required. This will save a significant amount of time, though you must cut armored cable carefully (See photo, right). Check with your local electrical inspector for appropriate applications where you use this material.

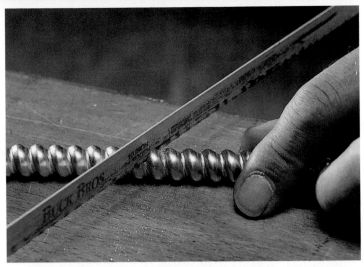

Cut through armored cable with a hacksaw. Hold the blade at a right angle to a ridge in the cable and cut through the raised center of the ridge and slightly into the edges. Make sure you do not cut into the wires or the bonding strip. Bend the cable at the cut and then twist sharply to break and remove the short end. You may want to make practice cuts on scrap pieces before beginning your project.

How to make connections with armored cable

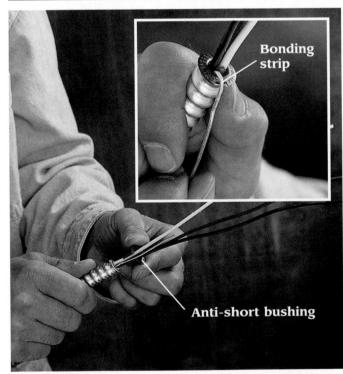

1 An anti-short bushing must protect the wires in armored cable from the rough edge of the cut cable. Slide the bushing over the wires and into the end of the cable. Push the bushing firmly into the end of the cable. Cut the bonding strip so there is about 2 in. remaining, then bend the strip over the bushing to hold it in place (See inset photo).

Bonding strip

Anti-short bushing

2 Attach the cable to a metal box with an armored cable connector. The holes in the end of the connector show that the bushing is properly in position.

Use auger bits to drill holes

Drill holes for each cable using a drill and a ⅝-in. auger bit. The screw-style tip of the auger bit pulls the cutting edge quickly through the wood. A right-angle drill, available at rental centers, makes drilling between framing members much easier. Long auger bits are used to drill at steep angles or through thick materials.

Install protector plates

A metal protector plate must be installed over each spot where there isn't at least 1¼ in. of wood protecting the cable from damage by nails or screws.

Make smooth 90° turns

Make a smooth curve when bending cable. Do not make sharp corners, which can crimp and damage the wires.

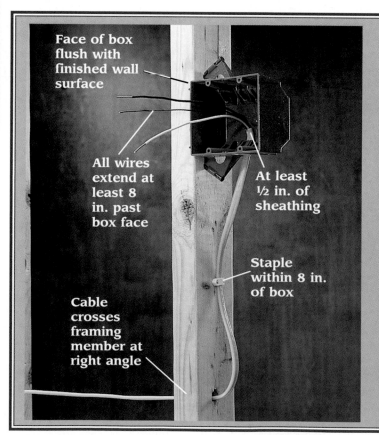

Face of box flush with finished wall surface

All wires extend at least 8 in. past box face

At least ½ in. of sheathing

Staple within 8 in. of box

Cable crosses framing member at right angle

Typical electrical box hook-up

Attach a plastic box to a framing member so the box face will be flush with the finished wall surface. Guidelines for common wall depths are on the sides of most boxes. Remove a knockout for each cable that will enter the box, using a hammer and screwdriver. Strip cable sheathing so 8-in. lengths of wire extend past the box face and at least ½ in. of sheathed cable extends past the cable clamping device. Anchor cable with cable staples within 8 in. of each box and also every 4 ft. where it runs along framing members.

Do not route cable diagonally between framing members. Cable should cross framing members at right angles. If you need more than one hole in a framing member, drill the holes along the length of the wood. Keep holes as close to the center of the wood as possible, with at least 1 in. of wood between them. Do not drill holes across the framing member's width, which can weaken it.

Working with conduit

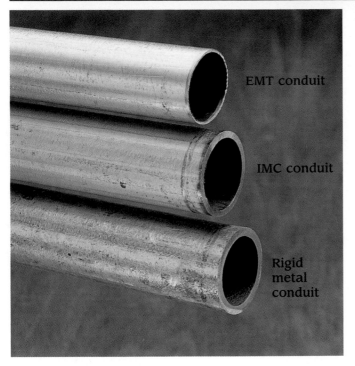

EMT conduit

IMC conduit

Rigid metal conduit

Types of metal conduit

Conduit is used to protect wires in exposed locations, such as on masonry surfaces in a basement. Conduit rated for exterior use can be used to install circuits outdoors. Check with your local electrical inspector to determine the type of conduit your project requires.

Metal conduit is available in three types. *EMT* (Electrical Metallic Tubing) is lightweight and easy to work with, but because of its thinner tubing, shouldn't be installed where it could easily be damaged. *IMC* (Intermediate Metallic Conduit) has thicker, galvanized walls to withstand rougher treatment. It also is a good choice for outdoor installations when used with weatherproof fittings. *Rigid metal* conduit provides heavy-duty protection, but is the most expensive and also requires threaded fittings. IMC or EMT should be adequate for most of your projects.

Metal conduit fittings

Metal fittings are available to make the installation of metal conduit quite easy. Rather than bend the conduit yourself with special tools, you can purchase these connectors pre-made to create the conduit layout your project requires.

Threaded couplings, connectors and sweeps are used to install rigid metal conduit.

Setscrew fittings are used with EMT and IMC. The removable cover on the *90° elbow* makes it easy to pull wires around the corner (See page 144). An *offset fitting* connects conduit, anchored flush against a wall, to the knockout on a metal electrical box.

The same metal electrical conduit boxes are used with all conduit types. An *L-body fitting* is used as a transition between vertical and horizontal lengths of conduit, such as when underground wires must enter a building. The cover can be removed, making pulling wires easier. Plastic bushings cover exposed conduit ends, protecting wires from damage by the rough metal edges. Metal pipe straps anchor conduit against masonry surfaces or wood framing members. Conduit should be supported within 3 ft. of each electrical box and fitting, and every 10 ft. otherwise.

Flexible metal conduit bends easily and can be used for short unsupported distances where rigid conduit is difficult to install. It is frequently used to connect appliances that are permanently wired, such as a water heater. Wires are pulled through flexible metal conduit in the same manner as with other conduit.

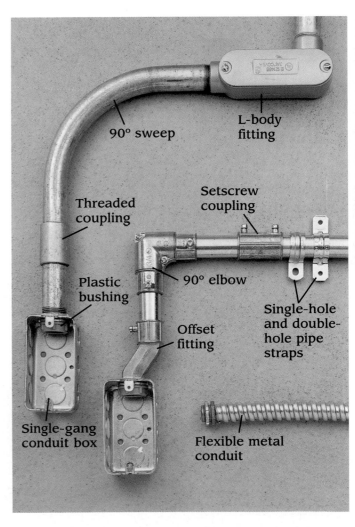

90° sweep

L-body fitting

Threaded coupling

Setscrew coupling

Plastic bushing

90° elbow

Offset fitting

Single-hole and double-hole pipe straps

Single-gang conduit box

Flexible metal conduit

Working with Conduit

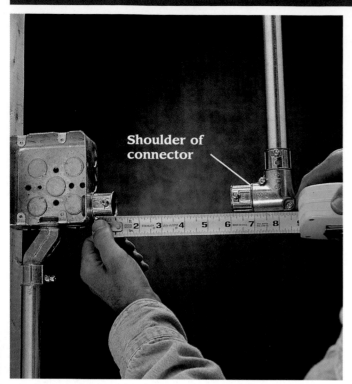

Measure from shoulder to shoulder

Use a tape measure to determine the length of conduit needed between locations. Measure to the shoulders of connectors to allow for the distance the conduit will require.

Shoulder of connector

Attaching hangers to masonry

Anchor conduit to masonry surfaces with self-tapping masonry screws and galvanized metal pipe straps. Conduit must be anchored within 3 ft. of each box or fitting and every 10 ft. otherwise. See page 61 for more information on anchoring to masonry.

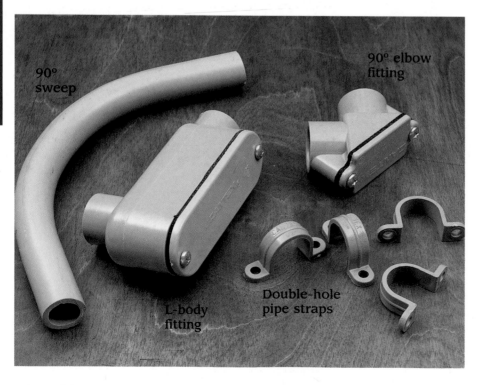

90° sweep

90° elbow fitting

L-body fitting

Double-hole pipe straps

Plastic conduit

A simple alternative to metal

Most local codes allow the use of PVC plastic conduit in installations requiring wire protection. Plastic conduit and fittings are lightweight and very easy to install. It is cut and assembled with solvent glue just like PVC plumbing pipe. Check with your local electrical inspector to find out if plastic conduit is okay for your project.

Plastic conduit must always be connected to plastic electrical boxes and fittings. These boxes and fittings are similar to those for metal conduit. Always run a green insulated grounding wire when using plastic conduit, as the conduit doesn't provide a grounding path.

Working with Conduit

1 Turn off the main breaker and remove the panel cover. Check for power using a circuit tester (See page 129). Open a knockout near the new breaker location. Cut cable to leave about 3 ft. of excess. (Wires must be routed around the inside perimeter of the panel.) Connect cable to the panel with a cable clamp. Remove sheathing, leaving at least ½ in. extending past the clamp.

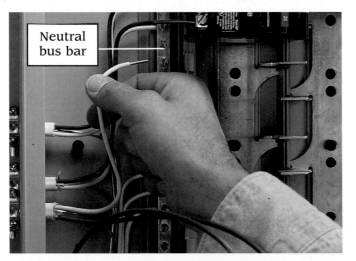

Neutral bus bar

2 Bend the cable grounding wire around the panel perimeter to the grounding bus bar, cut it to length and connect it to an open setscrew terminal. Route the white wire to the neutral bus bar and cut it to length. Strip ½ in. of insulation from the end and connect it to an open terminal.

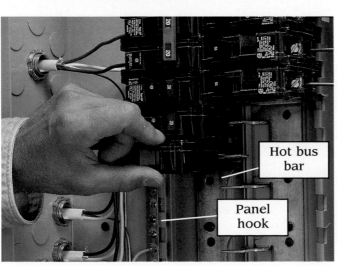

Hot bus bar

Panel hook

3 Route the black wire to the location where the new breaker will be installed. Cut wire to length, strip ½ in. of insulation from end and attach it to the set-screw terminal on the new single-pole breaker. Place one end of the breaker under the panel hook and snap breaker onto the hot bus bar. Replace panel cover.

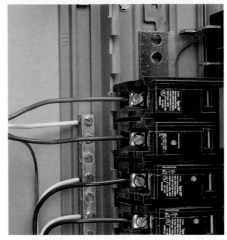

How to connect a 120/240-volt circuit

The red wire and black wire from a 3-wire cable are connected to the terminals on a double-pole breaker. The white wire is connected to the neutral bus bar and serves as a shared neutral for both circuits. The grounding wire is connected to the grounding bus bar.

Adding a 240-volt circuit

Connect the black and white wires from a 2-wire cable to the terminals on a double-pole breaker. Tag the white wire with black tape to indicate it is serving as a 'hot' wire. There is no neutral bus bar connection for this circuit. Connect the grounding wire to the grounding bus bar.

Adding & Expanding Circuits

Adding & Expanding Circuits 141

How to prepare a fishtape for running cable

1 Remove about 3 in. of sheathing from the end of the cable. Insert the wires through the hook at the end of the fishtape, then bend them back onto the cable. Begin wrapping electrical tape on the fishtape above the hook.

2 Continue wrapping electrical tape tightly around the fishtape and wires and onto at least 2 in. of cable past the connection. The junction should be as thin and smooth as possible.

Helpful tips for running cable

Cut out for wall-to-ceiling access

To route cable from one finished room to the room above, cut a 3 × 5-in. opening in the wall surface near the ceiling. Drill through the top plate using a long auger bit at as steep an angle as possible. If you need to route the cable into the ceiling, cut another 3 × 5 in. opening in the ceiling near the wall. You may need to drill another hole to make a path for the cable into the joist cavity. Patch the wall and ceiling with wallboard.

Creating wall-to-floor access

To route cable from one finished room to the room below, cut a 3 × 5 in. hole in the wall surface near the floor, behind the baseboard if possible. Drill through the bottom plate using a long auger bit at as steep an angle as possible.

How to run cable with a fishtape

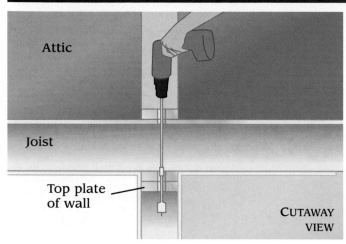

Drilling from above a wall

Routing cable through a wall is much easier if you have access to the attic space above the wall. Measure carefully from a structural member common to both levels to determine where to drill. This same method is used when drilling up into the wall cavity from the basement below the wall.

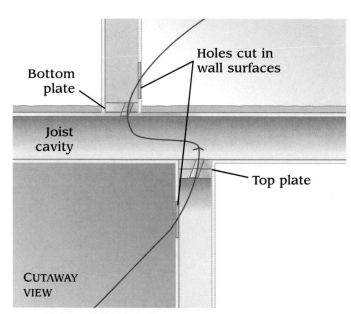

Routing cable through offset walls

Routing cable through offset walls in finished rooms is difficult. You will need two fishtapes and a helper. Cut holes in appropriate wall surfaces and drill holes in the bottom and top plates of the walls (See page 142). Have your helper run one fishtape down through the holes in the room above. Push the other fishtape up through the holes in the lower room and catch the first fishtape with the hook on yours. Pull your fishtape until the hook from the other fishtape emerges from the holes. Attach cable to the fishtape and have your helper pull it to the room above.

Fishing alternative

You can use mason's string and a lead weight to fish cable through a wall. You must have access to the space above and below the wall to do this. After drilling holes in the bottom and top plates, have a helper lower the weighted string from above. Bend a hook in the end of a piece of stiff wire and push it through the lower hole to snag the string. Attach the string to the cable as if it were a fishtape (See page 142).

Cut a baseboard channel

Routing cable behind baseboard and door casing is a simple method for adding new cable within a finished room. Carefully remove the baseboard or casing so it can be re-installed. Remove enough wall surface behind the trim pieces so you can work but make sure the trim will cover the work area. You won't need to patch holes in the wall surfaces that are covered by trim pieces. Create a route for the cable, cutting notches in the wall studs that the cable must cross. Once the cable is in place, cover each notch with a metal protective plate. Re-install the trim pieces. You may need to fill gaps between the trim pieces and framing members caused by wall surface removal, using scrap lumber spacers.

Fishing through conduit

Push a fishtape through the conduit until the hook appears at the end of the conduit where the wires need to enter. Connect the wires to the fishtape (See page 142). Pull all wires through the conduit together. At 90° corners, remove the fitting cover and use the fishtape to pull through each length of conduit rather than trying to make one pull around the tight corner.

How to create an opening to run cable down from the attic

1 Drill a ⅜-in.-dia. access hole in each end of the length of floor board you need to remove, at the inside face of the joists. Cut across the board along the edge of the joist, using a jig saw.

2 Cut 1 × 2-in. cleats and attach them with screws. When the electrical work is finished, re-attach the piece of floor board to the cleats.

Connecting a light fixture

All standard light fixtures are attached to the electrical box and the cable wires in a similar fashion, whether they are ceiling or wall mounted. To replace a light fixture, remove the globe, light bulb and mounting screws and carefully pull the old fixture away from the electrical box. Turn off the power and test with a circuit tester (See page 129). Disconnect the wire connections. Attach the mounting strap that came with the new light fixture, if the electrical box does not already have one. Connect the black lead from the new fixture to the black cable wire. Connect the white lead to the white cable wire and the cable grounding wire to the green grounding screw on the mounting strap. Tuck the wires into the box. Position the new fixture and attach it to the mounting strap with the mounting screws.

A ceiling fan requires more support than a standard light fixture. When replacing a light fixture with a fan, the electrical box must be attached to a framing member or to a heavy-duty brace. This brace comes with an electrical box with special mounting hardware.

Tips for installing & connecting a ceiling fan

Install a mounting bar between ceiling joists

Turn off the power and check with a circuit tester (See page 129). After removing the light fixture and existing electrical box, insert the brace through the hole in the ceiling. Use an adjustable wrench to extend the ends of the brace until they are firmly seated against the joists.

Hook up the fan

Insert the cable into the electrical box provided with the brace, then position the box and attach it to the brace with the special hardware. Attach the fan mounting plate to the electrical box. Hang the fan from the hook on the mounting plate. Connect the fan wire leads to the cable wires as directed in the instructions. Make sure the grounding wires are pigtailed to the grounding screw on the mounting plate. Finish the fan assembly following manufacturer's directions.

Installing canister-style recessed light fixtures

You can replace a standard light fixture with a recessed light fixture. Recessed fixtures have a self-contained electrical box. Retrofit units are designed to fit through an opening in the ceiling; other units must be installed from above. Make sure you purchase a unit designed for contact with insulation if your project requires it. NOTE: If you don't have access to the ceiling from above, you must attach the cable to the electrical box and make all wire connections before you insert the unit through the hole in the ceiling.

1 Turn off the power and check with a circuit tester (See page 129). Remove the old light fixture and electrical box. Insert the recessed fixture through the hole in the ceiling and attach it to the ceiling surface with the mounting clips provided.

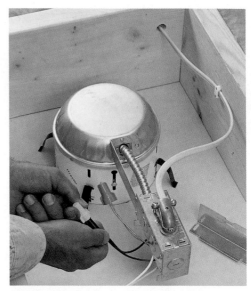

2 Attach the cable to the recessed fixture's electrical box with a cable clamp. Remove cable sheathing, leaving at least ½ in. of sheathing extending past the clamp. Connect the black fixture lead to the black cable wire, white lead to the white wire and the cable grounding wire to the grounding screw on the box. Attach the box cover.

Installing a vent fan

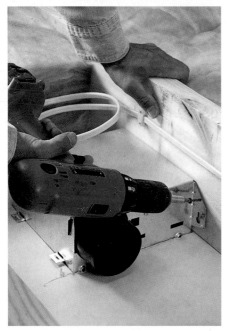

1 Drill a small hole near the center of the planned fan location. Push a length of stiff wire through the hole, into the attic. Locate the wire from the attic, then use the fan box to adjust the position of the opening so the box can be attached to a joist. Cut the opening for the box, then use screws to mount it to the joist.

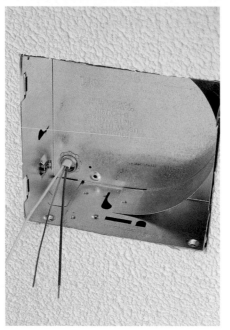

2 Mount the vent cover on the roof or through an exterior side wall and attach the vent hose to the tailpieces on the fan and the vent cover. Remove a knockout on the fan box, then attach cable to the box with a cable clamp. At least ½ in. of sheathing should extend past the cable clamp.

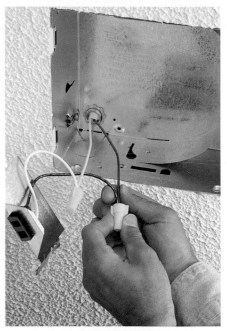

3 Connect the black lead from the fan's wire connection box to the black cable wire, the white lead to the white wire and the cable grounding wire to the grounding clip or screw on the box. Attach the wire connection box to the fan box. Mount the fan motor unit and plug it into the receptacle on the wire connection box. Attach the fan grill.

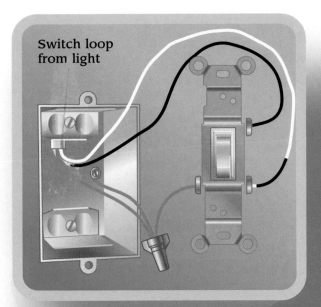

Switch loop
from light

Switch connections

Wires from either one or two cables will be connected to a single-pole switch. More cables may be present in the electrical box containing the switch but will not have any wires connected to the switch.

One cable connected to switch (left) means that current is first routed to the light fixture electrical box and then a cable brings current to the switch box for the switch to control. This is often called a switch loop. The neutral white wire serves as a hot wire and must be tagged with black electrical tape.

Two cables connected to switch indicate that current comes to the switch box before being routed to the light fixture.

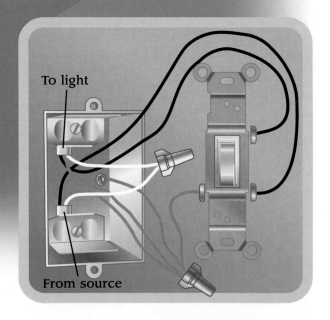

To light

From source

Silver terminals

Brass terminals

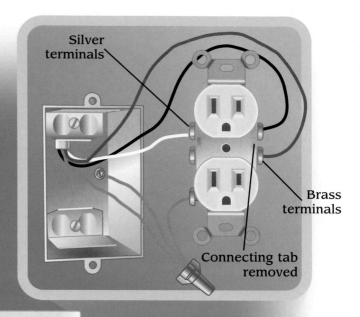

Silver terminals

Brass terminals

Connecting tab removed

Receptacle connections

There are four basic receptacle wiring patterns. Always connect neutral wires to silver terminals and hot wires to brass terminals.

One 2-wire cable connected to the receptacle (above left) indicates the receptacle is at the end of the circuit run.

Two 2-wire cables connected to the receptacle (below left) mean the receptacle is in the middle of the run.

One 3-wire cable attached to the receptacle (above right) indicates a split receptacle, with each half of the unit serving a separate circuit or use, such as when one half is controlled by a switch. Note: The connecting tab between the brass terminals must be removed on a split receptacle.

A two-slot receptacle (below right) is often found in older homes. There is no grounding screw on the unit. Do not replace a two-slot receptacle with a 3-slot receptacle unless a grounding path is created.

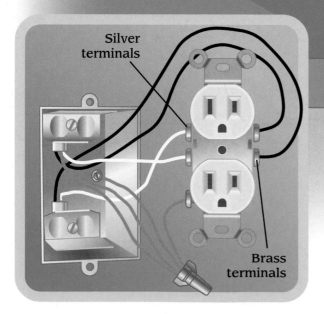

Silver terminals

Brass terminals

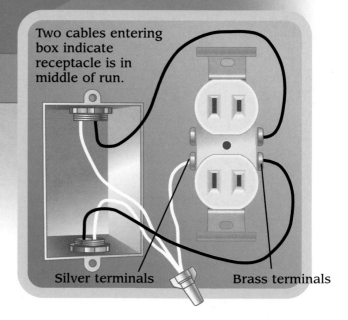

Two cables entering box indicate receptacle is in middle of run.

Silver terminals

Brass terminals

Standard single ceiling fixture

Wires from either one or two cables in a light fixture box will connect to the light fixture. Cables from other circuits may be present in the box but will not connect to the fixture.

One cable connected to the light fixture indicates that current is routed to the switch box before coming to the light fixture.

Two cables connected to the light fixture indicate that current is routed to the fixture's electrical box through one cable and is then routed to the switch through the other cable, often called a switch loop (See page 147). The white wire in the switch loop must be tagged with black electrical tape because it serves as a hot wire.

If your project has two or more light fixtures controlled by one switch, see page 152 for wiring connections.

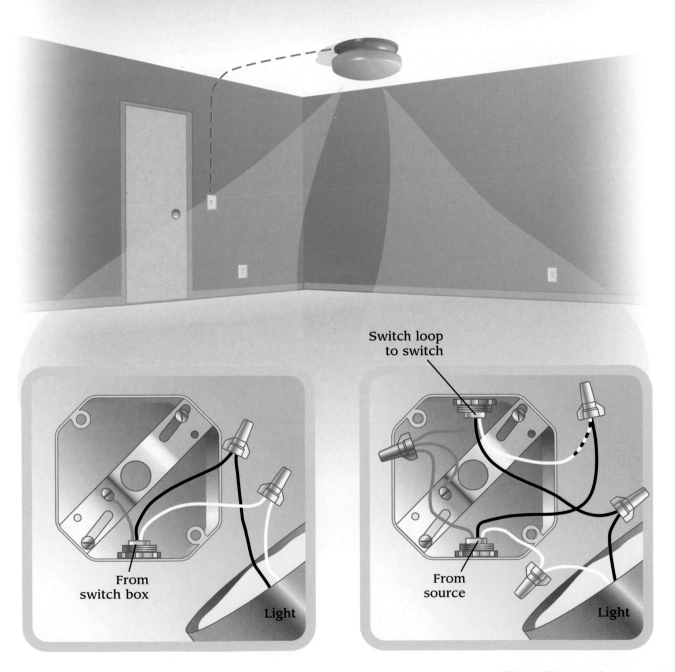

Switch loop
to switch

From
switch box

Light

From
source

Light

Adding a new receptacle

When adding a new receptacle, it is usually easiest to access power from an existing receptacle. An existing receptacle will be in the middle of the circuit run or at its end (See page 148). This illustration shows obtaining power from a receptacle at the end of the circuit. If you need to access power from a middle-of-run receptacle, use the wiring diagram on page 148 as a guide.

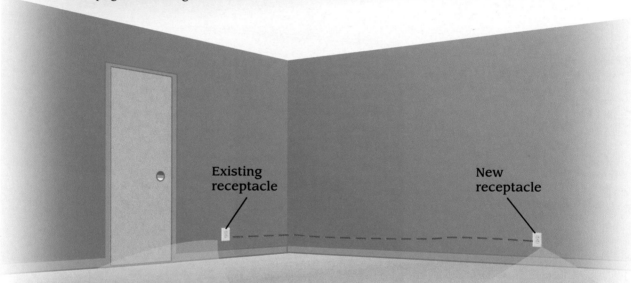

Existing receptacle

New receptacle

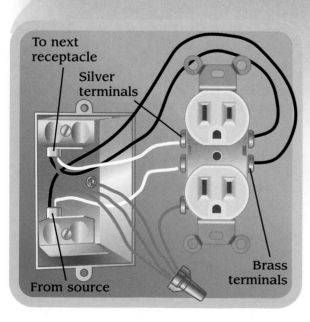

To next receptacle

Silver terminals

From source

Brass terminals

Silver terminals

Brass terminals

Illustrations & Diagrams

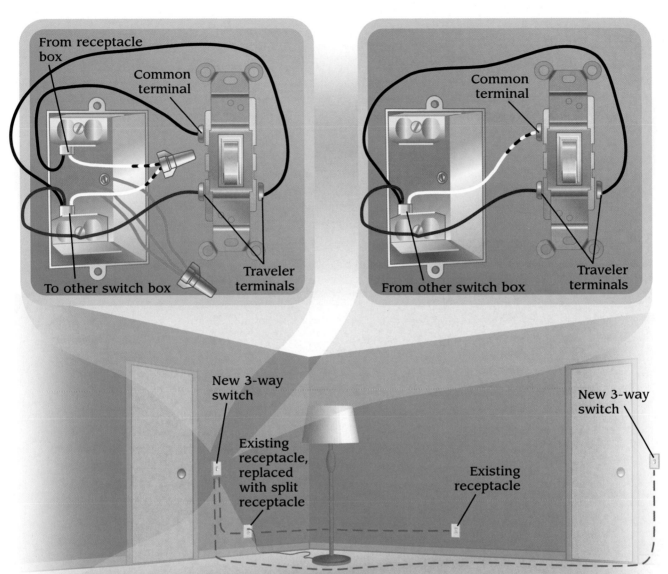

From receptacle box

Common terminal

To other switch box

Traveler terminals

Common terminal

From other switch box

Traveler terminals

New 3-way switch

Existing receptacle, replaced with split receptacle

New 3-way switch

Existing receptacle

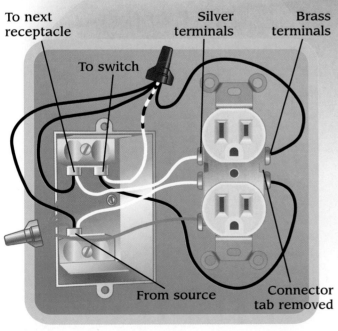

To next receptacle

To switch

Silver terminals

Brass terminals

From source

Connector tab removed

Switched outlet controlled by 3-way switches

Adding a switched light fixture to a finished room can be done by replacing an existing receptacle with a split receptacle where one half is controlled by a switch. A light fixture, such as a floor lamp, is plugged into this half of the receptacle. This is a good method for rooms where access above the ceiling isn't available to install a ceiling fixture.

In this illustration, 3-way switches are installed at both entryways. One type of 3-way switch installation is shown. Every 3-way installation must follow this pattern: The common terminal on one switch is connected to the power source, the common terminal on the other switch is connected to the hot lead of the fixture (in this case the hot terminal on the receptacle), and the traveler terminals on both switches are connected together. All neutral wires connected to switches must be tagged with black electrical tape to indicate they are serving as hot wires.

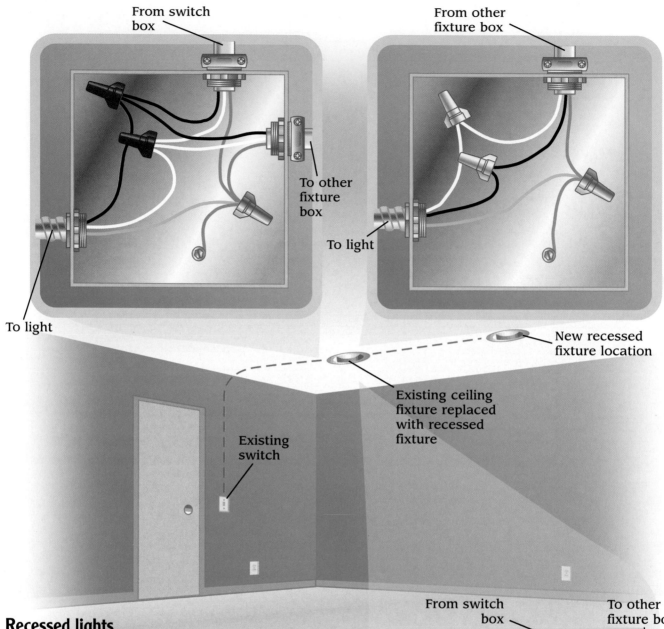

From switch
box

From other
fixture box

To other
fixture
box

To light

To light

New recessed
fixture location

Existing ceiling
fixture replaced
with recessed
fixture

Existing
switch

Recessed lights

Replacing an existing ceiling fixture with a recessed
light fixture is relatively easy. You can add additional
recessed fixtures at the same time. These wiring
diagrams show the self-contained electrical boxes
found on recessed fixtures. The armored cable
connects the electrical box to the light.

Either one or two cables are connected to the
existing ceiling fixture. If there is one cable, power is
routed to the switch box first. The diagram above, left
shows wire connections for replacing the fixture with a
recessed light while adding another recessed light.

If there are two cables, power is routed to the fixture
box before going to the switch. The diagram at right
shows wire connections for this, again adding another
recessed light.

The diagram above, right, shows wire connections
for the additional recessed fixture in either situation.

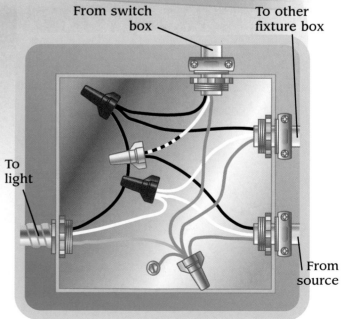

From switch
box

To other
fixture box

To
light

From
source

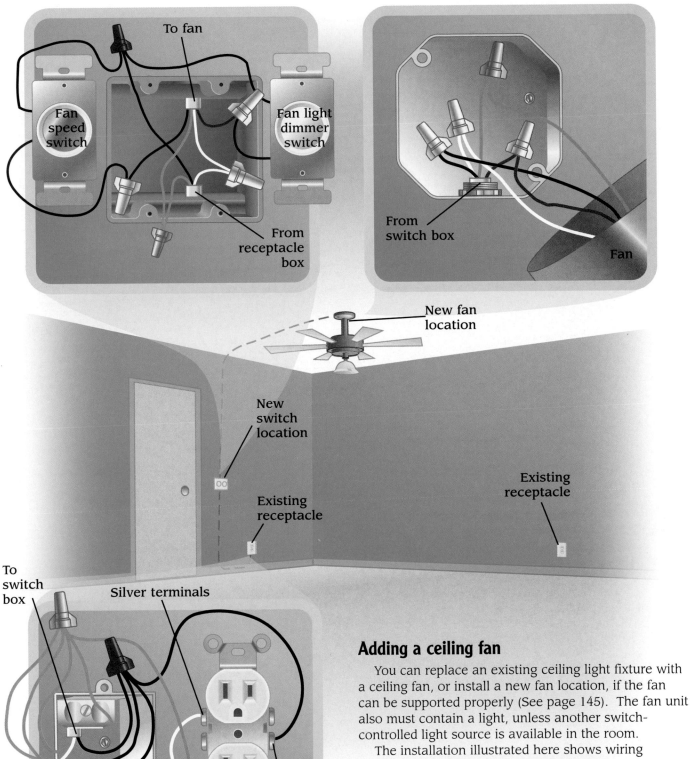

Fan speed switch

To fan

Fan light dimmer switch

From receptacle box

From switch box

Fan

New fan location

New switch location

Existing receptacle

Existing receptacle

To switch box

Silver terminals

Brass terminals

To next receptacle

From source

Adding a ceiling fan

You can replace an existing ceiling light fixture with a ceiling fan, or install a new fan location, if the fan can be supported properly (See page 145). The fan unit also must contain a light, unless another switch-controlled light source is available in the room.

The installation illustrated here shows wiring connections when accessing power from an existing receptacle. You must have a 3-wire cable between the switch box and the fan location if you wish to control the light and fan speed with wall switches. Otherwise, you must control the light with a wall switch. Fan speed is controlled by a pull chain at the fan.

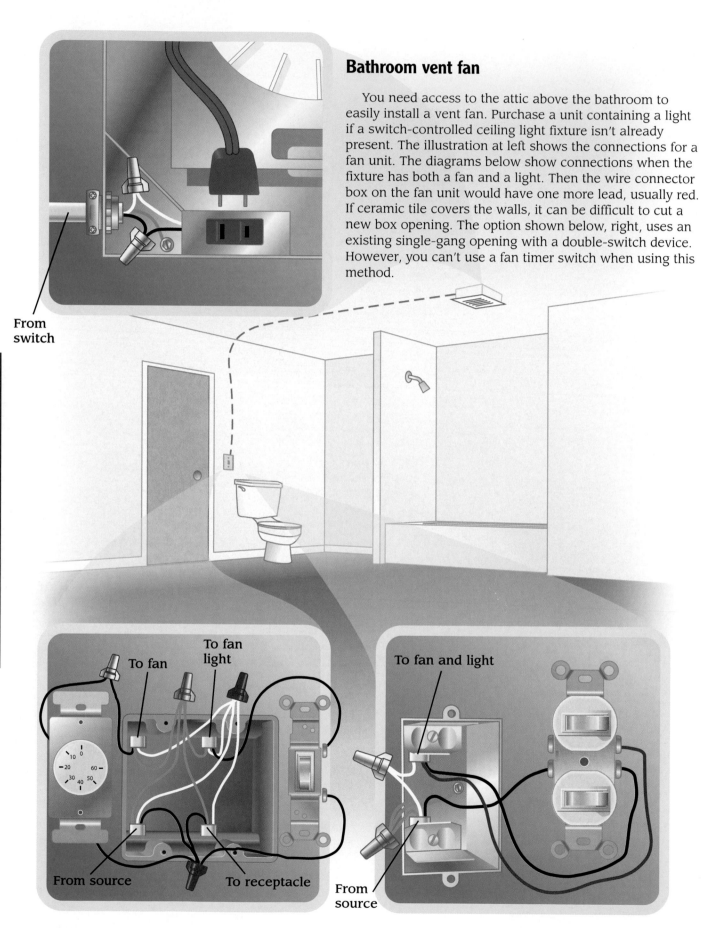

Bathroom vent fan

You need access to the attic above the bathroom to easily install a vent fan. Purchase a unit containing a light if a switch-controlled ceiling light fixture isn't already present. The illustration at left shows the connections for a fan unit. The diagrams below show connections when the fixture has both a fan and a light. Then the wire connector box on the fan unit would have one more lead, usually red. If ceramic tile covers the walls, it can be difficult to cut a new box opening. The option shown below, right, uses an existing single-gang opening with a double-switch device. However, you can't use a fan timer switch when using this method.

From switch

To fan

To fan light

From source

To receptacle

To fan and light

From source

Illustrations & Diagrams

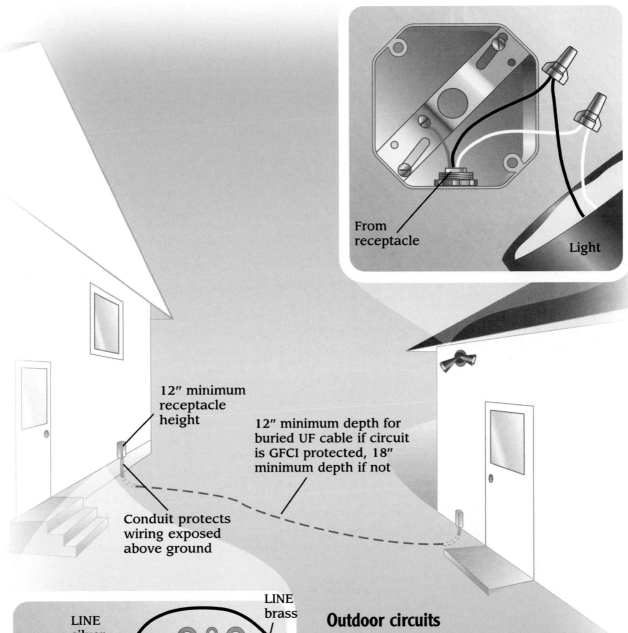

12" minimum receptacle height

12" minimum depth for buried UF cable if circuit is GFCI protected, 18" minimum depth if not

Conduit protects wiring exposed above ground

From receptacle

Light

LINE silver

LINE brass

From source

To garage

LOAD silver

LOAD brass

Outdoor circuits

All outdoor receptacles should be GFCI-protected devices. The terminals on these receptacles are marked LINE and LOAD. The LINE terminals are connected to the power source and to the rest of the circuit if it doesn't require GFCI protection. Connecting to the LOAD side of the GFCI receptacle provides GFCI protection for the circuit from that point on. Check with your local electrical inspector to determine your project requirements. The security light installed on the garage in this illustration would contain light and motion sensors. You could also install a switch to control the fixture manually.

Index